D11193823

HENRY KNOX

A Da Capo Press Reprint Series

THE ERA OF THE AMERICAN REVOLUTION

GENERAL EDITOR: LEONARD W. LEVY

Claremont Graduate School

C E

HENRY KNOX
A SOLDIER OF THE REVOLUTION

by
Noah Brooks

DA CAPO PRESS • NEW YORK • 1974

Universitas
BIBLIOTHECA
Ottaviensis

16 8478

Library of Congress Cataloging in Publication Data

Brooks, Noah, 1830-1903.
   Henry Knox, a soldier of the Revolution.

   (The Era of the American Revolution)
   Reprint of the 1900 ed. published by Putnam, New
York.
   1. Knox, Henry, 1750-1806. I. Title.
E207.K74B8   1974   973.3'092'4 [B]   74-8496
ISBN 0-306-70617-2

E
207
.K74B8
1974

This Da Capo Press edition of *Henry Knox* is an
unabridged republication of the first edition
published in New York and London in 1900.

Published by Da Capo Press, Inc.
A Subsidiary of Plenum Publishing Corporation
227 West 17th Street, New York, N.Y. 10011

All Rights Reserved

Manufactured in the United States of America

Οὐ τείχη οὐδὲ ᾠδεῖα οὐδὲ στοαὶ οὐδὲ ὁ τῶν
ἀψύχων κόσμος αἱ πόλεις εἰσίν, ἀλλ' ἄνδρες
αὐτοῖς εἰδότες θαρρεῖν.

AILIOS ARISTEIDES (129-189 A.D.).

NEITHER WALLS, THEATRES, PORCHES, NOR SENSE-
LESS EQUIPAGE, MAKE STATES, BUT MEN WHO ARE ABLE
TO RELY UPON THEMSELVES.

TRANS. BY ARTHUR WILLIAMS AUSTIN.

HENRY KNOX

Henry Knox

A SOLDIER OF THE REVOLUTION

MAJOR-GENERAL IN THE CONTINENTAL ARMY, WASHINGTON'S
CHIEF OF ARTILLERY, FIRST SECRETARY OF WAR
UNDER THE CONSTITUTION, FOUNDER OF
THE SOCIETY OF THE CINCINNATI

1750–1806

BY

NOAH BROOKS

Author of " Abraham Lincoln, and the Downfall of American Slavery "
"Washington in Lincoln's Time," etc.

ILLUSTRATED

G. P. PUTNAM'S SONS
NEW YORK & LONDON
The Knickerbocker Press

1900

Copyright, 1900
BY
G. P. PUTNAM'S SONS

The Knickerbocker Press, New York

To

THE SOCIETY OF THE CINCINNATI

WHOSE ENDURING PATRIOTIC INFLUENCE AND BENEFICENCE

JUSTIFY THE WISDOM OF ITS ORIGINATORS

THIS MEMORIAL OF ONE OF ITS MOST ILLUSTRIOUS FOUNDERS

IS RESPECTFULLY DEDICATED

PREFACE

HE author of this volume has drawn his materials from a considerable number of sources; but his principal storehouse has been the Knox Manuscripts, now in the possession of the New England Historic Genealogical Society, Boston. This valuable collection, comprising nearly twelve thousand letters and other documents, has been mounted on sheets of durable paper and bound up in fifty-five massive folio volumes; its preservation, after years of exposure to the vandalism of autograph-hunters and to divers vicissitudes, is due to the loving care and thoughtfulness of a grandson of General Knox, the late Admiral Henry Knox Thatcher, U. S. N. The papers were for a time in the custody of Mr. Charles S. Davies, of Portland, Maine, who began a memoir of Knox, but whose failing health interrupted his work before it was well begun. In like manner, Mr. Joseph Willard, of Boston, began but did not finish a similar work, in the preparation of which he was to have used these papers. Finally, a brief biography of Knox was prepared by Mr. Francis S. Drake for the *Memorials of the Massa-*

chusetts Society of the Cincinnati, the Knox papers
being the foundation of the book, of which only
three hundred copies were printed.   Besides these
papers and Mr. Drake's work, the author is indebted
to the documents collected by Mr. Davies, aforementioned, and now in the possession of Mr. David
G. Haskins, Jr., of Cambridge, Mass.   The Davies
papers are in the custody of the New England Historic Genealogical Society, by the courtesy of Mr.
Haskins, a grandson of their zealous collector.
Eaton's *History of Thomaston, Rockland, and South
Thomaston, Maine,* Thacher's *Military Journal,* and
the collections of sundry historical societies of Maine
and Massachusetts have also been of great use in the
preparation of the book.

The establishment of Montpelier, as Knox's
family seat was called, in the township of Thomaston, Maine, was an event of importance in the history of that region.   To this day the counties of
Knox, Lincoln, and Waldo perpetuate the memories
that cluster around the name of the illustrious
soldier, who, as Washington's Chief of Artillery and
his trusted friend and companion, achieved fame
and added lustre to the titles which he bore.   As
the family of the author was allied to that of Knox,
tales and traditions of Knox's greatness, of the
state which he maintained at Montpelier, and of the
generous public spirit which he manifested in his
Maine home formed a part of the author's earliest
recollections.   To gather up the main facts in
Knox's life and energetic public service has therefore been a labour of love; and the author ventures

the hope that this labour will serve its purpose and give to his fellow-countrymen a tolerably clear picture of the personality and the career of General Henry Knox.

Castine, Maine, October, 1899.

CONTENTS

CHAPTER I

PAGE

THE SCHOOLING OF A SOLDIER I

Henry Knox, a Boston tradesman—Descended from the Knoxes of the North of Ireland—Migration of his father's family to Boston—Adventures of his boyhood—The " Boston Massacre "—Brewing of the storm—Knox opens a bookstore—Curiosities of the time and trade—The port of Boston closed to commerce—Knox's invoices of books imported—His bookstore pillaged—His enlistment in a train-band—Formation of militia companies—Early love passages—He marries a daughter of a Tory house—An Epithalamium.

CHAPTER II

THE BREAKING OF THE STORM 27

Lord Percy's excursion from Boston—Battle of Lexington —Knox volunteers—He meets Washington at Cambridge —Lack of trained engineers—John Adams's friendship for Knox—A glimpse of the American volunteer officers— Knox's adventurous journey to Fort Ticonderoga and his return with artillery—Entertaining letters en route—Dorchester Heights fortified—The British driven out of Boston—Poetic tribute to Knox's feat.

CHAPTER III

MILITARY OPERATIONS AROUND NEW YORK . . 49

Doings of " The Sons of Liberty "—Knox plans defences for the coast of Connecticut—A pen picture of Admiral

PAGE

Hopkins—Washington's generals at New York—The battle of Long Island—Flight of Mrs. Knox—An embassy
from Lord Howe to "George Washington, Esq."—Depression in the American ranks—Trial of a torpedo boat—
Evacuation of New York—Fall of Fort Washington—
Greene's sorrow—The fight transferred to New Jersey.

CHAPTER IV

THE FIGHT FOR THE JERSEYS 75

A British proclamation of amnesty—The famous American
crossing of the Delaware—Trenton, Princeton, and Morristown—Knox's plans for an arsenal and military school—
Arrival of French volunteer officers—Knox threatened
with being superseded—Protest of American officers—
Ducoudray provided for—The plague of deserters and
"bounty-jumpers."

CHAPTER V

THE CONTEST MOVES SOUTHWARD 96

Howe sails for Philadelphia—Washington follows—The
battle of the Brandywine—Battle of Germantown—News
of Burgoyne's surrender cheers the American camp—
Valley Forge—The "Conway cabal"—Washington's com-
posure—Darkest days.

CHAPTER VI

IN THE DARKEST DAYS OF THE WAR . . . 116

Military operations wait on diplomacy—Another British
proposal for terms of peace—Howe's evacuation of Philadelphia—The Americans take possession of the city—
Battle of Monmouth—Arrival of D'Estaing's fleet—Knox's
privateering ventures—Charges against Benedict Arnold
—Celebration of the French alliance—Knox's family

PAGE

bereaved by death—Arrival of Rochambeau—Treason of
Arnold and execution of André—Mutiny of the Pennsyl-
vania line—Rochambeau's march to the Hudson from
Connecticut.

CHAPTER VII

THE BRITISH SURRENDER AT YORKTOWN . . 146

Washington's grand strategy—Knox's artillery brought
into action—His letters home—Junction of American and
French forces—Elation of the people along the line of
march—The enemy beleaguered in Yorktown—Final surrender and capitulation of Cornwallis and his army.

CHAPTER VIII

THE END OF THE WAR 163

Preliminary Treaty of Peace signed—Irritating delay of
the British—Fruitless negotiation for exchange of prisoners—Knox appointed to command of West Point—Dissen-
sions and discontent in the army—The famous " Newburgh
addresses "—Knox as a peacemaker—He organises the
Society of the Cincinnati—Unfriendly criticisms of the
Order—Knox in command of the army—Final departure
of the British from New York—Knox heads the column
taking possession of the city—Washington's farewell.

CHAPTER IX

A TRYING INTERREGNUM 180

Knox's plans for the maintenance of the army—Correspondence between Washington and Knox on this subject
—Congress appoints Knox Secretary of War—Shays's rebellion—Proposals for a new Federal Constitution by
Knox—His plan for a general government—Ratification
of the new Constitution—Knox's care of General Greene's
son—The lad sent to Lafayette.

Contents

CHAPTER X

PAGE

IN WASHINGTON'S FIRST ADMINISTRATION . . 211

Knox's plan for a national militia—Popular fears of a
standing army—Treaties with Indian tribes—Friction between the Executive and Legislative Departments—Secretary Knox's brief speech in the Senate—His life in New
York—He retires from office—Personal characteristics of
General and Mrs. Knox.

CHAPTER XI

THE RETURN OF CINCINNATUS 232

Knox fixes his place of residence in Maine—His plans for
vast undertakings—Troubles with squatters—Financial
embarrassments—War with France imminent—Knox mortified by being placed below Hamilton and Pinckney in
military rank—He fills sundry civil offices.

CHAPTER XII

A BUSY LIFE ENDED 255

Death by an untoward accident—A military funeral—
General expressions of grief—His last will and testament
—His munificence and public spirit—Estimate of his
character.

ILLUSTRATIONS

PAGE

MAJOR-GENERAL HENRY KNOX . . *Frontispiece*
From the painting by Gilbert Stuart, in the Museum of Fine Arts, Boston.

BIRTHPLACE OF HENRY KNOX, BOSTON, MASS. . 2
Redrawn from an old print.

THE BOSTON MASSACRE 8
From the painting by Alonzo Chappel.

ARRIVAL OF KNOX WITH ARTILLERY . . . 12
From a design by F. O. C. Darley.

FACSIMILE OF AUTOGRAPH OF HENRY KNOX . . 18

STATUE OF ISRAEL PUTNAM 32
J. Q. A. Ward, Sculptor.

THE JUMEL MANSION, WASHINGTON HEIGHTS, NEW
YORK 40

ALEXANDER HAMILTON 54

MAJOR-GENERAL JOHN SULLIVAN 60

MAJOR-GENERAL PHILIP SCHUYLER . . . 62
From a painting by Col. John Trumbull.

JOHN ADAMS 64

AARON BURR 68

Illustrations

PAGE

STATUE OF NATHAN HALE 70
 By Frederick Macmonnies.

MAJOR-GENERAL CHARLES LEE 76
 From an English engraving published in 1776.

WASHINGTON'S HEADQUARTERS, POMPTON, N. J. . 78

BATTLE OF PRINCETON—DEATH OF MERCER . . 84
 From the painting by Col. John Trumbull.

MAJOR-GENERAL HENRY KNOX [1] 92
 From the study for the original painting by Gilbert Stuart.

THE MARQUIS DE LAFAYETTE 104
 From a French print, 1781.

THE CHEW HOUSE, GERMANTOWN, PA. . . . 108

WASHINGTON AT MONMOUTH 124
 From a design by F. O. C. Darley.

BENEDICT ARNOLD CARRIED IN EFFIGY . . . 136

THE CAPTURE OF ANDRÉ 138
 From a print in the possession of Dr. Coutant.

COUNT DE GRASSE 144

WEST POINT AT THE TIME OF THE REVOLUTION . 158
 Redrawn from Barber's " Historical Collection."

MAJOR-GENERAL NATHANAEL GREENE . . . 162
 From the painting by Col. John Trumbull.

HEADQUARTERS OF MAJOR-GENERAL KNOX AT VAIL'S
 GATE, NEWBURGH, N. Y. [2] 174

[1] Reproduced with permission from the original painting in the possession of
Mrs. C. W. Stimpson.
[2] Reproduced with permission from *King Washington*, by Adelaide Skeel and
William H. Brearley.

Illustrations

XV

PAGE

WASHINGTON'S FAREWELL TO HIS OFFICERS . . 178
    From the painting by Alonzo Chappel.

MAJOR-GENERAL HENRY KNOX [1] 212
    From the painting by Edward Savage.

"MONTPELIER," THE HOME OF GENERAL KNOX,
    THOMASTON, MAINE [2] 232

MAJOR-GENERAL BENJAMIN LINCOLN . . . 238

THE GRAVE OF HENRY KNOX AT THOMASTON, MAINE 256

THOMAS FLUCKER 260
    From the painting by John Singleton Copley, in
    the art collection in Bowdoin College.

[1] Reproduced from Drake's *Life and Correspondence of Henry Knox.*
[2] From an oil painting in possession of Wm. A. Walker.

GENERAL HENRY KNOX

CHAPTER I

THE SCHOOLING OF A SOLDIER

IT is not easy to understand why a figure so commanding and a character so exalted as the figure and character of General Henry Knox should have been so inconspicuous in the written history of the Republic. Even a cursory examination of the record of the times in which Knox lived and wrought will disclose his energetic personality, his pre-eminent abilities, his lofty patriotism, and his winning manners. Above all, one who won and held the affection and esteem of Washington, as Knox did, could have been no common man.

As Washington's grand character was perfected, if not evolved, by the wonderful events of the first great crisis in the affairs of the American people, so, in the storm and stress that accompanied the birth of the Republic, the person of Henry Knox, noble

and majestic, was gradually detached from the less
distinguished of his fellow-men, and he became, by
the force of his nature, one of the foremost of that
glorious company of military heroes whose genius
and prowess guided the American people from a
condition of colonial dependence to one of national
sovereignty. The hour struck, and the man
emerged from obscurity to eminence. The young
tradesman, devoting his abundant energies to the
service of his country, and sacrificing ease, comfort,
and the prospects of affluence, was transformed into
a soldier well versed in the art of war, familiar with
camps, a master of strategy. His merits in these
pursuits, so unexpectedly opened before him, were
very great. As a slight reward, he gradually rose
to the highest military rank then known in the
American army establishment. He began his public
career as a modest militiaman; he ended as a major-
general and as the chief officer of the departments
of the Army and the Navy of the United States.

At this distance of time, the career of such a man,
so filled with activity, so closely connected with the
history of his country, and so brilliant in the rapid
and picturesque development of a famous and lov-
able personality, may well furnish a fascinating subject for the pen of the biographer and the study of
any who admire manly generosity and singleness of
purpose in a good cause. The life of Henry Knox
may be commended to future generations of American citizens as one not only worthy of imitation but
also endued with a certain atmosphere of romance
which allures and gratifies the student.

BIRTHPLACE OF HENRY KNOX, BOSTON, MASS.

REDRAWN FROM AN OLD PRINT.

The name of Knox * has been made forever famous by the stern reformer who bore it in the stormy times of Henry VIII., Elizabeth, and Mary Queen of Scots. John Knox, the reformer, was a native of the district of East Lothian, Scotland, and the family of Henry Knox originated, so far as the family records have been traced, in the adjacent Lowlands. During the early part of the eighteenth century, the migration of many Scotch Presbyterians to the north of Ireland resulted in the establishment of a colony whose descendants are known in England and America as the Scotch-Irish. Later in the century, considerable numbers of these crossed the seas and settled in various portions of the New England States. During the revolutionary struggle these people were identified with the cause of human liberty, into which they threw themselves with devotion; and their descendants have unto this day proved the sturdy worthiness of the stock from which they sprang.

---

* One of the Knox family, residing on the family estate, County Tyrone, north of Ireland, was raised to the peerage by George II., first as Baron, Lord Wells, and subsequently as Lord Viscount Nothland. This personage, after the American Revolution was over and the independence of United States acknowledged, courteously offered to General Henry Knox the family coat-of-arms, his lordship thinking that the distinguished American had ample right to armorial bearings. Knox declined the offer, saying that he was "not certain that he was entitled to be regarded a cadet of a distinguished house." He preferred to bear no cognisance but his own. His daughter, Mrs. Thatcher, says: "It was his pride to prefer the position which he acquired in his own proper sphere and become, so far as Providence should please, the head of his own house."

A party of these desirable emigrants, under the spiritual leadership of the Rev. John Morehead, landed at Boston in 1729. They founded a religious society in Bury Street, and it is a curious historical fact that the first two names on the baptismal records of the parish are the characteristic ones of Knox and Campbell. These two families were destined to be united; for William Knox was married at Boston, in February, 1735 (old style), to Mary, daughter of Robert Campbell. William Knox was a shipmaster, and, for a time at least, was in comfortable circumstances, owning as he did some wharf property and the house in which his children were born, a two-story wooden building with a gambrel roof, situated on Sea Street, near the foot of Summer Street and opposite the head of Drake's Wharf. Henry was the seventh of ten sons, and was born July 25, 1750. Only four of these ten boys arrived at the years of maturity; of these the two elder, John and Benjamin, went to sea, but never returned home, and their ultimate fate is unknown. William, the youngest of the family, was born in 1756, and was subsequently associated with his more distinguished brother in various ways until his death, which took place in 1797. The father of the family was overtaken by financial misfortune about the time of the birth of his youngest son; he was obliged to sell his house on Sea Street, and he soon after went to St. Eustatius, in the West Indies, where he died in 1762, aged fifty years. His widow survived him nine years, dying in Boston, December 14, 1771, aged fifty-three years.

Henry Knox appears to have been a stalwart youngster, fond of manly sports, devoted to his mother's welfare, active in affairs that engaged the attention of the neighbourhood in which he lived, and yet withal addicted to the study of books as well as of men and business. Left fatherless just as he was about to be graduated from the Boston grammar-school, young Knox found himself, with his brother William, then only six years old, the sole support and stay of his mother. Leaving school, he took a place in the book-store of.Messrs. Wharton & Bowes, in Cornhill, doubtless considering himself very fortunate in being able to secure any kind of employment in those troublous times; for discontent and dissatisfaction with the Imperial Government was beginning to seethe in the colonies, and signs of political disturbance were multiplying in the land.

But, although apprenticed to a master who required strict attention to business, young Knox contrived to acquire a considerable stock of knowledge while in the employment of the booksellers' firm. Surrounded by useful books, he dipped into them with the eagerness of an active and inquisitive mind. He deeply studied the pages of Plutarch, became well versed in the history of famous generals and warriors, and not only made himself tolerably familiar with the classics as he found them translated into English, but he learned to speak and write the French language, an accomplishment which he found very useful in his after-life.

But the young student was no milksop. We find

him an active figure in the pastimes and diversions
of his day and generation. An entertaining incident
is related to show his stalwart strength and his spirit.
Boston, then a small town, was divided into two
rival factions — the Northenders and the South-
enders, the rivalry and the division being more
especially apparent among the boys of the respective
localities. The young Bostonians followed the example of their English progenitors in the celebration of Guy Fawkes Day, the 5th of November,
their manner of celebration being known as Pope's
Night. Effigies of the Pope and the Devil were
borne through the streets on wheeled platforms, or
floats, saluted with derisive shouts and burning gunpowder. When the procession had paraded to the
satisfaction of the mock celebrants, the effigies were
committed to the flames of a bonfire with prodigious
acclaim. As a matter of course, the rivalry of the
North End and the South End made it necessary
that there should be two pageants of this kind; and
also, as a matter of course, the two processions finally
encountered each other on some neutral ground mid-
way between the two sections of the town. On one
occasion, a broken wheel disabled the vehicle on
which the effigies of Knox's party were borne, and,
rather than submit to the disgrace of withdrawing
this feature of their celebration, Knox put his
shoulder under the load and so carried it through
the night until the rival procession was met with,
when the customary pitched battle was precipitated
and the show ended in the capture of one party's
paraphernalia by its rival faction. It was character-

istic of Knox that he early learned to put his
shoulder to the wheel of any enterprise in which his
abundant zeal was enlisted.

Knox was twenty years old and not yet " out of
his time " of service when the sanguinary affray
known in history as the Boston Massacre took place.
The citizens of Boston had been greatly irritated by
the establishment of an armed garrison in their city.
Altercations between the soldiery and the people
were frequent, and the spirit of bitterness that prevailed might be compared to a fire that smouldered
beneath the surface, ready to break out on the
slightest provocation. A squabble had taken place
on the night of March 5, 1770, near the barracks in
which the British soldiers were quartered, in the
heart of the city. A sentry had been set upon by
a citizen, and other soldiers, rallying to the support
of their comrade, armed themselves with any weapon
that came handy (shovels and tongs, it is said);
sufficient excuse for the gathering of a mob was
evident, and a vast concourse of excited people soon
assembled. An attack was made upon a sentry in
front of the custom-house on King Street (now State
Street), and a squad of six men was sent to the relief of the beleaguered soldier. This action still
further inflamed the mob, who assailed the soldiers
with such epithets as " lobster-backs " and " bloody-
backs," and the red-coated infantrymen were de-
risively invited to fire. Captain Preston, who
commanded the post, was absent from the barracks,
but was sent for in haste, and when he arrived upon
the ground he took six more men with him to the

support of the soldiers who were on duty in front of the custom-house.

At this juncture, young Knox, who had been visiting friends in Charlestown and was now on his way home, came upon the scene. He exerted his powerful influence in favour of peace and attempted to restrain the crowd from rushing upon the soldiers. When Captain Preston appeared, Knox passionately seized him by the coat and implored him " for God's sake " not to fire upon the people but to take his men back into the barracks, urging that the officer's life must answer for any life that might be taken in the event of an armed conflict. Every intelligent man knew perfectly well that, according to English law, the soldiers must not fire unless an order to that effect had first been issued by a civil officer to their commanding officer. While the agitated Preston listened to the remonstrances of Knox, fully aware of the justice of the young man's position, a soldier was struck with a club in the hands of a citizen. Enraged by the blow, the soldier levelled his piece and fired without orders. This was the signal for random firing by the other soldiers, and the mob fled in wild disorder. As a result of the volley, three men were killed instantly, two others were mortally wounded, and six men were less severely wounded. The Boston Massacre passed into history.

The ultimate result of this affray was the removal of the British troops from the city, and the postponement of the final conflict for at least five years. But these were years of uneasiness and uncertainty in the American colonies, years in which the already

THE BOSTON MASSACRE.

FROM THE PAINTING BY ALONZO CHAPPEL.

exasperated feelings of the people were still further exacerbated by offensive displays of the power and authority of the Crown. Undismayed by the stormy aspect of the political sky, however, Knox, having attained his majority, resolved to go into business on his own account. His modest establishment received the somewhat pretentious name of The London Book-Store, and its opening was announced in Edes & Gill's *Gazette*, July 29, 1771, in the following terms:

"This day is opened a new London Book-Store by Henry Knox, opposite Williams' Court, in Cornhill, Boston, who has just imported in the last ships from London a large and very elegant assortment of the most modern books in all branches of Literature, Arts, and Sciences (catalogues of which will be published soon), and to be sold as cheap as can be bought at any place in town. Also a complete assortment of stationery."

Among the papers of Knox are the original invoices of goods shipped from London to him during the few years that intervened between his opening his book-store and his departure to join himself to the patriot army. Some of these are curiously interesting as indications of the sort of literary pabulum which was served out to our forefathers. For example, an invoice dated at London, October 12, 1771, sets forth the fact that there has been shipped that day " on board the *Pasti*, Capt. Isaac Cazneau, for Boston, in New England, by Tho's Longman, Bookseller in London, Three Trunks of Merchandize on the account and risque of Mr. Henry Knox, Merchant in Boston." The total amount of the bill is £196 17s. 13d. The books appear to be chiefly

devoted to law, medicine, and politics, with a plentiful sprinkling of works on divinity; and the polemic
disposition of the New Englanders of that age is
evinced in the items of printed sermons ordered by
the young bookseller in Boston.

His invoice contains twelve copies of Dodd's *Sermons to Young Men*, an item which is balanced by
four copies of *The Fool of Quality*, four of *The London Songster*, one of Smollett's *Quixote*, one of *The
Vicar of Wakefield*, two of *Grandison*, one of Vol-
taire's *Lewis the XVth*, and twenty-five copies of
Armstrong's *Œconomy of Love*. Twelve Bibles
figure in this unique list, and the considerable item
of one hundred and twenty copies of Salmon's
Grammar would suggest that young Knox had
secured a contract to furnish books for a public
school. A later invoice contains fifty copies each
of *Pamela*, *Joseph Andrews*, *Tom Jones*, *Clarissa*,
and *Grandison*, items that clearly indicate the character of the fiction read by the staid people of New
England in those days.

Knox added stationery to his stock of books, and
in an invoice from Wright & Gill, of London, dated
February 17, 1772, the total amount of which was
£656 19s. 8d., we find German flutes, bread-baskets,
telescopes, "protractors," dividers, paper hangings,
"moguls," and standishes. On the back of this
invoice is the following endorsement: "Messrs.
Wright & Gill rely upon Mr. Knox's punctual Re-
mittances, and he may be assured of being served
on the best of terms." It is worthy of note that
the titles *Fool of Quality* and Baxter's *Saint's Rest*

appear in nearly every one of the invoices shipped from London to Knox and his successor. The works of Philip Doddridge also appear to have been greatly in demand in New England about that time.

Another illustration of the literary taste of the times is found in a letter addressed to Henry Knox by Henry Sherburne, who, writing from Portsmouth, N. H., November 4, 1773, asks to know the prices of " such books of the story-telling sort " as he may have for sale, the prices being fixed to meet the requirements of " any person who buys 20 vols., 12 mos." Mr. Sherburne warns Mr. Knox that he has been already offered some books at very reasonable rates. His list includes

" 1 *Batchelor of Salamanca*, 1 *Anacreon*, 1 *Dickey Gotham and Doll Clod*, 1 *Tristram Shandy*, 1 *Peregrine Pickle*, 1 *Collection of Stories* —2 vols., 1 *Collection of Dodsley's Letters*, printed about the end of the last century, in which are Rochester's Letters to his friend, Henry Saville."

The primitive commerce in books was to some extent reinforced by exchanges among the dealers in such wares doing business in American towns. Thus we find James Rivington writing from New York, March 17, 1774, offering Knox a bargain. After asking Knox to get Paul Revere's prices for engraving certain plates, Rivington says: " I am printing many little Children's Books & send you a specimen of *Rob'n Crusoe* with your name in the title. These I will send you cheaper than you can import them."

But the time was coming when such pleasing fictions as *Rob'n Crusoe* and *Peregrine Pickle* should not wholly interest the American colonists. It is instructive to note the gradual change in public sentiment and thought, as the times wore on, to more exciting themes. Men's minds were directed to the study of politics, and the invoices and advertisements of Knox and others showed that the rights and privileges of Parliament, the duties of citizens, English law, and the prerogatives of the King engrossed the attention of readers.

One can readily imagine that Knox's London book-store, stocked as we know it to have been with the best books then extant, and with many elegant trifles of the day, such as could be included in the very elastic category of " stationery," was likely to become popular with " the quality " of the good old town of Boston. Harrison Gray Otis, who knew Knox with some degree of intimacy, said of his establishment: " It was a store of great display and attraction for young and old, and a fashionable morning lounge." And General Henry Burbeck, one of Knox's contemporaries, said: " Knox's store was a great resort for the British officers and Tory ladies, who were the *ton* at that period."

One of the frequent customers of the handsome and gallant-looking young bookseller was Miss Lucy Flucker, a bright and lively member of the fashionable Tory circles of Boston. Her father, Thomas Flucker, who is described as " a high-toned loyalist of great family pretensions," was the royal secretary of the province, and, as a matter of consequence, a personage of high social dignity. Mr. Otis says

ARRIVAL OF KNOX WITH ARTILLERY.

FROM A DESIGN BY F. O. C. DARLEY.

that Miss Lucy " was distinguished as a young lady of high intellectual endowments, very fond of books, especially of the books sold by Knox, to whose shelves she had frequent recourse, and on whose premises was kindled, as the story went, ' the guiltless flame ' which was destined to burn on the hymeneal altar, ' despite of father and mother and all of my kin.' " The Fluckers were of a French Huguenot family who came to America from England.

Knox found time to indulge in outdoor sports with moderation, notwithstanding his busy life as bookseller, stationer, and bookbinder, for he added this latter branch of industry to his already crowded store and shop. In the summer of 1773, while gunning on Noddle's Island, now occupied by East Boston, he lost the third and fourth fingers of his left hand by the bursting of his fowling-piece. He was afterwards wont to conceal the maiming of his hand by the skilful winding of a silk handkerchief around the member. Gilbert Stuart, when he painted the half-length portrait of Knox which is now the property of the city of Boston, artfully placed the left hand of his sitter on a piece of artillery in such a position as to hide the loss of the two fingers.

When Knox remitted to the surgeons who dressed and cared for his wounded hand the generous sum which he thought should recompense them (three guineas to one and five guineas to another), he could not refrain from expressing his gratitude in the somewhat stilted language of the day.

"Sir," he wrote, "the mariner, when the danger is past, looks back with pleasure and surprize on the quicksands and rocks which he has escaped, and if perchance it was owing to the skillfulness of the pilot or great activity of some brother seaman on board, the first ebullitions of his gratitude are violent, but afterwards settle to a firm respect and esteem for the means of his existence. So, Sir, gratitude obliges me to tender you my most sincere thanks for the attention and care you took of me in a late unlucky accident"—with more to the same purport.

Political troubles thickened in the devoted country that was so soon to become the theatre of a long and exhausting war. Governor Hutchinson, wearied and disgusted with the popular opposition to his administration, resigned his office and went to England; he was succeeded by General Thomas Gage, whose attitude was that of a military, rather than a civil, functionary. The attempt to force upon the colonies the importation of cargoes of tea on which high duties were to be paid for the benefit of the British East India Company, still further exasperated the people and hastened the crisis that was blackly advancing upon the sullen belligerents. Knox, writing to his London correspondents, Wright & Gill, under date of May 30, 1774, said: "If the act to block up this harbour should continue in force any length of time, it must deeply affect every person in Trade here, and consequently their Correspondents on your side of the water. But it is expected the British merchants will see their own interest so clearly as to induce them to exert their whole influence in order to get so unjust and cruel an edict repealed." This appeal to the evident interest of the British business men, as we know, was ineffective, although others than Knox addressed themselves to their business correspondents in London.

James Rivington, the well-known Tory printer, bookseller, and newspaper editor, of New York, was one of Knox's correspondents, and that worthy sent Knox, in July, 1774, a consignment of five chests of the hated and proscribed Chinese tea. Knox declined the commission, and the consignment was subsequently turned over to another person. Writing to Rivington about this time, Knox, after closing the business portion of his letter, adds a postscript in which he says:

"I forgot my politics—or rather, I have none to communicate at present. Things seem to be pretty much at a stand, since I wrote you. The troops encamped on the common keep up a most excellent discipline, and seem cautious that no affray begins on their part. The Citizens, taught by experience to be quiet, are equally cautious to avoid any disturbance. The Non-Consumption agreement or the solemn league and covenant has made a very rapid progress since the Governor's proclamation forbidding it; by the last accounts I have been able to collect, it will be general throughout this Province, New Hampshire, and Connecticut. The New Acts for regulating this Government will, I perfectly believe, make great difficulties. The people are in no disposition to receive an act pregnant with so great evils. What mode of Opposition will be adopted, I do not know; but it is the general opinion that it will be opposed; hence the key to the formidable force collecting here."

By the enactment into law of the obnoxious Boston Port Bill, the Home Government had endeavoured to close the port of Boston against all commerce except that directly licensed by the imperial authorities. The colonists promptly answered this by

entering into a solemn league and covenant to ab-
stain from the consumption of all goods imported
from England. This action on the part of the
colonists, of course, immediately affected the business of Knox. Accordingly, in a letter from him
to his London correspondent, Thomas Longman,
bookseller, in November, 1774, the harassed Boston-
ian writes:

" Sir,—I have received yours, per Capt. Callahan, and the books
in good order, also the Magazines to August inclusive. I am sorry
it is not in my power to make you remittance per this opportunity,
but shall do it very soon. This whole Continent have entered into
a General non-Importation agreement until the late acts of Parliament respecting this Government, &c., are repealed, which will prevent my sending orders for any Books until this most desirable end
is accomplished. I cannot but hope every person who is concerned
in American trade will most strenuously exert themselves in their
'respective stations for what so nearly concerns themselves. I had
the fairest prospect of entirely balancing our account this fall, but
the almost total stagnation of Trade in consequence of the Boston
Port Bill has been the sole means of preventing it, and now the non-
consumption agreement will stop that small circulation of Business
left by the Boston Port Bill—I mean the internal business of the
province. It must be the wish of every good man that these unhappy differences between Great Britain and the Colonies be speedily
and finally adjusted ; the influence that the unlucky and unhappy
mood of the Politicks of the times has upon trade, is my only excuse
for writing concerning them. The Magazines and the new publications concerning the American dispute are the only things which I
desire you to send at present, which I wish you to pack together well
wrapped in brown paper as usual."

Knox's first bill for books purchased of Longman
amounted to £340, and the total amount of his
purchases from that house, up to the close of 1772
(four months less than two years), was £2066. The

political troubles alluded to in the foregoing letter
caused such a falling-off in Knox's orders that Longman's sales on American account may be said to
have almost entirely ceased. It was in vain that English merchants sought to modify the severity of the
imperial treatment of the American colonies, hoping
that such an amelioration would redound to their
own advantage. The British Government was irre-
trievably committed to the fatal policy of force and
oppression. Meanwhile in the colonies there was
by no means an undivided front presented by those
who, although they had not begun to see clearly
even a hope of independence, were resolved upon
opposition to British rule. It was an age of pam-
phleteering; the press, both in this country and in
England, constantly threw off thousands of broad-
sides and pamphlets—satiric, argumentative, humor-
ous, and ponderously logical, and all designed to aid
the cause of the long-suffering colonists, or that of
the British loyalists. James Rivington, although
fully aware of the fact that Knox had thrown himself with ardour into the struggle of the colonists for
some concession of their rights, wrote to the bookseller, under date of December 1, 1774, offering to
send him copies of the Tory pamphlets for sale;
but, as if reflecting that Knox's patriotic impulses
might interfere with his commercial instincts, he
said:

" My reasons for not troubling you with these very warm, high-
seasoned pamphlets is that your very numerous friends of the patriot
interest may be greatly disgusted at your distributing them ; but
if you are not so very nice, as I supposed, from the state of your

2

interest, &c., and are willing to have these sort of articles, I will
secure them for you from time to time. Pray explain yourself on
this head directly, for I mean to show every expression of my attention to you."

It is to be regretted that Knox's answer to this insidious proposition has not been preserved; it was
undoubtedly as " high-seasoned " as any of Rivington's Tory pamphlets.

While we are on the topic of Knox's business
affairs, we may as well anticipate the final downfall
of his bookselling establishment. After Knox had
left Boston to enter the patriot army, his business
was conducted by his younger brother, William.
But as the war cloud deepened, Boston was occupied
by British troops and the civil rule was displaced by
martial law; complete license was allowed the soldiers and the Tories in their treatment of the property of the recalcitrant colonists. Among others,
the absent Knox was a sufferer from the violence of
those who were for the time holding rule in the city.
His store was plundered and pillaged, and his stock
ruined. Long after the war was over and the independence of the States had been acknowledged,
Knox made a payment on his account with Longman, the amount paid being 11,000 guilders, or
about £1000. This did not square the account,
however, and, owing to grave financial embarrassments that overtook him late in his life, the book-
seller-general left a portion of that debt unpaid when
sudden death cut short all his plans. In his letter
enclosing a draft for the last payment made by Knox
to Longman, dated December 15, 1793, he wrote:

FACSIMILE OF AUTOGRAPH OF HENRY KNOX.

"It is but justice to myself to say that, while I experience the strongest sensations of gratitude for your forbearance and liberality, it is with extreme inconvenience that I pay so heavy an arrear for property destroyed by events which I could no more control than I could the great operations of nature, nor am I more responsible for them : I mean the war. In paying you, I feel inclination and duty blended together. Had my pecuniary situation admitted the measure, you should long ago have received the amount due."

The patriot who resented the war brought on to subject the colonies to imperial rule was yet sensitive to obligations due a British subject, although the property represented by those obligations had been destroyed in the British interest.

One dangerous feature of the times was the activity of the colonial militia. In the piping times of peace the British Government had encouraged a martial spirit among the colonists. Several companies of militia had been organised in Boston. The earliest of these was " The Ancient and Honourable Artillery Company," organised in 1638. Next in order of age came the Cadets, organised about 1754, and composed of young men belonging to the higher circles of Boston society. The Cadets were popularly known as " The Governor's Guards," as they acted as escort to that functionary on all occasions of ceremony. Knox, at the age of eighteen, had joined the artillery company, commonly known as " The Train." This organisation was largely composed of men from the South End, and, in contradistinction to the Cadets, its members were chiefly drawn from the ranks of mechanics and shopkeepers. The artillery was commanded by Major Adino Paddock, a chair-maker, whose shop was on

Common (now Tremont) Street, opposite Boston
Common. Paddock was a useful and efficient drill-
master, and his company received valuable instruction from the officers of a company of British artillery,
which, having entered Boston *en route* for Quebec
too late to finish the journey in the winter of 1766,
remained in quarters at Castle William, Boston
Harbour, until the following May. Unwittingly,
the British officers were schooling the militiamen
whom they were afterwards to meet on the field of
battle; for a majority of the officers of Paddock's
command were afterwards enrolled in the patriot
army, and served under Knox, Gridley, and Crane.

Paddock's company had three fine brass pieces,
3-pounders, that were probably those mentioned in
the chronicles of the time as having been brought
over from England on the brigantine *Abigail*, about
the date of the formation of " The Train." These
guns were cast in England from two old cannon sent
over for that purpose by the General Court of Massachusetts. They bore the arms of the province, and
were spoken of as " new pieces " when, on the
King's Birthday, in 1768, they were fired in a royal
salute during a parade in King Street. At the final
breaking out of the War of the Revolution, these
guns were stored in a gun-house on West Street.
The building and a public schoolhouse were surrounded by a high fence and, after the times grew
more and more stormy, a sentry was stationed at
the door of the gun-house. General Gage had expressed his intention of seizing all the arms of the
militia of Boston, and had actually begun to seize

the military stores and weapons of the people of the
province.   It was suspected that Paddock, who was
a Tory, was more than willing to surrender the brass
pieces of his company; accordingly, six bold young
patriots, one of whom was the schoolmaster, Abraham Holbrook, took advantage of the temporary
absence of the sentinel at the gun-house to remove
the guns from their carriages and hide them in the
schoolhouse, whence they were subsequently taken
in the night and conveyed to the American lines.
They were in actual service during the entire war,
and, while General Henry Knox was Secretary
of War, he had two of the pieces, then dubbed
" Hancock " and " Adams," suitably inscribed to
indicate their pedigree.   In the course of time, the
guns were taken to the chamber at the top of the
monument on Bunker Hill, where they remain unto
this day.

A further contribution to the history of the artillery company in which Knox received his first les-
sons in gun practice may be found in the records of
the Committee of Safety, which, in February, 1775,
instructed Dr. Joseph Warren, who was subsequently killed at the battle of Bunker Hill, to ascertain how many of Paddock's men " could be
depended upon to form an artillery company when
the Constitutional Army of the Province should take
the field, and that without loss of time."   The
answer to Warren's inquiry is not a matter of record,
but the rosters of the Army of the Revolution disclose the names of a large majority of Paddock's
militiamen.   As for Paddock, that worthy artillery-

man stayed in Boston, an active Tory, until its
evacuation by the royal troops, when he sailed with
them to Halifax. He was afterwards rewarded by
an appointment as Inspector of Artillery Stores,
with the rank of Captain, in the British Army.

Meanwhile, an offshoot from Paddock's company
was formed in 1772 by the organisation of another
militia troop, known as the " Boston Grenadier
Corps," commanded by Captain Joseph Peirce.
Knox, who was now twenty-two years old, was one
of the founders of the new organisation, and was
second in command to Peirce. The uniform of the
corps was unusually handsome, and the bearing of its
ranks on parade was the subject of universal praise.
Even the British officers were warm in praise of the
corps, the members of which were from five feet and
ten inches to six feet in height. We may be sure
that Knox, the second in command, who was of
lofty stature, and who, according to the local chronicle of the time, was " a splendid figure in uniform,"
attracted the admiring glances of many a fair maiden
besides those of Miss Lucy Flucker, who is reported
as having been more than ever enamoured of the
handsome and gallant young bookseller when she
beheld him clad in the glorious panoply of Mars, his
wounded hand " handsomely bound with a scarf,
which, of course, excited the sympathy of the
ladies."

Even in the midst of alarms, the love-making of
the pair went bravely on, notwithstanding the opposition of the aristocratic Tory family of Miss Lucy.
Knox was an acknowledged " rebel "; he had cast

in his fortunes with a cause which the Fluckers felt
to be doomed to certain loss and defeat; the young
swain was a tradesman, and an alliance with one of
plebeian origin and seditious inclinations was clearly
to be regarded as not only obnoxious to the family
but fraught with misery to the young lady. She
was told that there could be but one issue to the
impending conflict; the rebellious colonies would
be overwhelmed by the vast power of the Imperial
Government; and she would be eating the bitter
bread of poverty while her wiser sisters would be
riding in their coaches. It was all in vain. Miss
Lucy, now eighteen years of age, had a will of her
own, and, although soundly rated by her parents,
continued to maintain to Knox the tender relation
of promised bride. It is evident that this was a
"love match," and both parties thereto maintained
toward each other the most loving and affectionate
relations during their subsequent life. We shall see
that, even up to the time when old age might be
supposed to dim the flame of man's ardour, Knox
habitually addressed his wife in terms which suggest
the devoted lover rather than the busy man of affairs,
the well-ripened husband and father.

It would appear that the pair were so determined
in their resolve to wed that an elopement would have
taken place if the parents of Lucy had not finally
been induced to yield their reluctant consent to the
union which they conscientiously thought to be
likely to turn out an unfortunate one for their
daughter. At one time, correspondence by letter
between the youthful swain and his inamorata was

made so difficult that the young lovers were obliged to resort to the undutiful device of a secret correspondence. In one of his notes, dated Monday evening, March 7, 1774, Knox wrote:

"I wish the medium of our correspondence settled, in order to which I must endeavour to see you, when we will settle it. What news? Have you spoken to your father, or he to you, upon the subject? What appearance has this (to us) grand affair at your house at present? Do you go to the ball to-morrow evening? I am in a state of anxiety heretofore unknown. My only consolation is in you, and in order that it should be well grounded, permit me to beg two things of you with the greatest ardency: never distrust my affection for you without the most rational and convincing proof— if you do not hear from me in a reasonable time, do not lay it to my want of love, but want of opportunity; and do not, in consequence of such distrust, omit writing to me as often as possible. . . . Don't distrust the sincerity of your Fidelio."

Knox, imbued with the high-flown sentiment of the time, addresses his love as " Speria."

The inevitable sequel to all this courting (the age-yellowed missives of which survive—pathetic and tender evidence of the ardour of the lovers, long since turned to dust) may be found in the following announcement in Edes & Gill's *Gazette* of June 20, 1774:

"Last Thursday (the 16th) was married, by the Rev. Dr. Caner, Mr. Henry Knox of this town, to Miss Lucy Flucker, second daughter to the Hon. Thomas Flucker, Esq., Secretary of the Province."

After a common custom of the times, a friendly poetaster composed these epithalamic lines to accompany the formal announcement of the marriage:

" Blest tho' she is with ev'ry human grace,
   The mien engaging, and bewitching face,
   Yet still an higher beauty is her care,
   Virtue, the charm that most adorns the fair ;
   This does new graces to her air inspire,
   Gives to her lips their bloom, her eyes their fire ;
   This o'er her cheek with brighter tincture shows
   The lily's brightness and the blushing rose.
   O may each bliss the lovely pair surround,
   And each wing'd hour with new delights be crown'd !
   Long may they those exalted pleasures prove
   That spring from worth, from constancy and love."

The young pair at once began housekeeping, watched, doubtless, by the curious eyes of the bride's family, who were certain that poverty and disaster were in store for one who had so rashly ventured upon the uncertain sea of matrimony with a rebel and a tradesman. Lucy Flucker's only brother was a lieutenant in the British Army, and, while he was serving the cause of the King, his newly made brother-in-law was zealously studying the art of war and schooling himself for the service into which he was so soon to enter. Large promises were held out to young Knox to induce him to take a commission in the royal cause; he was regarded as too desirable a man to be lost from the military service of the King. The British officer who had observed with admiration the evolutions of the artillery company of which Knox was second in command, and had said that a country which produced such " boy soldiers " as he could not readily be brought under subjection, only gave voice to the sentiment that pervaded the ranks of the determined colonists. Knox was one of many well-equipped young men who waited for the signal to spring to the defence of the country's rights and serve in the field the cause of civil liberty. In due time the hour struck. The soldier was ready when the signal sounded.

CHAPTER II

THE BREAKING OF THE STORM

1775–1776

NOX'S business in Boston was in a fairly prosperous condition, notwithstanding the stormy aspect of the times. Although the sales of books fell off greatly in amount and importance, the profits of the stationery, printing, and binding departments of his trade must have been considerable. He was almost without a competitor in these lines of business. Paul Revere, the North End coppersmith and engraver, was one of a committee of young mechanics who cautiously patrolled the streets by night to watch and report to the patriots outside of the city all suspicious movements of the Royal Government and troops. Knox, as a well-known sympathiser with the rebellious colonists, was kept under surveillance, and was forbidden to leave Boston. Although there is no record of the fact, it is certain that he was actively engaged with others in watching the enemy and communicating with friends in the region roundabout; Cambridge,

Lexington, and Concord being then centres of "rebel" activity.

As the tension between the colonists and the royal authorities was increased, the towns collected their stores of powder, lead, and musketry. To intimidate the country and exercise his little army, Governor-General Gage sent out from Boston to Jamaica Plain, a village about four miles from Boston, five regiments of troops under the command of Lord Percy (afterwards Duke of Northumberland), the route selected being purposely circuitous, and covering about ten miles. It was expected that these troops would attack the magazines of the Massachusetts villages, and lively anticipations of fighting in earnest were entertained by the patriots both inside and outside of Boston. But the military diversion, for such it proved to be, came to an end without any collision of arms. Dr. Joseph Warren, of the Committee of Safety, sagely reported of Percy's expedition that it marched without baggage or artillery. "But," he adds, "had they attempted to destroy any magazines, or to abuse the people, not a man of them would have returned to Boston." The storm was ready to break. The lines were drawn closer and yet closer. For a time, the exodus from Boston of persons who identified themselves with the patriot cause had been rather encouraged than forbidden; only men who, like Knox, might add real value to the gathering force of the malcontents in the rural districts, were detained by special orders. Now, however, the Tories complained that the flight of "rebels" had become so formidable in numbers that there was danger that none but loyalists and the royal troops would be left in the town, and the destruction of the place would be attempted by the host outside. A positive prohibition of all migration from the town was accordingly issued by the Governor-General.

Percy's expedition of observation was undertaken on the 30th of March, 1775. On the 18th of April, Gage sent a force of eight hundred men to seize and destroy the military stores collected at Concord and Worcester. The order was to be executed with secrecy and celerity, the expedition setting forth in the night. How the surrounding country was warned of the approach of the redcoats has been celebrated in song and story. Paul Revere's midnight ride to rouse the people, as described in Longfellow's immortal lyric, was undertaken from Charlestown, in obedience to the signal of two lanterns swung in the belfry of the old North Church, one light being agreed as notice that the British had set forth by land, and two lights indicating that the route was by water. John Hancock and John Adams were housed in Lexington, and when Paul Revere, waking the captains of minute-men on his way, had told them of the impending crisis, he rode on to Concord to notify the patriots there assembled. Falling in with Dr. Prescott, who was destined to play an important part in the military drama then opening, Revere swept on his way. He was surrounded by a party of British officers, taken prisoner, and carried back to Lexington, where he arrived only a little while before the column of troops whose approach he had signalled came upon the scene. Prescott escaped and rode on, accompanied by William Dawes, to rouse the countryside, which was speedily in arms. At last "the shot heard round the world" was fired. The long, long struggle was begun.

The march of the minute-men began that night, and before the 20th of the month arrived, the towns of Massachusetts, Rhode Island, Connecticut, and New Hampshire had concentrated at Cambridge a little army of resolute and determined men. On the 19th of April, just one year after his marriage, Knox, unable longer to tarry in Boston inactive while his brother patriots were in arms and eager for the fray, secretly left the town, accompanied by his wife. His departure was undertaken in the night, special interdiction on his movements having been laid by Gage. Generous offers had been made to him to induce him to take service in the royal forces. But, turning his back upon all such blandishments, he made his way directly to the colonial headquarters at Cambridge. The sword which he had worn in the militia service went with the young pair, cunningly secreted in the quilted lining of Mrs. Knox's cloak. With this weapon alone was the young soldier to carve out his fortunes. For better or for worse, he was now with the defenders of the patriot cause.

Repairing to the headquarters of General Artemas Ward, who was then in command of the "rebel" troops about Boston, Knox offered his services as a volunteer, declining any special commission.

Virtually, the siege of Boston now began, and Knox, whose studies in military science and engineering were now made available for the good cause, planned and superintended a line of fortifications round the town. But, while the movements which finally culminated in the battle of Bunker Hill were in progress, he was occupied in reconnoitring services in the vicinity of Charlestown. It was upon his reports that the orders of General Ward were subsequently issued. After the battle of Bunker Hill, hostilities having now begun in earnest, Mrs. Knox was taken to Worcester, the better to escape the perils and dangers of a residence near the scene of hostile action around Boston. It was at this time that Knox's talents as an engineer and artillerist were called into active requisition. Skilled engineers were greatly in demand in the patriot army, and Knox, who appears never to have ceased his study of the military science most requisite to his purposes and the needs of his country, was clearly the master spirit in the execution of the formidable works that now began to surround the beleaguered town of Boston. The most important of these was a fort on Roxbury Neck, known as Roxbury Fort, commanding the sole land exit from the besieged town.

Even while the smoke of the battle of Bunker Hill was rising on that hot 17th of June, 1775, the Continental Congress, assembled in Philadelphia, unwitting of the tremendous events that were happening in the North, appointed George Washington, of Virginia, to be General and Commander-in-chief of the armies raised for the maintenance and defence of American liberty. At the same time, Artemas Ward, of Massachusetts, was appointed to be first Major-General under Washington; Horatio Gates, of Virginia, was appointed Washington's Adjutant-General, with the rank of Brigadier-General; and Charles Lee, an English half-pay officer, was made second Major-General. Before the month ended, the list of general officers was filled out by the appointment of Philip Schuyler and Israel Putnam to be Major-Generals, and Seth Pomeroy, Richard Montgomery, David Wooster, William Heath, Joseph Spencer, John Thomas, John Sullivan, and Nathanael Greene as Brigadier-Generals.

Knox still remained in the volunteer service—a volunteer in the very strictest sense of the word, desiring and seeking no commission. Immediately after his arrival at Cambridge, where he took command of the army, Washington made an inspection of the works erected about the beleaguered town of Boston, and extracts from Knox's letters, written at that time, indicate the admiration with which the new commander viewed the fortifications in the construction of which Knox had so important a share. Writing to his wife under date of " Roxbury (Lemuel Child's), Thursday morning, 6 o'clock, July 6, 1775," Knox says:

"Yesterday, as I was going to Cambridge, I met the generals, [Washington and Lee] who begged me to return to Roxbury again, which I did. When they had viewed the works, they expressed the greatest pleasure and surprise at their situation and apparent utility, to say nothing of the plan, which did not escape their praise."

STATUE OF ISRAEL PUTNAM.

J. Q. A. WARD, SCULPTOR.

In a later letter, Knox expresses his pleasure at beholding the " ease and dignity " with which Washington filled his exalted station as Commander-in-chief; and he incidentally mentions that he has an important appointment to keep with the General. Writing under date of July 11th, Knox refers to a foray which " our people " had lately made upon Boston Neck; and he adds that the British regulars were in such a state of trepidation that it was likely that seven hundred and fifty men could have then taken full possession of the town. He adds: " The new generals are of infinite service in the army. They have to reduce order from almost perfect chaos. I think they are in a fair way of doing it. Our army still ' affect to hold the army besieged '; and will effectually continue to do so." The phrase " affect to hold the army besieged," in this note, is a quotation from an angry proclamation issued by General Gage, June 12, 1775, which caused much merriment in the American camp.

Writing to his brother William, who still remained in Boston, September 25, 1775, Knox says:

" Last Friday, Lucy [Mrs. Knox] dined at General Washington's. Last Saturday, let it be remembered to the honour and skill of the British troops, they fired 104 cannon-shot at our works, at not a greater distance than half pointblank shot,—and did what? Why, scratched a man's face with the splinters of a rail-fence ! I have had the pleasure of dodging these heretofore engines of terror with great success ; nor am I afraid they will hit me, unless directed by the hand of Providence."

Writing to Governor Trumbull, of Connecticut, November 2, 1775, Washington complains of the lack of trained officers in the engineer corps, and says: " Most of the works thrown up for the defence of our several encampments have been planned by a few of the principal officers of the army, assisted by Mr. Knox, a gentleman of Worcester." And on the 8th of the same month, the Commander-in-chief wrote to the President of the Continental Congress, as follows:

" The council of officers are unanimously of opinion that the command of the artillery should no longer continue in Colonel Gridley ; and, knowing no person better qualified to supply his place, or whose appointment will give more general satisfaction, I have taken the liberty of recommending Henry Knox to the consideration of Congress."

Richard Gridley, formerly a captain in the Paddock artillery organisation, was a veteran of the French and Indian war, but was now, by reason of age and infirmities, incapacitated for further active service. Next in rank to Gridley was David Mason, who offered to serve as lieutenant-colonel of Washington's artillery if Henry Knox might be commissioned colonel. A number of active and meritorious officers in the artillery generously united with Mason in urging the appointment of Knox as colonel. He was accordingly appointed, and his commission, dated November 17, 1775, reached him some time later, when he had returned from an arduous expedition to Fort Ticonderoga.

In these later days of strict military discipline and schooling, it seems singular that a man who had never had the advantages of a military education should have been selected for the trying post of chief of the artillery of the army. The Boston bookseller suddenly became, not only a colonel, but the head of an arm of the service requiring the most thorough and practical knowledge of military science. The wisdom of Washington's appointments was justified by the after-experience of the men whom he selected for important positions. In the case of Knox, it may be said, his appointment proved to be one of profound wisdom.

The force under Knox's immediate command, however, was not very large. According to a return made in November, 1776, his regiment consisted of twelve companies with 635 men on the rolls. The field officers were Henry Knox, Colonel; William Burbeck, first Lieutenant-Colonel ; David Mason, second Lieutenant - Colonel ; John Crane, first Major; John Lamb, second Major. All these, made subsequently, gave a good account of themselves.

John Adams, who had known Knox in Boston as a young man who had attracted his attention by " his pleasing manners and inquisitive turn of mind," was so gratified by Knox's determination to take an active part in the war as a commissioned officer, that he wrote to him from Philadelphia, under date of November 11, 1775, as follows:

"I had the pleasure of a letter from you a few days ago, and was rejoiced to learn that you have at last determined to take a more important share than you have done hitherto in the conduct of our military matters. I have been impressed with an opinion of your knowledge and abilities in the military way for several years, and of late have endeavoured, both at camp, at Watertown, and at

Philadelphia, by mentioning your name and character, to make you more known, and consequently in a better way for promotion.

" It was a sincere opinion of your merit and qualifications which prompted me to act this part, and therefore I am very happy to be able to inform you that I believe you will very soon be provided for according to your wishes ; at least, you may depend upon this, that nothing in my power shall be wanting to effect it. It is of vast importance, my dear sir, that I should be minutely informed of everything which passes at the camp while I hold a place in the great Council of America ; and therefore I must beg the favour of you to write me as often as you can by safe conveyances. I want to know the name, rank, and character of every officer in the army ; but more especially of every officer who is best acquainted with the theory and practice of fortification and gunnery. What is comprehended within the term of Engineer ? and whether it includes skill both in fortifications and gunnery ; and what skilful engineers have you in the army ; and whether any of them, and who, have seen service, and when and where ?

" I want to know if there is a complete set of books upon the military art in all its branches in the library of Harvard College, and what books are the best upon those subjects."

This interesting letter from Adams marks the beginning of a long and intimate friendship and correspondence between the two patriots. In later years, as we shall see, John Adams reposed in the discretion of Knox the most complete and unwavering confidence; and his confidence was united to an esteem that never once halted during the trying times of the Revolution and the formative period that succeeded the armed struggle. From this period, too, dates the lifelong and affectionate friendship that bound together Knox and Washington. We should bear in mind that although Washington, the Virginian aristocrat, had at once been taken into the affection of the people of New England, the traditions of the social caste to which he had belonged were not likely to incline him unquestioningly to intimacy with one who, like Knox, had been born and bred a tradesman, no matter what his military merit might promise for him.   But the fact remains historical that Henry Knox won the affection of Washington as no other man (if we may possibly exclude Alexander Hamilton) ever did.   The letters that passed between Washington and Knox, from this time forth, breathe a spirit of sincere devotion that is not common among men.   If " the cold heart of Washington," of which some historians make mention, had no warm place for any others, it is certain that the two patriots to whom allusion has just been made were very dear to the Commander-in-chief. There must have been something fine and grand in the character of Henry Knox that inspired so exalted an admiration and so deep an affection as that in which Washington held Knox.

Just here we may anticipate the chronology of our story to quote a pleasant passage from a letter written by Miss Dorothy Dudley, at Cambridge, April 19, 1776, to her friend Miss Esther Livingstone.   Describing in her piquant way the military celebrities then assembled in Cambridge, the writer says of Gen. Nathanael Greene *:

" He is rather a large man, with a face indicating fire and firmness, tempered by the innate goodness which looks out of his clear, quiet eyes.   General Harry Knox is his most intimate and trusted friend. The two were almost constantly together in the days when both

---

* From *Cambridge in 1776*, compiled by D. G. Haskins, Jr., and others.

were studying the art of war, and Mr. Knox kept a book-store on Cornhill. He, like his friend, is the soul of honour, and possessed of a manly heart brimming with benevolence."

The siege of Boston had now (November, 1775) begun in earnest. But the need of siege-guns was severely felt by the patriot army, and men began to cast about in their minds for some means to procure guns of sufficient weight and range to throw shot into the beleaguered town. The fertile and inventive mind of Knox conceived the daring enterprise of sending to Fort Ticonderoga, on Lake Champlain, not far from the Canadian frontier, to drag thence the supply of ordnance captured by Ethan Allen and then lying there unused. Knox's plan was submitted to Washington, who, after careful scrutiny, gave his approval to the difficult and hazardous undertaking. Cannon must be had or the siege would be indefinitely prolonged, if not ultimately abandoned. Knox's plan was to make the journey to Fort Ticonderoga while the snow and ice combined to render streams passable and roads feasible for sleds and sleighs. In open water, he urged, boats could be employed, and the total expense of the expedition on which so much depended, and which could be successfully carried out, need not be more than one thousand dollars. This sum was fixed as the limit of immediate and needful expenditure; but in one of Knox's account-books we find this brief and comprehensive entry: " For expenditures in a journey from the camp round Boston to New York, Albany, and Ticonderoga, and from thence, with 55 pieces of iron and brass ordnance, 1

THE JUMEL MANSION, WASHINGTON HEIGHTS, NEW YORK.

barrel of flints, and 23 boxes of lead, back to camp (including expenses of self, brother, and servant), £520.15.8¾.'' In his final instructions to Knox, Washington said that the want of cannon was so great that '' no trouble or expense must be spared to obtain them.''

Knox was accompanied on his long and difficult journey by his brother William, then about nineteen years old. The lad, who had been left in charge of his brother's business in Boston, had made his escape to the insurgent lines, the shop and stock in trade of the bookseller on Cornhill having been looted by the British and Tory residents. He was to return to the wreck sooner than he probably thought.

Gen. Philip Schuyler, of New York, had been instructed by Washington to render to Knox every possible assistance in his expedition to Ticonderoga; and when Knox, after securing sundry small stores of ordnance in the city of New York, wrote to his wife that he was thankful to leave so '' expensive '' a city, he made his way to Albany, where Schuyler was then living. From New York Knox wrote to Washington recommending that an establishment for the casting of brass and iron cannon be fixed there, '' where it could be expeditiously and cheaply done.'' He reached Albany December 1, and was cheered on his way by General Schuyler, who rendered great assistance then and afterwards in the way of securing transportation. The winter was severe, the roads unbroken, and the snows deep. Oxen in large numbers were necessary for the hauling of the cannon and these animals were secured at considerable trouble in the thinly inhabited regions through which Knox travelled.

He reached Ticonderoga on the 5th of December, and, at once collecting the coveted ordnance, began his homeward journey. His inventory of the arms shows that he took away eight brass mortars, six iron mortars, one howitzer, thirteen brass cannon, thirty iron cannon, a barrel of flints, and a quantity of lead. The heaviest of the artillery were brass 18- and 24-pounders, and iron 12- and 18-pounders; truly a noble acquisition for the expectant besiegers of Boston. A letter from Knox to Washington, dated at Fort George, December 17th, gives us a vivid picture of some of the difficulties encountered on the homeward trip. He says:

" I returned to this place on the 15th, and brought with me the cannon, it being nearly the time I computed it would take us to transport them here. It is not easy to conceive the difficulties we have had in transporting them across the lake, owing to the advanced season of the year and contrary winds ; but the danger is now past. Three days ago it was very uncertain whether we should have gotten them until next spring, but now, please God, they must go. I have had made 42 exceeding strong sleds, and have provided 80 yoke of oxen to drag them as far as Springfield, where I shall get fresh cattle to carry them to camp. The route will be from here to Kinderhook [New York], from thence to Great Barrington [Mass.], and down to Springfield. I have sent for the sleds and teams to come here, and expect to move them to Saratoga on Wednesday or Thursday next, trusting that between this and then we shall have a fine fall of snow, which will enable us to proceed farther, and make the carriage easy. If that shall be the case, I hope in sixteen or seventeen days' time to be able to present to your Excellency a noble train of artillery."

One of the difficulties encountered on the way to

Albany from Fort Ticonderoga was the necessity of ferrying the heavy cannon across pieces of open water. This was accomplished by means of " gondolas," as the flat-bottomed scows then in use were called. The modern " gundalow " of the New England coast is the scow that has derived its name from the sweep-propelled craft of Venice. Knox's hindrances are further hinted at in a letter which he wrote to Washington from Albany, January 5, 1776, as follows:

" I was in hopes that we should have been able to have the cannon at Cambridge by this time. The want of snow detained us for some days, and now a cruel thaw hinders from crossing the Hudson River, which we are obliged to do four times from Lake George to this town. The first severe night will make the ice sufficiently strong; till that happens, the cannon and mortars must remain where they are. These inevitable delays pain me exceedingly, as my mind is fully sensible of the importance of the greatest expedition in this case."

The route of this novel expedition, it will be seen, lay over the Green Mountains and the wild passes of that range and down through the hill country of New England, by " roads that never bore a cannon before and have never borne one since." On his way up to Ticonderoga from Albany, Knox passed a stormy night sleeping on the floor of a rude log-cabin which served as a wayside inn for chance travellers through that sparsely populated region. His bedfellow was Lieut. John André, who had been taken prisoner by Gen. Richard Montgomery at St. John's, and was now on his way to Lancaster, Pennsylvania, to await an exchange.

It was a strange chance that brought together these
two men under the same blankets in a remote cabin
in the wilderness. Years later, Henry Knox was to
serve on the military tribunal which sentenced
André to the ignominious death of a spy. Now, all
unconscious of what Fate had in store for them,
they passed the greater part of the night in conversation. Between the two men there were many
points of resemblance. Says a biographer * of
André:

> "Their ages were alike; they had each renounced the pursuits
> of trade for the profession of arms, each had made a study of his
> new occupation, and neither was devoid of literary tastes and habits.
> Much of the night was consumed in pleasing conversation on topics
> that were rarely, perhaps, broached in such circumstances; and the
> intelligence and refinement displayed by André, in the discussion of
> subjects that were equally interesting to Knox, left an impression on
> the mind of the latter that was never obliterated. The respective
> condition of the bedfellows was not mutually communicated till the
> ensuing morning when they were about to part; and when Knox, a
> few years later, was called on to join in the condemnation to death
> of the companion whose society was so pleasant to him on this occa-
> sion, the memory of their intercourse gave additional bitterness to
> his painful duty."

From Albany, under date of January 5, 1776,
Knox wrote to his wife a lively and entertaining
narrative of his return journey up to that point.
After a brief account of his adventures amidst ice,
snow, forests, and blind roads, he makes this digres-
sion:

> "A little about my travels. New York is a place where I think
> in general the houses are better built than they are in Boston. They

* Winthrop Sargent, *Life and Career of Major John André*.

are generally of brick, and three stories high, with the largest kind of windows. Their churches are grand ; their college, workhouse, and hospitals most excellently situated, and also exceedingly commodious ; their principal streets are much wider than ours. The people,—why, the people are magnificent : in their equipages, which are numerous ; in their house furniture, which is fine ; in their pride and conceit, which is inimitable ; in their profaneness, which is intolerable ; in the want of principle, which is prevalent ; in their Toryism, which is insufferable, and for which they must repent in dust and ashes. The country from New York to this place [Albany] is not very populous,—not the fifth part so much so as in New England, and with much greater marks of poverty than there. The people of this city, of which there are five thousand or six thousand, are, I believe, honest enough, and many of them sensible people,— much more so than any part of the government which I 've seen. There are four very good buildings for public worship, the remains of capital barracks, hospital, and fort, which must in their day have been very clever.

" Albany, from its situation, and commanding the trade of the water and the immense territories westward, must one day be, if not the capital, yet nearly to it, of America. There are a number of gentlemen's very elegant seats in view from that part of the river before the town ; among them I think General Schuyler's claims the preference, the owner of which is sensible and polite, and I think has behaved with vast propriety to the British officers who, by the course of war, have fallen into our hands. Certain of them set out for Pennsylvania yesterday, among whom was General Prescott, who by all accounts behaved exceedingly ill to Colonel Allen of ours, who was taken at Montreal. Here also is Major Gamble, who wrote the letters from Quebec which were published last summer. There are in all about sixty commissioned officers, besides about twenty of the Canadian noblesse, who appeared as lively and happy as if nothing had happened. One or two of the officers I pitied, the others seemed concerned, but not humbled. The women and children suffer amazingly at this advanced season of the year. It is now past twelve o'clock, therefore I wish you a good night's repose, and I will mention you in my prayers."

All of Knox's letters to his wife breathe the sincerest and most affectionate devotion of the married lover. One of his letters, written while on this arduous journey, begins in this fashion:

" MY LOVELY AND DEAREST FRIEND :—Those people who love as you and I do never ought to part. It is with the greatest anxiety that I am forc'd to date my letter at this distance from my love, and at a time too when I thought to be happily in her arms."

We may be sure that the arrival of Knox in camp, with the " noble train of artillery " which he had promised to Washington, was hailed with prodigious acclaim. From that moment the speedy end of the British occupation of Boston was determined. Gage had been recalled to England in August of the previous year, virtually in disgrace, and his departure from Boston in the following October was regarded by the patriots in the light of a victory over a man whom they most cordially hated. General Howe was now in command, and the British army of occupation was harassed by sea and land. A little navy had been improvised by the New England colonies, and a series of reprisals had taken place between the American privateersmen and the British men-of-war. The burning of the open and unprotected town of Falmouth (now Portland), Maine, by the infamous Captain Mowatt, had convinced the patriots of other parts of the colonies that although contumacious Boston was to be severely punished for its stubborn resistance to the royal mandates, war was to be carried into every part of the colonies on the continent. The first naval battle of the war, as it is usually called, took place near Machias, Maine, in the summer of 1775, when John Knight, afterwards an admiral in the British navy, and several other officers,

were taken prisoners and sent to Washington's
headquarters at Cambridge. While Knox was on
his memorable expedition to Fort Ticonderoga, the
patriots captured the British brigantine *Nancy*,
bound to Boston from London, with military stores,
among which were two thousand muskets, one hundred and five thousand flints, thirty-one tons of
musket-shot, three thousand round shot for 12-
pounders and four thousand for 6-pounders. Guns
of this calibre were in the train brought to camp by
Knox.

General Ward was placed in command of a movement upon Dorchester Heights, commanding the
harbour of Boston, which was determined upon now
that the supply of artillery was so amply reinforced
that the line of circumvallation around the doomed
town was well-nigh complete. The immediate
charge of details was intrusted to General Thomas,
and, a formidable breastwork having been thrown
up, a vigorous cannonading opened from the American works to the north of the town, on the night of
March 2, 1776, and was continued during the next
two ensuing days. The ground was frozen, and four
hundred yoke of oxen, under cover of the night,
drew the ordnance and stores needed for the new
batteries, passing unheeded amidst the din, with the
British sentries on Boston Neck, scarcely a mile
away.

The British were utterly confounded when, by the
light of early morning, they found the harbour and all
of the southern part of Boston lying under the "rebel"
guns on the heights of Dorchester. Evacuation

was forced upon Howe, and, after using indirect and irregular means of communicating to his besiegers his intention to leave the place which had been made too hot to hold him, he embarked his troops, nearly nine thousand, all told, and sailed away to Halifax. He took with him eleven hundred loyalists, or Tories, who had been subjected to persecutions from their neighbours and who fled from the greater wrath to come. Most of these made homes for themselves in Nova Scotia and New Brunswick; others eventually returned to England. Among these latter were the Flucker family. But Secretary Flucker long after drew his salary as a royal functionary of the province from which he was a fugitive. In a letter written by his daughter Lucy (Mrs. Knox) to her husband, in July, 1777, the dutiful wife but rebellious daughter says: " By a letter from Mrs. Tyng to Aunt Waldo, we learn that papa enjoys his £300 a year as secretary of the province. Droll, is it not ? "

Howe's evacuation of Boston took place on the morning of Sunday, March 17, 1776. At the head of his army, Washington entered the town by the long street that passes down " the Neck," an avenue which now bears the name of the great commander whose strategy and prowess had freed the town from its invader. Howe's troops had been sorely distressed during their long confinement in the besieged town. Even fuel was scarce; several churches had been used for secular purposes, and the old North Church, from whose belfry had been shown the signal lights of Paul Revere, had been taken down

and used for firewood.   Knox rode with the army
into the town of his birth, and we are led to believe
that his brother William then returned to Boston
and endeavoured to gather up some of the remnants
of the ruined business on Cornhill.   At any rate, the
letters passing between the two brothers from this
time forward indicate William's residence in Boston.

Great was the rejoicing of the colonists, from New
England to Georgia, over the wonderful news that
the British had been driven out of Boston.   But
even most of the colonists did not know how imminent was the danger, up to a very late period of the
siege, that lack of ammunition and a demoralisation
of the patriot troops would compel an abandonment
of the operations around Boston.   Knox's letters
disclose the fact that there was a great scarcity of
powder, and that the disposition of some of the
troops, whose time of enlistment had expired, or
was about to expire, was little short of mutinous.
But all this was forgotten in the contemplation of
the signal victory which had been achieved over the
enemy.   The " Union Flag," as Washington called
the standard first hoisted at Cambridge, January 2,
1776, now floated over the forts and public buildings
of Boston and its harbour.

The first medal in the numismatic history of the
American colonies was ordered by Congress to be
struck in honour of Washington's victory.   It was of
gold and bore upon its face a representation of
Washington and his generals watching from Dorchester Heights the exit of the British fleet; American troops and ordnance are in the middle distance

below; and the proud motto of " HOSTIBUS PRIMO
FUGATIS " is engraved over the scene. The date
beneath is "Bostonium Recuperatum, XVII.
Martii, MDCCLXXVI." Knox's share in this
famous victory was duly celebrated, some years
later, in a poem descriptive of the war, written by
Mrs. Sarah Morton. These are some of the lady's
lofty lines:

> " And now the strong Artillery claims its birth,
> Terrific guardian of the trembling earth,
> With voice of vengeance, and tremendous breath,
> That wake the fiends of ruin, flight, and death :—
> What daring arm directs its dangerous way !
> What Chief beloved, ye brave Columbians, say !—
> 'T is thine, intrepid Knox, on Glory's car
> To shield the ranks, and guide the vollied war,
> And thine the clime of Freedom's early boast,
> Where the cold isthmus joins the stormy coast ;—
> What time thy much-enduring country draws
> Thy active valour to her suffering cause,
> Warmed at her call, in winter's dreary reign
> Thy hardy step explored the northern plain ;—
> I see thee dauntless tread the trackless way,
> Where frowning forests quench the glimmering day,
> Through the bleak wild, and up boreal steeps
> Where, wrapped in frost, the stilled artillery sleeps,
> I see that arm its ponderous weight prepare
> And call its thunder to the distant war."

CHAPTER III

MILITARY OPERATIONS AROUND NEW YORK

1776

HE scene of active operations was now transferred to New York and New Jersey. Since the autumn of 1775, it had become known that it was the intention of the British Government to seize New York and the Hudson River. While a large part of Lord Howe's fleet proceeded to Halifax to refit and recruit after the evacuation of Boston, the naval vessels were detained in the outer harbour to notify incoming English craft of the abandonment of Boston by the British forces. It was confidently and reasonably expected that a descent upon Long Island and New York Harbour would now be made, and Washington at once despatched General Charles Lee to take command of all forces available to withstand the anticipated invasion, and to fortify the place.

Intense excitement had pervaded the city of New York when the news of the evacuation of Boston reached there. "The Sons of Liberty," as the

4

more active of the patriot volunteers were called, had already begun to harass the small British force then lying in the city, the tidings from Concord and Lexington having roused them to a fever heat. Isaac Sears and John Lamb, two of the leaders of these devoted patriots, had made themselves specially obnoxious to the Tories, the first named of these having headed a band of one hundred men who, riding in from New Haven, Conn., trotted down Broadway and wrecked the printing-office of Rivington, the Tory printer, to whose correspondence with Henry Knox we have already had occasion to refer. Rivington's type was carefully saved and moulded into bullets for future use. So great was the disorder and tumult that Tryon, the royal Governor, fled to one of the English men-of-war lying in the harbour.

While the little army that had been occupied in the siege of Boston was being hurried to New York, Knox was ordered to Connecticut and Rhode Island to lay out fortifications for points along the coast that had been already molested or threatened by the enemy. His wife accompanied him a part of the way and was afterwards sent to Norwich and subsequently to Fairfield, for safety; a child, Lucy Flucker, had been born to the young couple, and was now with its mother in Connecticut. Meanwhile, the ill-starred American expedition to Quebec had been undertaken; it was abandoned in the early summer, but not until the gallant General Thomas had lost his life by smallpox and General Richard Montgomery had been killed in battle.

Writing to Washington from Norwich, Conn., under date of April 21, 1776, Knox says:

" In passing through Providence, Governor Cooke and a number of principal people were very pressing for me to take Newport in my way, in order to mark out some works of defence for that place. The spirited conduct of the colony troops posted there, in driving away the king's ships, alarmed the whole colony for the safety of its capital. Knowing your Excellency's anxiety for the preservation of every part of the continent, I conceived it to be my duty to act in conformity to their wishes, especially as I could get to Norwich as soon as the stores that set out on the 14th. Accordingly, I went to Newport, and marked out five batteries, which, from the advantageous situation of the ground, must, when executed, render the harbour exceedingly secure.

" Lieutenant-Colonel Burbeck declined complying with your Excellency's orders, alleging that the province had settled on him four shillings sterling per day during life, after the war was over, which, if he went out of the province, he might perhaps lose. Lieutenant-Colonel Mason, who came with the ordnance to this town, being in ill-health, I have permitted to go by land."

William Burbeck, it will be remembered, was chosen first Lieutenant-Colonel of Knox's artillery regiment at the time of Knox's appointment. David Mason, who now succeeded Burbeck, had been second Lieutenant-Colonel. Burbeck's demur, which so much resembles the protests of modern militia officers who decline to pass beyond the borders of their respective States when called by national authority, threw him out of Washington's army. He never rejoined Knox's regiment, but remained in the employment of Massachusetts, being in command of Castle William, Boston Harbour, for many years. He died in Boston, July 22, 1785. Knox proceeded on his way to New York, and

wrote to Washington from New London, Conn.,
April 24, 1776, as follows:

" In consequence of your Excellency's directions, I am employed
in looking at and getting the necessary information respecting the
harbour, in which I shall spare no pains.   I mentioned to your Excellency Newport harbour, which, in conjunction with this, will,
when fortified, afford a safe retreat to the American navy and their
prizes in any wind that blows.   They are equally convenient for
ships coming from sea ; and if the wind is not fair to go into one
harbour, they may go into the other.   The artillery and stores are
all embarked [for New York] together with the remaining company
of my regiment, and have been waiting for a fair wind two days.

" Admiral Hopkins is still in this harbour, and I believe he will
be obliged to continue here for some time.   He has this day received
intelligence that four ships and two brigs are off Montauk Point and
Rhode Island, stationed in such a manner that but one appears at a
time and each is able to come up to the assistance of the others.
The captain of the *Cerberus* was on Block Island yesterday, and
told a man there that he was waiting for Admiral Hopkins, and
expected in four days to be joined by Captain Wallace and his
squadron."

Admiral Hopkins, to whom Knox refers in this
letter, was the famous Esek of that ilk.   Made
commander-in-chief of the fleet organised under the
orders of the Continental Congress, he now nominally ranked as Admiral.   In a letter to his wife,
written from New London, at this time, Knox gives
this bit of description:

" I have been on board Admiral Hopkins's ship, and in company
with his gallant son, who was wounded in the engagement with the
Glasgow.   The Admiral is an antiquated figure.   He brought to my
mind Van Tromp, the famous Dutch admiral.   Though antiquated
in figure, he is shrewd and sensible.   I, whom you think not a little
enthusiastic, should have taken him for an angel, only he swore now
and then."

There were many points of resemblance between Knox and Hopkins; both were men of pluck and energy, and both were born fighters. But Hopkins early came to grief and was dismissed from the service.

The forces under Washington's command with which he was to protect New York and its immediate environs consisted of about ten thousand men of all branches of the service. These were scattered all along the south shore of Long Island, Brooklyn Heights, Governor's Island, and Harlem on the one side of the city, and as far north as Fort Washington on the New York side of the Hudson, and Fort Lee on the Jersey side of that stream. Most of the cannon were old, honeycombed, and defective. On the 10th of June, 1776, Knox's report to Washington showed that he had fit for action one hundred and twenty-one cannon, both light and heavy, requiring for their service twelve hundred men. His regiment, present and fit for duty, numbered five hundred and twenty, officers and men; and he recommended that a draft be ordered to raise the regiment to its required numerical strength.

Congress had divided the military district of the Atlantic seaboard into two military departments, General Charles Lee being ordered to the command of the southern department, and Lord Stirling left in the north to carry out the plans so ably mapped out by his predecessor.

Lord Stirling, whose fortunes were to be so closely identified with those of Knox and other American patriots, and who served with them until

the close of the war, was a native of New York, his
family name being William Alexander. His title
was claimed by him through his Scotch descent, an
earldom being his by lineal right. Among the other
famous men with whom Knox was now associated
in the defence of New York was Alexander Hamilton, not yet twenty years old. He was captain of a
local artillery company, and he subsequently distinguished himself by covering the retreat of the
American army to Harlem Heights after the battle
of Long Island, and by his masterly activity in the
construction of the works at that point. He was
subsequently appointed aide and private secretary
to Washington, with the rank of Lieutenant-Colonel.
Of the Major-Generals commanding was Israel Putnam, who had left his plough in the furrow on his
farm in Pomfret, Conn., when tidings of the fight
at Lexington had reached him, and had taken a
leading part in the battle of Bunker Hill. He was
appointed a Brigadier-General by the government of
Connecticut, in April, 1775, and was made a Major-
General by the Continental Congress, June 17, 1775.
Major-General Heath had for his brigadiers Thomas
Mifflin and George Clinton, the last named of whom
had served in Canada and was subsequently Governor
of the State of New York, and Vice-President of the
United States. Major-General Spencer's brigadiers
were S. H. Parsons and James Wadsworth. Lord
Stirling and Alexander McDougall were brigadiers
under Major-General Sullivan, and Brigadier-Gen-
erals Nix and Heard were next in command to
Major-General Greene. The restless and ambitious

ALEXANDER HAMILTON

Aaron Burr had at first attached himself to the military family of Washington, but a mutual dislike having sprung up between the two, Burr withdrew and joined the staff of General Putnam, whom he served as aide for four years, with the rank of Lieutenant-Colonel. What varied fortunes were to befall most of the men whose names have here been cursorily mentioned as marshalled on the feeble line of New York's defences!

Lee's plans for the defence of the Hudson and the East River were considerably enlarged. A line of sunken hulks was set in the channel between Governor's Island and the Battery, and similar obstructions were laid across the river from Fort Washington (at what is now the foot of 183d Street) to Fort Lee, on the Jersey side of the river.

On the 25th of June, the long-expected arrival of the enemy actually took place, Lord Howe coming first in advance of his Boston army, then on its way from Halifax. He was followed by his brother, Admiral Howe, with troops from England; and next came the Hessian mercenaries, eight thousand in number, under General De Heister. When the Boston army had arrived in the bay, Howe's total command numbered about thirty-two thousand men, of whom not quite twenty-five thousand were reported fit for duty. The Hessians, however, did not arrive until the middle of August, although they are included in the above statement of General Howe's forces. At the lowest estimate, Howe's forces outnumbered those of Washington by at least six thousand men.

Learning that the Americans were strongly entrenched on Long Island, Howe landed on Staten
Island, where he was warmly welcomed by Governor
Tryon, who had so long been a fugitive from the
capital city of the province over which he had been
set to govern.   For a time there was a lull before
the storm that was so soon to break; but even this
deceptive tranquillity was occasionally disturbed by
false alarms.   It was momentarily expected that the
enemy would make a descent upon the city or upon
the south shore of Long Island, and the Narrows
were watched with feverish anxiety by the expectant patriots along the shores above.   During the
final preparations for resisting the invader, Knox had
permitted his wife to join him at his headquarters,
which were at the point now known as No. 1 Broadway.   Here they passed such hours of affectionate
intercourse as Knox could snatch from his arduous
duties.   A letter from Knox to his brother William,
then in Boston, dated July 11, 1776, describes one
of the panics that overtook the residents of New
York, in consequence of which Mrs. Knox was sent
post-haste to Connecticut:

"DEAR BILLY,—I received your affectionate letter by the post,
for which I thank you.   In consequence of a false report, my Lucy
and her babe are at Stamford, or Fairfield, where she writes me that
she is very unhappy, and wants to return here again, which would
make me as unhappy in contemplating the idea which you had of her
flight, as if it were real.   Indeed, the circumstances of our parting
were extremely disagreeable.   She had, contrary to my opinion,
stayed too long.   From the hall window, where we usually break-
fasted, we saw the ships coming through the Narrows, with a fair
wind and rapid tide, which would have brought them up to the city

in about half an hour. You can scarcely conceive the distress and anxiety that she then had. The city in an uproar, the alarm guns firing, the troops repairing to their posts, and everything in the height of bustle ; I not at liberty to attend her, as my country called the loudest. My God, may I never experience the like feelings again ! They were too much ; but I found a way to disguise them, for I scolded like a fury at her for not having gone before."

Mrs. Knox, we shall see, followed the General into even more critical phases of his military life than this. It was difficult for her to remain long away from her beloved husband. Another alarm in the city was caused, a few days later, by the manœuvres of a portion of the English fleet. As if to assure his wife that her presence in New York would be to her and to him a cause of constant apprehension, Knox wrote to her this account of the panic of July 12th:

" I thank heaven you were not here yesterday. Two ships and three tenders of the enemy, about twenty minutes past three, weighed anchor, and in twenty-five minutes were before the town. We had a loud cannonade, but could not stop them, though I believe we damaged them much. They kept over on the Jersey side too far from our batteries. I was so unfortunate as to lose six men by accidents, and a number wounded. This affair will be of service to my people ; it will teach them to moderate their fiery courage."

Lord Howe was willing, if possible, to stop the war here and avoid the further shedding of blood; and he essayed various expedients to open communication with General Washington for the purpose of ascertaining the basis upon which peace could be negotiated. But the Continental Congress had made its solemn declaration of the independence of the United States, and there was no authority on this side of the Atlantic to concede that independence as a basis of terms of peace. In a letter to his wife, dated at New York, July 15, 1776, Knox thus relates one of the famous historic incidents in which he had part:

" Lord Howe yesterday sent a flag of truce up to the city. They came within about four miles of the city, and were met by some of Colonel Tupper's people, who detained them until his Excellency's pleasure should be known. Accordingly, Colonel Reed and myself went down in the barge to receive the message. When we came to them, the officer, who was, I believe, captain of the *Eagle* man-of-war, rose up and bowed, keeping his hat off: ' I have a letter, sir, from Lord Howe to Mr. Washington.' ' Sir,' says Colonel Reed, ' we have no person in our army with that address.' ' Sir,' says the officer, ' will you look at the address?' He took out of his pocket a letter which was thus addressed :

" ' GEORGE WASHINGTON, ESQ.,
" ' NEW YORK.
" ' HOWE.'

" ' No sir,' says Colonel Reed, ' I cannot receive that letter.' ' I am very sorry,' says the officer, ' and so will be Lord Howe, that any error in the superscription should prevent the letter being received by *General Washington*.' ' Why, sir,' says Colonel Reed, ' I must obey orders.' ' Oh, yes, sir, you must obey orders, to be sure.' Then, after giving him a letter from Colonel Campbell to General Howe, and some other letters from prisoners to their friends, we stood off, having saluted and bowed to each other. After we had got a little way, the officer put about his barge and stood for us and asked by what particular title he chose to be addressed. Colonel Reed said, ' You are sensible, sir, of the rank of General Washington in our army?' ' Yes, sir, we are. I am sure my Lord Howe will lament exceedingly this affair, as the letter is quite of a civil nature, and not a military one. He laments exceedingly that he was not here a little sooner'; which we suppose to allude to the declaration of independence ; upon which we bowed and parted in the most genteel terms imaginable."

But Howe was evidently determined to have audience with Washington through some of his own subordinate officers. On the 22d of July Knox wrote to his wife as follows:

"On Saturday I wrote you we had a capital flag of truce, no less than the adjutant-general of General Howe's army. He had an interview with General Washington at our house. The purport of his message was in very elegant, polite strains, to endeavour to persuade General Washington to receive a letter directed to George Washington, Esq., etc., etc. In the course of his talk every other word was, ' May it please your Excellency,' ' if your Excellency so please '; in short, no person could pay more respect than the said adjutant-general, whose name is Colonel Paterson, a person we do not know. He said the etc., etc. implied everything. ' It does so,' said the General, ' and anything.' He said Lord and General Howe lamented exceedingly that any errors in the direction should interrupt that frequent intercourse between the two armies which might be necessary in the course of the service. That Lord Howe had come out with great powers. The General said he had heard that Lord Howe had come out with very great powers to pardon, but he had come to the wrong place ; the Americans had not offended, therefore they needed no pardon. This confused him. After a considerable deal of talk about the good disposition of Lord and General Howe, he asked, ' Has your Excellency no particular commands with which you would please to honour me to Lord and General 'Howe ? ' ' Nothing, sir, but my particular compliments to both '— a good answer.

"General Washington was very handsomely dressed, and made a most elegant appearance. Colonel Paterson appeared awe-struck, as if he was before something supernatural. Indeed, I don't wonder at it. He was before a very great man indeed. We had a cold collation provided, in which I lamented most exceedingly the absence of my Lucy. The General's servants did it tolerably well, though Mr. adjutant-general disappointed us. As it grew late, he even excused himself from drinking one glass of wine. He said Lord Howe and General Howe would wait for him, as they were to dine on board the *Eagle* man-of-war : he took his leave and went off."

On the 11th of August, Knox, who was an exceedingly busy man at this time, wrote as follows to his wife:

" You wish to know how I pass my time. I generally rise with or a little before the sun, and immediately, with a part of the regiment, attend prayers, sing a psalm, and read a chapter [in the Bible] at the Grand Battery. General Putnam constantly attends. I despatch a considerable deal of business before breakfast. From breakfast to dinner I am broiling in a sun hot enough to roast an egg. Sometimes I dine with the generals, Washington, Putnam, Stirling, etc., but I am mortified that I have n't had them to dine with me in return. However, that cannot be. I go to bed at nine o'clock or before, every night."

A few days later, having received from Mrs. Knox a letter in which she made some rather severe criticisms of the manners and speech of the Connecticut people among whom she was temporarily sojourning, Knox thought it needful that he should restrain her freedom of comment. It will be recollected that the lady was described by those who knew her as a person of exceeding lofty manners. In these later days she would have been described by the irreverent as " stuck-up." Her sensible and loving husband wrote:

" Take care, my love, of permitting your disgust to the Connecticut people to escape your lips. Indiscreet expressions are handed from town to town and a long while remembered by people not blessed with expanded minds. The want of that refinement which you seem to speak of is, or will be, the salvation of America ; for refinement of manners introduces corruption and venality. . . . There is a kind of simplicity in young States, as in young children, which is quite pleasing to an attentive observer."

It was during this time of pressure and anxiety

MAJOR-GENERAL JOHN SULLIVAN.

that Knox was obliged to carry on a vigorous correspondence with John Adams, who appears to have
taken very seriously to heart the condition of the
army and the apparent neglect of Massachusetts men
in the selection of general officers. On the 13th of
August, Adams, who was an inveterate grumbler,
writes from Philadelphia to Knox as follows:

"I am very much chagrined that the Massachusetts has not its
proper proportion of General Officers. I wish I was better acquainted
with the Persons and Characters of the Colonells from that State.
It will never do for the Massachusetts to furnish so many Men, and
have so few Generals while so many other States furnish so few Men
and have so many Generals."

On the 21st of August, Knox, writing to Adams,
asks when it is proposed to re-enlist the army; he
also laments the weakness of the artillery arm of the
service and says that all may be lost in consequence
of the failure to supply these deficiencies. Again,
as in other letters, he urges that the army must be
paid. " When their homes were invaded," he says,
" they fought for self-preservation. Now that they
are moved away from these, they naturally consider
that those who do not fight should pay."

Replying to this letter, Adams, writing on the
25th of the same month, says: " Able officers are
the soul of an Army. Gentlemen of sense and
knowledge, as well as of valour, must be advanced.
I wish you would give me in confidence a list of the
best Officers from Massachusetts with their characters. This may be delicate, but it will be safe."
Descending to details, Mr. Adams asks Knox to give
him the " characters " of " Coll Shepherd, **Coll**

Henshaw, and Major Brooks''; he also asks if '' Austin deserves promotion or note.'' These letters from Adams indicate to some degree the confidence which that sturdy patriot had in Knox, as well as Adams's desire to be kept intimately informed concerning the personnel of the army, Massachusetts interests being more especially his charge.

On the 22d of August, the British forces had been transferred from Staten Island to the opposite shore of Long Island, the landing being effected at Gravesend Bay, under cover of the guns of the fleet. On the 27th of the month began the series of military movements which are known in history as the battle of Long Island. It would be superfluous to narrate here the events of those unfortunate engagements; and we may content ourselves with quoting the brief account of the disaster given by Knox in a letter to his wife, written on the 28th:

'' About two o'clock in the morning (yesterday), the enemy attacked the woods in front of our works on Long Island, where our riflemen lay. They attacked with a chosen part of the Hessians, and all the light infantry and grenadiers of the army, and after six or seven hours' smart skirmishing, our people fell back in front of our works. The enemy lost nearly one thousand killed. We lost about the same number, killed, wounded, and taken prisoners, among whom are General Sullivan and Lord Stirling. General Parsons was missing until this morning, when he returned. I met with some loss in my regiment : they behaved like heroes, and are gone to glory. I was not on the island myself, being obliged to wait on my Lord Howe and the navy gentry who threatened to pay us a visit.''

Previous to the opening of this series of engagements, however, it appears that Knox's habit was

MAJOR-GENERAL PHILIP SCHUYLER.

FROM A PAINTING BY COL. JOHN TRUMBULL.

to cross over to the Long Island shore with Washington every day to inspect and direct the lines of defences that were being thrown up by the Americans. The retreat of the American troops to New York, conducted under the immediate direction of Washington, is briefly described as follows by one of Knox's contemporaries, Dr. Thacher *:

"After this unfortunate skirmishing, our army retreated within their lines at Brooklyn, and were exposed to the greatest hazard ; our troops fatigued and discouraged by defeat, a superior enemy in their front, and a powerful fleet about to enter the East River, with a view of effectually cutting off their retreat ; but an interposition of Providence, and the wisdom and vigilance of the Commander-in-Chief, preserved our army from destruction. Having resolved to withdraw his army from its hazardous position, General Washington crossed over to the Island in the night of the 29th of August, and personally conducted the retreat in so successful a manner, under the most embarrassing circumstances, that it is considered a remarkable example of good generalship. A circumstance which is remarked as manifestly Providential, is that a thick fog enveloped the whole of Long Island in obscurity about two o'clock in the morning, while on the side of the enemy at New York, the atmosphere was perfectly clear. Thus, by a Providential interposition of an unusual fog, our army, consisting of nine thousand men, in one night embarked under great disadvantages, and with their baggage, provisions, stores, horses, and the munitions of war, crossed a river, a mile or more wide, and landed in New York undiscovered and without material loss. The enemy were so near, that they were heard at work with their pickaxes, and in about a half an hour later, the fog cleared off, and the enemy were seen taking possession of the American lines."

Sullivan and Stirling, taken prisoners in these operations, were subsequently exchanged, and Sullivan was charged by Lord Howe with a mission to the Continental Congress. The British General

* Thacher, *Military Journal*, p. 56.

could not treat with the "rebel" Congress for terms of peace, but he asked that a number of private gentlemen should be commissioned to confer with him, such commissioners to be members of the body to whom he addressed his message. Benjamin Franklin, John Adams, and Edward Rutledge were accordingly appointed to serve on such commission, and these gentlemen had an interview on Staten Island with Lord Howe, the issue being, of course, resultless. The commissioners firmly insisted that Congress had no power to agree that the people "should return to their former dependent state."

During these trying times the depression in the American ranks was very great. Washington retained his serene temper, so violently disturbed while the disorderly and blundering retreat to the shores of Long Island was in progress. Knox's letters written at this time disclose the fact that his discouragements were chargeable to the low standard of efficiency among the subordinate officers of the army and to the disorderly and unmilitary character of the enlisted men. On the 5th of September, he wrote to his wife:

"We want great men, who, when fortune frowns, will not be discouraged. God will I trust in time give us these men. The Congress will ruin everything by their stupid parsimony, and they begin to see it. It is, as I always said, misfortunes that must raise us to the character of a *great people*. One or two drubbings will be of service to us; and one severe defeat to the enemy, ruin. We must have a standing army. The militia get sick, or think themselves so, and run home; and wherever they go they spread a panic."

Washington's faith in the militia had been shaken

JOHN ADAMS.

by recent experiences on Long Island, and he was disinclined to undertake the further defence of New York with troops so untrustworthy and so restive under their conditions.   The men were " badly paid and wretchedly fed," according to the statement made to Congress by Brigadier-General John M. Scott. Even when Congress, yielding to the remonstrances of the general officers of the army, consented to " raise a standing army to consist of about seventy-five thousand men, to serve for a term of three years, or during the war," the pay of a private soldier was only $6.67 per month, and that of the field officers varied from fifty to seventy dollars a month.   To encourage enlistments, however, bounties in the shape of land warrants were offered in addition to small sums in the currency of the times.   These land warrants varied in extent, the privates receiving warrants for one hundred acres for service during the war, and the officers receiving land in proportion to their respective ranks, from two hundred to five hundred acres.

The unstudied letters of Knox to his wife, min-gling as they did matters of war and marital affection and confidence, are entertaining reading.   It was Knox's habit then and afterwards to preserve all letters that came into his hands; and, after the war, when the correspondence which had passed between him and his wife could be arranged and docketed, nothing seems to have escaped his careful attention. Here is the opening paragraph of a letter dated at New York, September 5, 1776: " My dearest hope, —I received your entertaining letter with all the

5

raptures of a young, passionate lover. The sentiments of my being are charming, and her Harry
blesses the moment which gave him such a rich
treasure." After dwelling upon certain domestic
affairs of much consequence to husband and wife,
but of no interest to the present generation of
readers, Knox passes to military matters in this
paragraph: " We must have a standing army," and
he proceeds to give good reasons why this is imperatively necessary.

Knox joined with Greene, Putnam, and perhaps
others in supporting Washington's determination to
abandon the further defence of New York. But a
majority of a council of war, on the 6th of September, voted to hold the city at all hazards. Congress
voted to leave the whole question to the decision of
the Commander-in-chief, and on the 12th of the
month the previous action of the council was re-
versed and preparations for an immediate evacuation
were carried out with celerity. This was not begun
a moment too soon. Howe, aware of the critical
situation of the American troops, had already moved
his ships to positions enabling them to bombard the
city and to cut off the retreat of the Americans up
Manhattan Island. On the 15th of September, the
British troops made a landing at Kip's Bay, about
three miles above the city, and the evacuation was
so hurriedly completed that Knox, who had been
busily engaged in removing ordnance and stores,
narrowly escaped capture. Encountering Silliman's
brigade of Connecticut militia retreating in great
confusion from Corlaer's Hook, which they had

been left, with other troops, to protect, Knox attempted to rally the demoralised forces, with whom he threw himself into a partly finished work (known as Fort Bunker Hill), where he hoped, as he said, "to make a gallant defence," further retreat being thought impracticable. But Colonel Aaron Burr, who was one of General Israel Putnam's aides, came riding up and assured the troops that retreat was still possible by the Bloomingdale road. He guided them to this line of retreat, and Knox, seizing a boat, made his way in safety up the East River. Arriving at Harlem, he was received with great acclaim by his brothers-in-arms, and Washington, who had given him up as lost, greeted him with an affectionate embrace. It was on this retreat that Mrs. Murray, whose name has been given to one of the hills that rise to the north of what is now Thirty-fourth Street, served well the patriot cause by entertaining and detaining Howe and his pursuing troops at her hospitable mansion. Putnam conducted the retreat, and while Howe dallied over the refreshments furnished liberally by Mrs. Murray, the Americans escaped an encounter with a greatly superior force. Thacher says: "Ten minutes, it is said, would have been sufficient for the enemy to have secured the road at the turn, and entirely cut off General Putnam's retreat. It has since been almost a common saying among our officers, that Mrs. Murray saved this part of the American army."

While the army remained on Harlem Heights, Knox's labours were arduous and incessant. Writing to his brother on the 19th of September he

he says: " My constant fatigue and application to
the business of my extensive department has been
such that I have not had my clothes off o' nights
for more than forty days." In the same letter he
says: " The rascally Hessians took my baggage
waggon, and I must therefore press you to buy me
some blue cloth, or, if that is not to be had, some
brown cloth superfine." One of the curious incidents of the time, which doubtless engaged the
attention of the overworked engineer and artillery
officer, was the testing of an invention of a machine
in the nature of a submarine torpedo, designed by
Mr. D. Bushnell, of Connecticut, who gave to his
machine the name of " the American Turtle, or
Torpedo." The invention was in the nature of a
submarine boat which was to be rowed horizontally
under water at any given depth, " and the advent-
urer concealed within might rise, or sink, as occasion
requires." A small magazine of powder was attached to the boat in such a manner that it might be
screwed to the bottom of an enemy's ship and then
exploded by means of a clockwork within the con-
trivance. It was determined to make an experiment
with Bushnell's torpedo on the British 64-gunship
Eagle, then lying in the East River. The experiment was not successful. The inventor being unable
to be present to manage his machine, a sergeant
who had volunteered to essay the undertaking, was
baffled by encountering an obstacle in the hull of the
ship.. Nevertheless, the magazine did explode and
" General Putnam and others who had waited with
great anxiety for the result, were exceedingly amused

AARON BURR.

with the astonishment and alarm which this secret explosion occasioned on board the ship.'' Thacher says that it was the general opinion that '' this wonderful machine '' was '' admirably calculated to execute destruction among the shipping ''; but no further mention of it is made in the chronicles of the time.

After a series of skirmishes with no important results, the army settled down to a condition of comparative quiet on Harlem Heights, which had now been tolerably well fortified. Washington's headquarters were established at the mansion of Colonel Roger Morris, now known as the Jumel Mansion, on 160th Street, east of Tenth Avenue. The British were in full possession of the city below, the Americans being entrenched on the southern crest of the heights. A great fire broke out in the city on the 21st of September, and the devastation was more widespread on account of the failure of the fire-engines, which were out of order; hand-buckets were the sole means of extinguishment of the flames; the alarm bells had been removed by order of the Provincial Congress. Nearly all that part of the city lying south of what is now bounded by Chambers and Barclay Streets was destroyed, and five hundred buildings, among them Trinity Church and the Lutheran Church, were burned. Incendiarism was charged upon the '' rebel '' residents, many of whom were arrested. In the midst of the excitement, a patriotic soldier, Nathan Hale, of Connecticut, was arrested, tried, convicted, and hanged as a spy. Captain Hale made no defence, and he regretted, he said, that he had but one life to give for his country. The cruel and inhuman treatment accorded to Hale by the British was cited, a few years later, as a certain precedent for the treatment of Major André, captured as a spy near West Point. But André's fate, though that of a spy, was far less abhorrent than that of Hale.

In scanning the letters of Knox, written about this time, one is struck by the anxious tone which pervades those in which he refers to the morale of the army. Again and again, he insists that the officers should be educated in some sort of a military school. He seems to have seen that the war would be long and wasteful of human life; his letters breathe the most confident spirit of ultimate victory, while they dwell on the urgent need of drill for the troops, a long-term service for the rank and file, and a military training school for the men who are to be placed in command. Thus, in a letter addressed to his brother William, and dated Harlem Heights, eight miles from New York, September 23, 1776, he says:

" The general is as worthy a man as breathes, but he cannot do everything nor be everywhere. He wants good assistants. There is a radical difficulty in our army,—the lack of officers. We ought to have men of merit in the most extensive and unlimited sense of the word. Instead of which, the bulk of the officers of the army are a parcel of ignorant, stupid men, who might make tolerable soldiers but who are bad officers ; and until Congress forms an establishment to induce men proper for the purpose to leave their usual employments and enter the service, it is ten to one they will be beat until they are heartily tired of it. We ought to have academies, in which the whole theory of the art of war shall be taught, and every encouragement possible be given to draw persons into the army that may

STATUE OF NATHAN HALE.

BY FREDERICK MACMONNIES.

give lustre to our arms. As the army now stands, it is only a re-
ceptacle for ragamuffins. You will observe I am chagrined, not
more so than at any time I 've been in the army ; but many late
affairs, of which I 've been an eye-witness, have so totally sickened
me, that unless some very different mode of conduct is observed in
the formation of the new army, I shall not think myself obliged by
either the laws of God or nature to risk my reputation on so cobweb
a foundation. . . .   The grounds on which we now rest are
strong, I think we can defend them : if we don't, I hope God will
punish us both in this world and in the world to come, if the fault is
ours."

The Boston bookseller had now been in the
military service one year, yet he appears to have
acquired the habit, if not the ability, of an accomplished and severe military critic.   But it should be
said here that most of the contemporaneous accounts of the doings of the American army at that
time fully bear out the newly fledged colonel in his
strictures.

Active movements were now resumed by Lord
Howe, whose tactics, however, were never very
vigorous, justifying the criticism of one of his own
friends that he " calculated with the greatest ac-
curacy the exact time necessary for his enemy to
make his escape.''   It was not until October 12th
that he moved against the position held by the
Americans on Harlem Heights.   His design was to
flank Washington's forces by moving through Westchester County ; but his dilly-dallying at less important points along the shores gave Washington ample
time to evacuate the heights and establish himself
at White Plains, where he held the roads leading to
the Hudson and to New England, which offered

him two available avenues for further retreat. On
the 28th of October, Howe sustained a severe loss
of men in killed and wounded in an engagement
which Knox thus describes in a letter to his brother,
dated " Near White Plains, 32 miles from New
York, 1 Nov., 1776." He says:

" Last Monday the enemy with nearly their whole force advanced
upon the hills above us ; and soon after ten o'clock in the morning,
with a large part of their army, began a most furious cannonade on
a hill [Chatterton's] on our right, where we had about one thousand
posted under General McDougall, which they carried with considerable loss. Our loss was not very great. Our men had no works,
and were not timely reinforced, owing to the distance they were from
the main body. The enemy's having possession of this hill obliged
us to abandon some slight lines thrown up at White Plains. This
we did this morning, and retired to some hills about half a mile in
the rear. The enemy are determined on something decisive, and we
are determined to risk a general battle only on the most advantageous
terms. We are manœuvring, in which we think they are somewhat
our superiors."

Still, Washington was left free to move, and he
accordingly fell back to Northcastle Heights, nearer
the Hudson, where he established himself in an im-
pregnable position. Howe's only recourse now was
in the direction of Fort Washington, the location of
which, opposite Fort Lee on the Jersey side of the
Hudson, gave it much apparent importance so long
as the Americans were to occupy any part of the
New York shore. It was a question that had given
Congress and the army much anxiety to determine
whether Fort Washington should be held. General
Greene, who believed that Howe's next move would
be into the Jerseys, urged that the fort be retained

as long as possible.   Washington, and probably some
of his generals, was anxious for the immediate trans-
fer of his troops into the Jerseys, carrying the
campaign in the direction of Philadelphia.

Howe's movement on Fort Washington was preceded by a demand for its immediate surrender, his
ultimatum being that if he were compelled to attack,
he would put the garrison to the sword.   The commanding officer, Colonel Robert Magaw, replied that
such a massacre as that threatened would be unworthy of a British officer, adding that he should
defend the fort to the last extremity.   After a
violent and furious assault, in which British and
Hessians participated, the Americans were overwhelmed and the fort was surrendered on honourable terms.   The loss of this important fortification
caused great mortification and grief to the patriots,
the moral effect of the disaster being greater than its
actual effect upon the military fortunes of the struggling colonists.

An interesting side-light is thrown upon this event
by a letter written by General Greene to his intimate
and confidential friend Knox, dated at Fort Lee,
November 17, 1776, as follows:

" Your favour of the 14th reached me in a melancholy temper.
The misfortune of losing Fort Washington, with between two and
three thousand men, will reach you before this, if it has not already.
His Excellency General Washington has been with me for several
days.   The evacuation or reinforcement of Fort Washington was
under consideration, but finally nothing concluded on.   Day before
yesterday, about one o'clock, Howe's adjutant-general made a demand of the surrender of the garrison in the general's name, but
was answered by the commanding officer that he should defend it to

the last extremity. Yesterday morning, General Washington, General Putnam, General Mercer, and myself went to the island to determine what was best to be done ; but just at the instant we stepped on board the boat the enemy made their appearance on the hill where the Monday action was, and began a severe cannonade with several field pieces. Our guards soon fled, the enemy advanced up to the second line. This was done while we were crossing the river and getting upon the hill. The enemy made several marches to the right and to the left,—I suppose to reconnoitre the fortifications and lines.

" There we all stood in a very awkward situation. As the disposition was made, and the enemy advancing, we durst not attempt to make any new disposition ; indeed, we saw nothing amiss. We all urged his Excellency to come off. I offered to stay, General Putnam did the same, and so did General Mercer ; but his Excellency thought it best for us all to come off together, which we did, about half an hour before the enemy surrounded the fort. The enemy came up Harlem River, and landed a party at headquarters, which was upon the back of our people in the lines. A disorderly retreat soon took place ; without much firing the people retreated into the fort. On the north side of the fort there was a very heavy fire for a long while ; and as they had the advantage of the ground, I apprehend the enemy's loss must be great. After the troops retreated in the fort, very few guns were fired. The enemy approached within small-arm fire of the lines, and sent in a flag, and the garrison capitulated in an hour. I was afraid of the fort : the redoubt that you and I advised, too, was not done, or little or nothing done to it. Had that been complete, I think the garrison might have defended themselves a long while, or been brought off. I feel mad, vexed, sick, and sorry. Never did I need the consoling voice of a friend more than now. Happy should I be to see you. This is a most terrible event : its consequences are justly to be dreaded. Pray, what is said upon the occasion ? A line from you will be very acceptable.

" I am, dear sir, your obedient servant,

" N. GREENE."

CHAPTER IV

HE island of Manhattan, from the Battery to Kingsbridge, was now in full possession of the British, and two days later, Cornwallis, commanding under Howe, passed up the Hudson with six thousand men and landed at a point nearly opposite Yonkers. The evacuation of Fort Lee became inevitable, and the retreat of Washington's little army across the Jerseys began. It was now late in November, and the retreat was conducted in a cold and inclement season; the Americans were almost constantly in sight of their pursuers, the rearguard of the retreating army burning and pulling down bridges which were speedily rebuilt by the British. The object of the Americans was to delay their pursuers as much as possible until impassable roads and the severities of winter should end the campaign. Putnam, Greene, Stirling, Mercer, and Knox were with Washington, whose entire force consisted of about four thousand men. The time

75

of enlistment for many of these was to expire in December, and Howe, who naturally expected and believed that the American force would now melt away, returned to winter quarters in New York, leaving Colonel Donop and his Hessians and a Highland regiment (the 42d) to hold the line across the Jerseys. Washington wrote to Governor Livingston, of New Jersey, to be prepared for an invasion, and he recommended that the people remove or destroy their stock, grain, and effects that would be of use to the enemy, reminding them that the ravages that had been committed by the British troops in Westchester, N. Y., would be repeated in the Jerseys. On the 30th of December, the two British Peace Commissioners, General Howe and Admiral Howe, issued a proclamation offering pardon and amnesty to " all who had taken up arms against their King," provided they returned to their homes within sixty days. At this time the panic in New Jersey and Pennsylvania was very great, and many availed themselves of the terms offered in the proclamation of the royal agents. Dark and gloomy was the prospect before the dwindling forces now falling back upon the Delaware.

But although even the well-balanced and calm mind of Washington was disturbed by visions of a a final and irretrievable defeat of his country's cause, Knox's letters continued to breathe the same spirit of resolute belief in the ultimate triumph of the patriots. Writing to his wife and brother and to his intimate friends, General Nathanael Greene and Harry Jackson, Knox persistently urged that the

MAJOR-GENERAL CHARLES LEE.

FROM AN ENGLISH ENGRAVING PUBLISHED IN 1776.

cause was too dear to the God of Nations to be allowed to fall, and too dear to humanity to suffer
long.   While he lamented the parsimony and the
meddlesomeness of the Continental Congress and
the short-sighted policy that permitted brief terms
of enlistment and the employment of officers un-
schooled in military science, he confidently predicted
the final victory of the arms of the nascent nation
now struggling in its earliest throes for existence.
It was Knox's cheery spirit and his calm belief in
ultimate success that strengthened the faith of the
Commander-in-chief.

The British were marching into Trenton, on the
8th of December while Washington was crossing the
Delaware into Pennsylvania.   Cornwallis's movements had been sluggish, or the Americans would
have been overtaken before they could have crossed
the river.   But Washington not only had time to
escape; he had availed himself of opportunity to
seize and carry off everything in the shape of floating craft for seventy miles and up and down the
Delaware at the place of his crossing, thus preventing the enemy from immediate pursuit and providing
himself with the means for a return.   Gen. Charles
Lee, left with Gates on the Jersey side of the river,
assumed that his separation from Washington gave
to himself the supreme command of his and Gates's
troops, without regard to the orders of the Commander-in-chief, which were many times repeated
to urge him to join his forces to those on the Pennsylvania side of the Delaware.   His treasonable conduct was finally terminated by his capture at Basking

Ridge, and he was hurried off to place him beyond
all possibility of rescue. His command now de-
volved upon Sullivan, who lost no time to carry out
Washington's orders to take his troops into Pennsylvania.

A bold stroke, designed to cripple the enemy and
cheer the despondent patriots, was resolved upon by
Washington. He had crossed the Delaware southward on the 8th of December, and now he made
ready to recross the river during the night following
Christmas Day. In the orders prescribing the details of the march to Trenton it was set forth that
the troops should " be assembled one mile back of
McKonkey's Ferry, and as soon as it begins to grow
dark, the troops to be marched to McKonkey's
Ferry, and embark on board the boats in the following order under the direction of Colonel Knox."
Then follows the order of crossing, and it is further
specified that, " Immediately upon their debarkation,
the whole to form and march in subdivisions from
the right. A profound silence to be enjoined, and
no man to quit the ranks on the pain of death.
Each brigadier to appoint flanking parties; the reserve brigade to appoint rear guards of the columns;
the heads of the columns to be appointed to arrive
at Trenton at five o'clock."

This historic military feat has often been described
by pen and pencil. The difficulties of the passage,
the roaring wintry storm, the stream obstructed by
masses of floating ice, and the ill-clad and ill-shod
troops suffering bitterly from the intense cold, are
features of the picture. But the gallant band of

WASHINGTON'S HEADQUARTERS, POMPTON, N. J.

heroes, cheered by the stentorian voice of Knox, who superintended the passage, and by their belief that they were pressing on to victory, minded none of these obstructions and went rejoicing on their way. There is in Knox's letter to Mrs. Knox, giving an account of the passage of the river and the battle of Trenton, a certain reserve that is characteristic of all of his official and unofficial reports of military events in which he had taken a leading part.

After describing the position of the enemy and the number of the contending forces, Knox says that the " hardy design " of attacking Trenton by storm was formed. The fact that the town was held by the foreign mercenaries, and not by the British troops, seems to have encouraged the hope that the " hardy design " might prove successful. The passage of the river was accomplished by the aid of a corps of New England men, recruited from the coast towns and accustomed to the management of water-craft. There were about three thousand men in the ranks that crossed the Delaware on that stormy Christmas night; and they carried with them eighteen field-pieces. According to Knox, " The floating ice in the river made the labour almost incredible. However, perseverance accomplished what at first seemed impossible." He continues: " About two o'clock the troops were all on the Jersey side; we were then about nine miles from the object. The night was cold and stormy; it hailed with great violence; the troops marched with the most profound silence and in good order."

After describing the march to Trenton, with the

icy storm beating upon the backs of the men, Knox
says that the advanced guard of the enemy, a half-
mile from the town, was forced and the American
army which had advanced in two columns, " entered
the town pell-mell." The scene of war which then
was drawn upon the wintry stage was one of great
confusion, the like of which the writer had never
seen before. He continues:

" The hurry, fright and confusion of the enemy was not unlike
that which it will be when the last trump shall sound. They endeavoured to form in streets, the heads of which we had previously
the possession of with cannon and howitzers ; these, however, in the
twinkling of an eye, cleared the streets. The backs of the houses
were resorted to for shelter. These proved ineffectual ; the musketry
soon dislodged them. Finally, they were driven through the town
into an open plain beyond. Here they formed in an instant. During the contest in the streets measures were taken for putting an entire stop to their retreat by posting troops and cannon in such passes
and roads as it was possible for them to get away by. The poor
fellows, after they were formed on the plain, saw themselves completely surrounded, the only resource left was to force their way
through numbers unknown to them. The Hessians lost part of
their cannon in the town : they did not relish the project of forcing,
and were obliged to surrender upon the spot, with all their artillery,
six brass pieces, army colours, &c. A Colonel Rawle [Rahl] commanded, who was wounded. The number of prisoners was above
1200, including officers,—all Hessians. There were few killed or
wounded on either side. After having marched off the prisoners,
stores, &c., we returned to the place, nine miles distant, where we
had embarked. Providence seemed to have smiled upon every part
of this enterprise. Great advantages may be gained from it if we
take the proper steps. At another post we have pushed over the
river 2000 men, to-day another body, and to-morrow the whole army
will follow. It must give sensible pleasure to every friend of the
rights of man to think with how much intrepidity our people pushed
the enemy, and prevented their forming in the town.

" His Excellency the General has done me the unmerited great honour of thanking me in public orders in terms strong and polite. This I should blush to mention to any other than you, my dear Lucy ; and I am fearful that my Lucy may think her Harry possesses a species of little vanity in doing it at all."

Knox was now appointed a brigadier-general, his commission being dated December 27, 1776, the day following the victory at Trenton; but the news of that famous fight had not reached Congress when the commission was ordered. In a letter dated at Trenton on the 2d of January, 1777, Knox thus informs his wife of his advancement:

" We are collecting our force at this place, and shall give battle to the enemy very soon: Our people have exerted great fortitude, and stayed beyond the time of their enlistment, in high spirits, but want rum and clothing. Will it give you satisfaction or pleasure in being informed that the Congress have created me a general officer— a brigadier—with the entire command of the artillery ? If so, I shall be happy. It was unsolicited on my part, though I cannot say unexpected. People are more lavish in their praises of my poor endeavours than they deserve. All the merit I can claim is my industry. I wish to render my devoted country every service in my power ; and the only alloy I have in my little exertions is, that it separates me from thee,—the dearest object of all my earthly happiness. May Heaven give us a speedy and happy meeting. . . . The attack of Trenton was a most horrid scene to the poor inhabitants. War, my Lucy, is not a humane trade, and the man who follows it as such will meet with his proper demerits in another world."

Evidently John Adams and other friends of Knox, who were solicitous that Massachusetts should have its full quota of general officers, had not been unmindful of the colonel of artillery. Nor can it be said that his promotion, however unsolicited, was either undeserved or rapid. Commissioned colonel

6

of Washington's sole regiment of artillery on November 17, 1775, and since entrusted with the command of all the artillery attached to that army, it
was not until two years had passed that he was
commissioned a general officer. And this, too, in a
time when men from civil life were rapidly raised to
high military rank, owing to the pressing exigencies
of the service; and it should not be forgotten that
three years had not passed since Brigadier-General
Knox was pursuing the peaceful vocation of a bookseller.

On his retreat across the Delaware, after the
battle of Trenton, Washington carried * " six excellent brass cannon, about one thousand two hundred small arms, and three standards, with a quantity
of baggage, etc." His prisoners were nearly fifteen
hundred in number, including thirty officers. This
signal victory greatly cheered the inhabitants of the
Jerseys and Pennsylvania, and reinforcements were
sent to the army from Virginia and Maryland. To
the honour of the patriotic citizens of Philadelphia,
it should be said that they had not waited for the
success at Trenton to send aid to the army, whose
efficient force was constantly changing. Fifteen
hundred citizens, although unused to the hardships
of military life, associated themselves together and,
marching to the relief of Washington's depleted
forces, endured cheerfully the vicissitudes of the inclement months of January and December, " sleeping in tents, barns, and sometimes in the open air."
The patriotic and wealthy Philadelphian, Robert

---

* Thacher's *Journal*.

Morris, raised the handsome sum of fifty thousand
dollars in specie which was sent to Washington's
camp to be used for pressing military purposes.

The New England regiments whose time had
expired were now persuaded to remain six weeks
longer, and these, with the recent acquisitions from
Philadelphia and elsewhere, brought Washington's
available force up to about six thousand men.
Emboldened by this prosperous turn of the tide,
Washington resolved on a brilliant stroke of strategy,
again crossing the Delaware and striking at the
British forces in the Jerseys. Hearing of this bold
movement, Cornwallis hurried to meet him. This
second crossing of the Delaware was successfully
accomplished on the 30th of December. The engagement that followed, known in history as the
battle of Princeton, is described in the following
letter from Knox to his wife:

"Morristown, Jan. 7, 1777.
" My Dearest Love,

" I wrote to you from Trenton by a Mr. Furness, which I hope you
have received. I then informed you that we soon expected another
tussle. I was not out in my conjecture. About three o'clock on
the 2nd of January, a column of the enemy attacked a party of ours
which was stationed about one mile above Trenton. Our party was
small, and did not make much resistance. The enemy, who were
Hessians, entered the town pellmell, pretty much in the same manner
that we had driven them a few days before.

" Nearly on the other side of Trenton, partly in the town, runs a
brook (the Assanpink), which in most places is not fordable, and
over which through Trenton is a bridge. The ground on the other
side is much higher than on this, and may be said to command Trenton completely. Here it was our army drew up, with thirty or forty
pieces of artillery in front. The enemy pushed our small party

through the town with vigour, though not with much loss. Their retreat over the bridge was thoroughly secured by the artillery. After they had retired over the bridge, the enemy advanced within reach of our cannon, who saluted them with great vociferation and some execution. This continued till dark, when of course it ceased, except a few shells we now and then chucked into town to prevent their enjoying their new quarters securely. As I before mentioned, the creek was in our front, our left on the Delaware, our right in the wood, parallel to the creek. The situation was strong, to be sure; but hazardous on this account, that had our right wing been defeated, the defeat of the left would almost have been an inevitable consequence, and the whole thrown into confusion or pushed into the Delaware, as it was impassable by boats.

" From these circumstances the general thought it best to attack Princeton twelve miles in the rear of the enemy's grand army, and where they had the 17th, 40th and 55th regiments, with a number of draughts, altogether perhaps twelve hundred men. Accordingly, about one o'clock at night, we began to march and make this most extra manœuvre. Our troops marched with great silence and order, and arrived near Princeton a little after daybreak. We did not surprise them as at Trenton; for they were on their march down to Trenton, on a road about a quarter of a mile distant from the one in which we were. You may judge of their surprise when they discovered such large columns marching up. They could not possibly suppose it was our army, for that they took for granted was cooped up near Trenton. They could not possibly suppose it was their own army returning by a back road; in short, I believe they were as much astonished as if an army had dropped perpendicularly upon them. However, they had not much time for consideration. We pushed a party to attack them. This they repulsed with great spirit, and advanced upon another column just then coming out of a wood, which they likewise put in some disorder; but fresh troops coming up, and the artillery beginning to play, they were after a smart resistance totally put to the rout. The 17th regiment used their bayonets with too much severity upon a party they put to flight; but they were paid for it in proportion, very few escaping. Near sixty were killed on the spot, besides the wounded. We have taken between three and four hundred prisoners, all British troops. They must have lost in this affair nearly five hundred, killed and wounded and prisoners. We lost some gallant officers. Brigadier-General

BATTLE OF PRINCETON—DEATH OF MERCER.

FROM THE PAINTING BY COL. JOHN TRUMBULL.

Mercer was wounded : he had three separate stabs with a bayonet. A Lieutenant-Colonel Fleming was killed, and Captain Neil of the artillery, an excellent officer. Mercer will get better. The enemy took his parole after we left Princeton. We took all their cannon, which consisted of two brass six-pounders, a considerable quantity of military stores, blankets, guns, etc. They lost, among a number of other officers, a Captain Leslie, a son of the Earl of Leven and nephew to General Leslie : him we brought off, and buried with the honours of war.

"After we had been about two hours at Princeton, word was brought that the enemy were advancing from Trenton. This they did, as we have since been informed, in a most infernal sweat,—running, puffing, and blowing, and swearing at being so outwitted. As we had other objects in view, to wit, breaking up their quarters, we pursued our march to Somerset Court House, where there were about thirteen hundred quartered, as we had been informed. They, however, had marched off, and joined the army at Trenton. We at first intended to have made a forced march to Brunswick ; but our men having been without either rest, rum, or provisions for two nights and days, were unequal to the task of marching seventeen miles further. If we could have secured one thousand fresh men at Princeton to have pushed for Brunswick, we should have struck one of the most brilliant strokes in all history. However, the advantages are very great : already they have collected their whole force, and drawn themselves to one point, to wit, Brunswick.

" The enemy were within nineteen miles of Philadelphia, they are now sixty miles. We have driven them from almost the whole of West Jersey. The panic is still kept up. We had a battle two days ago with a party of ours and sixty Waldeckers, who were all killed or taken, in Monmouth County in the lower part of the Jerseys. It is not our interest to fight a general battle, nor can I think under all circumstances it is the enemy's. They have sent their baggage to Staten Island from the Jerseys, and we are very well informed they are doing the same from New York. Heath will have orders to march there and endeavour to storm it on that side. ' There is a tide in the affairs of men, which taken at the flood leads on to victory.' For my part, my Lucy. I look up to heaven and devoutly thank the great Governor of the Universe for producing this turn in our affairs ; and the sentiment I hope will so prevail in the hearts of the people as to induce them to be a people chosen of

Heaven, not to give way to despair, but at all times and under all circumstances never to despair of the Commonwealth."

Knox, who had made a diligent and careful study of the topographical situation of the Jerseys, strongly advised the march to Morristown and the establishment of winter quarters at that place. The strategical advantages of the position at Morristown were considerable, and by taking it, the army was on the flank of the enemy and could change its base, in case of any emergency arising, without serious difficulty. Washington's ruse of keeping up watchfires in his deserted camps while he stole around to Princeton from Trenton, his masterly conduct of all the movements that had ridded the Jerseys of nearly all the enemy's troops, were evidence to the world that the head of the American army was a soldier of indomitable courage, vast patience, and unlimited military expedients. Brunswick and Amboy were now the only points in Jersey that were held by the British, who had so recently proclaimed themselves masters of the situation. Thacher, on the 30th of January, says: " It it with infinite satisfaction we learn that the royal army has been compelled to quit almost every part of the Jerseys, and that our army is pursuing them from post to post, and they find no security but in the vicinity of their shipping."

A season of comparative quiet for the army encamped at Morristown now ensued. That army, however, was again reduced to a mere handful of men; and from their winter quarters, consisting of an assemblage of huts, an occasional foray was made

upon the enemy, who had drawn in their outposts
to the borders of New York and Staten Island.
Meanwhile, Knox was sent to New England to
oversee the casting of cannon and the establishment
of laboratories for the manufacture of powder and
other material.   He visited his wife, who was then
in Boston, and from that town he writes as follows
to Washington, under date of February 1, 1777:

" After my letter to General Greene from Springfield, of the 26th
ult., I set out for this place, in order to provide such materials as
were necessary to carry on the various branches connected with the
laboratories and ordnance establishment.   Upon my arrival here, I
was much surprised at the very extraordinary bounty offered by the
State (\$86 2/3) for recruits for the service.   Part of a regiment, con-
sisting of four hundred men with a detachment of one hundred and
fifty artillery, marches to-morrow and next day for Ticonderoga.
The enlistments in this town have been exceeding rapid.   General
Ward is here, but whether he acts as councillor of the Massachusetts,
or a continental general, is difficult to say.   There must be one battalion of artillery raised in this State, for all the old artillery-men,
who have been two years in the service, and acquired some experience, are from this town and colony.   If Congress should still ad-
here to Brookfield in preference to Springfield, it will delay everything
for three or four months.   I wrote to General Greene from Springfield that it was the best place in all the four New England States
for a laboratory, cannon foundry, etc., and I hope your Excellency
will order it there."

Knox's advice was followed and the establishment
of the works which are to-day represented by the
United States arsenal at Springfield was the result
of his wise and well-directed labours.   It may be
said that to his incessant urging upon Congress was
due the ultimate establishment of sundry other
foundries and laboratories and the foundation of the

Military Academy at West Point, New York. A committee of the Continental Congress visited Washington's camp on Harlem Heights, in September, 1776, and Knox, with others of the army leaders, was requested to furnish the committee with such suggestions for the information of Congress as might occur to him. His paper was headed " Hints to Congressional Committee now in camp, Headquarters, Harlem Heights, Sept. 27, 1776," and is filled with shrewd and practical suggestions, some of which were destined, in later years, to justify the wisdom of the able officer who made them. In this interesting document he recommends laboratories for the manufacture of materials for gunpowder and fulminants, ordnance stores, gun-carriages and equipments, foundries for brass cannon, etc. He adds: " And as officers can never act with confidence until they are Masters of their profession, an Academy established on a liberal plan would be of the utmost service to America, where the whole Theory and practice of Fortifications and Gunnery should be taught." He refers to the military school at Woolwich, England, as a good example of an institution designed as a training school for army officers.

Returning to New Jersey, Knox was next engaged, with General Greene, in laying out a new series of defensive works on the Jersey side of the Hudson, an attack by the enemy from that direction being among the possibilities against which provision should be made. Letters from his wife and brother, written about this time, give some indication of the personal business cares that were intruded upon his attention while he was so deeply immersed in military labours. William Knox had succeeded in renting the building formerly occupied by his brother as a bookstore and was now carrying on the business under the advice of Mrs. Knox, who constantly wrote to him when she was not in Boston, giving many practical hints for his guidance. Among other useful suggestions, Mrs. Knox advised William not to confine himself exclusively to the book trade, but to look up other bargains which might prove equally advantageous. In a letter written to Knox, March 18, 1777, she says that William had gone to Newbury to purchase a cargo of stationery, " by which he thinks he shall make money." And a few days later, William writes to his brother that he has bought quills, foolscap paper, sealing-wax and wafers, the cost of which is two hundred pounds sterling, " of which," he hopefully adds, " I shall make a very pretty profit."

Knox was back again in Morristown for a short time, a few days later, and, elated by recent acquisitions to his artillery stores, some of which were secretly furnished from France, he writes on the last day of March to his wife as follows: " The enemy and we are laying upon our oars. What think you of the care of Providence to America in bringing in so many ammunitions, notwithstanding the care of our very malignant enemies ? For my own part, I bow with Gratitude to that High Power who putteth up and putteth down. America, under His smiles, shall win."

At this time Mrs. Knox was sojourning at Sewall's Point (now Brookline), near Boston, with Mrs. Heath, wife of the major-general. Mrs. Knox and her infant, her second child, had been inoculated for smallpox, and were suffering from the consequent effects thereof. The good lady was also exceedingly lonely, as appears from a letter written at this time to her husband in which she says: " I have no company but Madame Heath, who is so stiff that it is impossible to be sociable with her, and Mr. Gardner the treasurer, so you may well think what I feel under my present anxiety."

As for the Flucker family, they appear to have cut off all communication with their daughter and sister, Mrs. Knox, who writes to her husband, in answer to inquiries from him, says that they have sent her no missive or message. Replying to this, Knox, writing from Morristown, on May 20th, says: " Though your parents are on the opposite side from your Harry, yet it 's very strange that it should divest them of humanity. Not a line! My God! what stuff is the human heart made of ? Although father, mother, sister, and brother have forgotten you, yet, my love, your Harry will ever esteem you the best boon of Heaven."

A little later than this, an unpleasant incident in Knox's career threatened to put an end to his invaluable service in the American army. Silas Deane, one of the commissioners sent to France by the Continental Congress to negotiate with France for terms of amity and assistance, somewhat exceeded his powers in engaging officers of rank to co-operate in this country with the Americans. The agreement was that the French officers who accepted service in the American army should have there the same rank that they held in the French army. Among those who took service was one Ducoudray, an engineer officer of great talent and ability. He arrived in Boston early in May, expecting to be assigned to duty as commander-in-chief of the artillery. Mrs. Knox, who was then in Boston, hearing of Ducoudray's pretensions, wrote thus to her husband, who had returned to the Jerseys:

" A French General (Ducoudray), who styles himself commander-in-chief of the continental artillery, is now in town. He says his appointment is from Mr. Deane, that he is going immediately to headquarters to take command, that he is a major-general, and a deal of it. Who knows but I may have my Harry again? This I am sure of, he will never suffer any one to command him in that department. If he does, he has not the soul which I now think him possessed of."

On his part, Knox, naturally feeling deeply injured by this unexpected attempt, as he regarded it, to supersede him by another and a foreign officer, addressed Congress in terms that were at once firm and respectful, declining to serve under Mr. Deane's appointee. To his wife he wrote from Camp Middlebrook, on the Raritan, ten miles from New Brunswick, New Jersey, on the 21st of June, as follows:

" We have the most respectable body of continental troops that America ever had, no going home to-morrow to suck,—hardy, brave fellows, who are as willing to go to heaven by the way of a bayonet or sword as any other mode. With the blessing of Heaven, I have great hopes in the course of this campaign that we shall do something clever. I think in five days there will not be an enemy in the Jerseys ; but I fear they will go up the North River, where perhaps they may plague us more. The inhabitants here appeared as one man, and as a people actuated by revenge for the many rapes and murders committed on them. The Congress have taken some precious steps with regard to Mr. Ducoudray. They have resolved that Mr. Deane has exceeded his commission, and that they cannot ratify his treaty with Mr. Ducoudray. Pretty this !—to bring a gentleman 1200 leagues to affront him."

Knox's letter to Congress was addressed to John Hancock, President of that body, and was dated at Camp Middlebrook, July 1, 1777, as follows:

" SIR,—From information I have received I am induced to believe that Congress has appointed a Mr. Ducoudray, a French gentleman, to the command of the artillery.

" I wish to know of Congress whether this information be true ; if it is, I beg the favour of a permission to retire, and that a proper certificate for that purpose be sent me immediately.

" I am, sir, your most humble servant,

" HENRY KNOX."

" Hon. JOHN HANCOCK, Esq."

General Washington wrote to President Hancock and to Richard Henry Lee, a member from Virginia, protesting against the superseding of Knox by Ducoudray, adding that Ducoudray's appointment would cause the retirement of General Knox, who was " one of the most valuable officers in the service, and who, combating almost innumerable difficulties in the department he fills, had placed the artillery upon a footing that does him the greatest honour " ; and he further described Knox as " a man of great military reading, sound judgment, and clear conceptions." General Nathanael Greene and General Sullivan united in a similar letter to Congress.

MAJOR-GENERAL HENRY KNOX.

FROM THE STUDY FOR THE ORIGINAL PAINTING BY GILBERT STUART.

The effect of these letters is thus described in a letter from Knox to his wife, dated at Camp Pompton Plains, 13 July, 1777:

" The letter which I wrote to Congress, to know whether they had appointed Mr. Ducoudray, has, in conjunction with the letters of Generals Sullivan and Greene, produced a resolve purporting 'the said letters to be an infringement on the liberties of the people, as tending to influence the decisions of Congress,' and expecting that we make acknowledgments to them for 'so singular an impropriety.' Conscious of the rectitude of my intention and of the contents of my letter, I shall make no acknowledgments whatever. Though my country is too much pressed at present to resign, yet perhaps this campaign will be the last. I am determined to contribute my mite to the defence of the country, in spite of every obstacle."

None of the officers thus loftily snubbed by Congress offered either apology or resignation. But Congress finally resolved that Mr. Deane's engagements could not in this particular be ratified, and the difficulty was thus removed. Ducoudray was subsequently (August 11, 1777) appointed inspector-general with the rank of major-general, and assigned to the duty of superintending the defensive works on the Delaware. These works, it is interesting to recall, were planned by General Knox and were described in a memorandum filed by him with the Commander-in-chief, August 9, 1777. Ducoudray's term of service was short. On the 11th of the following September, while hastening to the battle of Brandywine, where he expected to serve as a volunteer, his horse became restive during the crossing of the Schuylkill, and, plunging from the ferryboat, carried with him his rider, who was drowned.

Although the quotas of men to be furnished to the army by the order of Congress were never quite filled, and recruits came in slowly, the hearts of the commanding officers were cheered by the prospect of a victorious summer campaign. Knox wrote to his wife from Morristown, on May 20th, in these hopeful terms:

" From the present information it appears that America will have much more reason to hope for a successful campaign the ensuing summer than she had the last. Our forces come in pretty fast and are disciplining for the war. We are well supplied with arms and amunitions of all species ; this, with the blessing of Heaven, will assist us much ; but, I am sorry to say it, we seem to be *increasing most rapidly in impiety*. This is a bad omen, but I hope we shall mend, though I see no immediate prospect of it."

As in more recent times, the American army was plagued with that class of scamps known as " bounty-jumpers." We have seen how large was the bounty offered in Massachusetts to volunteer recruits. The Continental authorities also held forth bounties in money and land to induce recruiting. It was found necessary, while Washington's headquarters were at Morristown, to issue a general order calling attention to the " frauds and abuses committed of late by sundry soldiers, who, after enlisting in one regiment and receiving the bounty allowed by Congress, have deserted, enlisted in others, and received new bounties." The Commander-in-chief proceeded to declare that " this offence is of the most enormous and flagrant nature, and not admitting the least palliation or excuse ; whoever are convicted thereof, and sentenced to die, may consider their execution certain and inevitable." What with the rawness of the recruits, their lack of discipline, their impiety, and their frequent inclination to obtain premiums for enlisting and then to desert, the task of making soldiers of the material offered must have been vexatious and difficult.

CHAPTER V

THE CONTEST MOVES SOUTHWARD

1777

THE events narrated in the preceding chapter were made to anticipate somewhat the chronological order of the history of the time. The movements of Howe, whose headquarters were in New York, remained a matter of anxious speculation among the American officers. It was uncertain whether he would return to New England, or make a descent upon Charleston, S. C., or Baltimore, or Philadelphia, or proceed up the Hudson and effect a junction with the invading army, which, under Burgoyne, was expected to move down from Canada, some ten thousand strong. The better to observe Howe and follow him, if practicable, Washington broke up his winter camp at Morristown and established himself in a strong position at Middlebrook, New Jersey, on the Raritan, on the 28th of May. But it was not until the 12th of June that the British general made any move whatever. At that time, he sent Cornwallis out to feel the American forces and to surprise General Sullivan at Princeton. The movement, however, was sluggish, as usual, and it was not until two days later that the entire army was in motion. How this design miscarried is described in a letter from Knox to his intimate friend, Henry Jackson. As Jackson's name occurs with great frequency in Knox's voluminous correspondence, it may be explained here that he was a native of Massachusetts and had been appointed colonel of the sixteenth additional Continental battalion raised in that State, his commission being dated January 12, 1777. He served with distinction in Sullivan's corps, and was appointed to the command of the last body of Continental troops that were disbanded in 1784. To him Knox was indebted for important financial aid in his later enterprises. Writing to him from " Camp Middlebrook, 21 June, 1777," Knox says:

" General Howe, on the 14th, put his whole army in motion. He had for a long time past been collecting his force from Rhode Island, New York, Staten Island, etc. The boats upon which he designed to cross the Delaware as a bridge were fixed on waggons, besides which he had a large number of flat-bottom boats fixed on waggons to transport to the Delaware. These boats with the necessary apparatus, waggons to convey the baggage and the ammunition waggons, etc., swelled the number of his waggons to perhaps 1000 or 1100, a great incumbrance to an army not very numerous. As I have before written, our position was exceeding good, and while we continued on it, the passage to the Delaware would be rendered extremely precarious, and to attack us in camp was an event much to be wished. However, something was to be done. General Sullivan was posted at Princeton with a force pretty respectable in itself but not sufficient to stop General Howe's army ; and he might, by a forced march, push a column between Princeton and us, and cut off General Sullivan's communications, at least ; but our intelligence being pretty

7

good, the General directed Sullivan to take post about four miles
from Princeton in such a manner that the surrounding of him would
be impracticable.   We also had a party at Milstone as a cover for the
ammunition to Princeton.   This was a dangerous post from its
proximity to the enemy, but rendered less so by the extreme vigilance
which we recommended and which the commanding officer particularly obeyed.   Matters were thus situated on the morning of the
14th, when we discovered that the party at Milstone was attacked.
Support was immediately sent to cover the retreat of the party, when
it was discovered to be the enemy's main body, as the same body of
observation posted there were obliged to retreat '*pretty quick*.' The
enemy took position.   Our whole army was immediately ordered
under arms, ready to be put in motion ; but the conduct of the
enemy rendered it unnecessary, for, instead of immediately pushing
for the Delaware, distant about twenty-five miles, or attacking General Sullivan, he sat down on the ground and instantly began to
fortify in a very strong position ; but it was not till the next day that
we discovered their work.   Their conduct was perplexing.   It was
unaccountable that people who the day before gave out in very gasconading terms that they would be in Philadelphia in six days should
stop short when they had gone only nine miles.   The intelligence
was pretty good with respect to their designs, yet it was too imperfect in respect to their numbers to warrant an attack on troops so
well disciplined, and posted as they were.   We also, in the course
of a day or two, discovered that they had not moved with any baggage, even tents and the most necessary, but had come out with an
intention of drawing us into the plain ; had left their immense number of waggons behind them ; but, even in this kind of ostentatious
challenge, they omitted not one precaution for their own safety.
They had Brunswick and the Raritan River on their right, secured
by eight or ten strong redoubts.   At Brunswick the Raritan bends
and runs a little way north and then turns nearly west.   This they
had in their front, secured by strong redoubts at Middlebrook.
Their left was secured by the river Milstone, which empties itself
into the Raritan near Bound Brook.   From their right to left was
about eight miles.

" In this situation they continued until early in the morning of
the 19th, continually at work throwing up redoubts.   We had a
large body of riflemen, under Colonel Morgan, perpetually making
inroads upon them, attacking their pickets, killing their light-horse ;

and beset them in such a manner that Mr. Howe, instead of marching to Philadelphia, found himself almost blockaded in an open,
flat country. Nothing could exceed the spirit shown on this occasion by the much injured people of the Jerseys. Not an atom of
the lethargic spirit that possessed them last winter,—all fire, all revenge. The militia of Pennsylvania likewise turned out universally,
so that, had Sir William put his attempt into execution, we should
probably have had twenty-five or thirty thousand militia upon his
back, besides the most respectable body of continental troops that
ever were in America.

"These things being fully represented to General Howe, he
thought it proper to take himself and light army back to Brunswick
again, and accordingly marched, about one o'clock in the morning
of the 19th, without beat of drum or sound of fife. When his army
had gotten beyond reach of pursuit, they began to burn, plunder
and waste all before them. The desolation they committed was
horrid and served to show the malice which marks their conduct.

"The militia light horse and riflemen exhibited the greatest marks
of valour, frequently taking prisoners within two hundred yards
of their encampment. Their loss must be at least one hundred
killed and wounded and taken prisoners, among whom are two lieu-
tenants of grenadiers of the 55th, and a cornet of light horse and a
number killed, two sergeants taken. This little march of General
Howe fully proved that no people or country can be permanently
conquered where the inhabitants are unanimous in opposition."

It appears from Knox's letter that Howe put his
whole army in motion on the 14th of June, thereby
impressing the Americans with the notion that an
active campaign was about to begin. He had been
drawing in his forces from Connecticut, New York,
and Staten Island, and had provided himself with a
pontoon train and other contrivances for crossing
streams. These, with the ammunition waggons
swelled his transportation to one thousand or twelve
hundred waggons. The main army of Washington
was posted along the Raritan, making the passage

of the enemy to the Delaware extremely hazardous. Sullivan, with a small force, was at Princeton, and another and smaller force was at Milstone, prepared to parry any blow that might be aimed at Sullivan's detachment.

Howe attacked the party at Milstone, and, covered on their retreat by a force from the Raritan, the Americans fell back upon Princeton. Washington ordered his whole army to be under arms and ready to move, but the British unaccountably paused and began to intrench themselves instead of pushing on to the Delaware, twenty-five miles distant, or attacking General Sullivan. Knox says: " Their conduct was perplexing. It was unaccountable that the people who, the day before, had given out, in very gasconading terms that they would be in Philadelphia in six days, should stop short when they had gone only nine miles." In a very good position for defence, the British remained, continually throwing up redoubts, until the morning of the nineteenth, when, finding himself blockaded in the midst of an open country by the Americans, who had gradually closed in upon him with much raiding and harassing, Howe thought proper to betake himself back to Brunswick. To Brunswick he accordingly went " about one o'clock in the morning of the 19th, without beat of drum or sound of fife. When his army had gotten beyond the reach of pursuit, they began to burn, plunder, and waste all before them. The desolation they committed was horrid, and served to show the malice which marks their conduct."

Knox pays a warm tribute to the spirit exhibited at this time by " the much injured people of New Jersey " and adds: " This little march of General Howe's fully proves that no people or country can be permanently conquered where the inhabitants are unanimous in opposition."

As a matter of fact, whatever may have been the original plans of Howe, he now withdrew once more from New Jersey, his entire army crossing to Staten Island on the 30th of June. From that time forward, for several weeks, his movements were veiled in such secrecy that the Americans were compelled to depend upon guesswork and probabilities for a solution of the military problem presented to them. Even when he finally set sail from New York, on the 23d of July, Washington was still left in doubt as to his ultimate destination. In a breezy letter to his wife, dated at " Beverhout, 8 miles north of Morristown, 26th July, 1777," Knox makes these comments on Howe's motions:

" General Howe has sailed from the Hook, we suppose for Phila-delphia, therefore we are now marching that way. If he is not going there, then Boston must be his object. We intercepted a letter from him to General Burgoyne, purporting that the expedition up the North River is given up for one to Boston. This letter was designed to fall into our hands, in order to deceive. We suppose he will be at Philadelphia near as soon as we : we are now four days' march from it. Upon the whole, I know he *ought*, in justice to his mas-ter, to either go up the North River or to the eastward, and endeavour to form a junction with Burgoyne ; therefore (if he is not a fool), he will operate accordingly ; but we are bound to Philadelphia upon this supposition, and it's very reasonable."

If Lord Howe had been as shrewdly advised as

he might have been by some strategist as competent
as Knox, the disasters that soon after overtook the
British army of invasion, east of the Hudson, would
probably have been averted. Howe's destination
was Philadelphia, and on the 30th of July, the fleet
appeared in the mouth of the Delaware. But that
stream was so obstructed that he again put to sea,
leaving his enemy still in doubt as to his ultimate
objective point. Washington's headquarters were
now established on Neshaminy Creek, about twenty
miles north of Philadelphia, where an enforced wait
of a fortnight kept the Commander-in-chief anxious
to ascertain the next move of his adversary. At
this camp Washington was joined by several volunteer foreign officers of distinction, among them being Lafayette, De Kalb, and eleven others. These
two first-named officers were commissioned major-
generals, after some delay, by Congress.

It was now supposed that Howe had either set
sail for Charleston, or that he had doubled on his
tracks and had gone to Boston. A council of war
in the American camp decided that Charleston was
the destination of the fleet, and that a retrograde
movement upon the Hudson, for the purpose of
heading off Burgoyne, was advisable. Just then the
British fleet was reported off the capes of the Chesapeake, and Washington's army, now numbering
about seven thousand men, was set in motion southward through Philadelphia. On the 25th of August,
Knox wrote as follows to his wife:

" The army yesterday marched through the city of Philadelphia.
Their excellent appearance and marching astonished the Tories, who

are very downcast on the respectability of the army. I was so unhappy as to be absent at this time. General Greene and myself begged the favour of his Excellency's permission to pay a visit to Bethlehem, distant about forty miles, to purchase some things for my dear, dear Lucy. The weather was extremely hot, and we set out about four o'clock in the afternoon and arrived the next morning at nine. An express from the general was waiting for us with orders to return immediately: he had rode all night. However, we first visited all parts of this singularly happy place, where all the inhabitants seem to vie with each other in humility and brotherly kindness. We joined the army, after a most fatiguing jaunt of a hundred miles yesterday, about an hour after they had passed through Philadelphia."

Washington's line of march took him to Wilmington, Delaware, and on the first day of September, Knox, writing from that town, announced the landing of the British in this letter:

"The enemy have landed at the head of the Elk, in Maryland, about twenty miles from this. Whether they intend to advance or not is at present uncertain. We shall remain here a few days; and if they will not come to us, we shall go to them. It is supposed that the enemy intend for Philadelphia; if so, they will meet with a stout opposition. I am at this moment president of a court-martial to try an officer of General Howe for recruiting in the Jerseys."

Howe's forces were now concentrated at Kennett Square, about seven miles south of the Brandywine River. Of the fighting at Chad's Ford, and the battle of Brandywine it is not necessary now to speak in detail. The efforts of the Continental army, heroic though they were, were not adequate to head off the British march upon Philadelphia. Knox's first letter, written after the battle, was addressed to his wife to assure her that he had not been whelmed in the great disaster. He says:

" My dear girl will be happy to hear of her Harry's safety; for, my Lucy, Heaven, who is our guide, has protected him in the day of battle. You will hear with this letter of the most severe action that has been fought this war between our army and the enemy. Our people behaved well, but Heaven frowned upon us in a degree. We were obliged to retire after a very considerable slaughter of the enemy: they dared not pursue a single step. If they advance, we shall fight them again before they get possession of Philadelphia; but of this they will be cautious. My corps did me great honour; they behaved like men contending for every thing that 's valuable."

A contemporary account says of Knox's men: " The regiment of artillery with their general behaved with their usual coolness and intrepidity. Some of them could scarce be prevailed on to quit their guns, even when surrounded by the enemy and forsaken by our infantry."

Knox's official account of the battle of Brandywine was sent to the President of the Council of Massachusetts.*

The American loss was set down at nearly three hundred killed, five hundred wounded, and ten field-pieces captured by the enemy. The British loss was reported to be something less than six hundred killed, wounded, and missing. The shattered army of Washington now fell back upon Philadelphia and Germantown, crossing the Schuylkill on the 13th of September. Howe advanced to meet it, and at one time a pitched battle seemed to be imminent, when a rainstorm of extraordinary violence set in and the ammunition of Washington's men was so damaged by water flowing into the cartridge boxes that a retreat was ordered and the army fell back to

* See Appendix.

THE MARQUIS DE LAFAYETTE.

FROM A FRENCH PRINT, 1781.

French Creek, Warwick Township, to repair and refit. These movement are thus described in a letter from Knox to his wife, dated at Pottstown, Sept. 24, 1777:

" I wrote you on the 13th. The same day we crossed the Schuylkill, in order to try the issue of another appeal to Him who directs all human events. After some days' manœuvring, we came in sight of the enemy, and drew up in order of battle, which the enemy declined ; but a most violent rain coming on obliged us to change our position, in the course of which nearly all the musket cartridges of the army that had been delivered to the men were damaged, consisting of above 400,000. This was a most terrible stroke to us, and owing entirely to the badness of the cartridge-boxes which had been provided for the army.

" This unfortunate event obliged us to retire, in order to get supplied with so essential an article as cartridges, after which we forded the Schuylkill, in order to be opposite to the enemy ; accordingly we took post at a place called Flatland Ford.

"A defensive war is the most difficult to guard against, because one is always obliged to attend to the feints of the enemy. To defend an extensive river when it is unfordable is almost impossible ; but when fordable in every part, it becomes impracticable. On the afternoon of the 21st the enemy made a most rapid march of ten or twelve miles to our right : this obliged us to follow them. They kindled large fires, and in the next night marched as rapidly back and crossed at a place where we had few guards, and pushed towards Philadelphia, and will this morning enter the city without opposition. We fought one battle for it, and it was no deficiency in bravery that lost us the day. Philadelphia, it seems, has been their favourite object. Their shipping has not joined them there. They will first have to raise the *chevaux de frise* in the Delaware, and defeat the naval force there, which is considerable.

" The troops in this excursion of ten days without baggage suffered excessive hardships,—without tents in the rain, several marches of all night, and often without sufficient provision. This they endured with the perseverance and patience of good soldiers. Generals Smallwood, Wayne, McDougall, and a considerable body of militia, will join us to-day and to-morrow. This day we shall move towards

Philadelphia, in order to try the fortune of another battle in which we devoutly hope the blessing of Heaven. I consider the loss of Philadelphia as only temporary,—to be recovered when expedient. It is no more than the loss of Boston, nor, in my opinion, half so much, when the present trade of the latter be considered. It is situated on a point of land formed by the rivers Delaware and Schuylkill, so that it would have been highly improper to have thrown ourselves into it.

" If the enemy do not get their shipping up soon, and go into Philadelphia, they will be in a very ineligible situation. I do not in the present circumstances consider Philadelphia of so much consequence as the loss of reputation to our arms ; but I trust in God we shall soon make up that matter. Billy * is well, and undergoes the hardships of the campaign surprisingly well, and they are neither few nor small."

Great was the panic in Philadelphia when the inhabitants of the capital were told that the British army was approaching and could be in the city within a few hours. The members of the Continental Congress were roused from their beds at midnight of the 19th of the month, Alexander Hamilton, of Washington's staff, being the bearer of the evil tidings. The delegates, who were under the royal ban as traitors of the deepest dye, set off in hot haste, and the exultant Tories made ready to receive the King's army with acclaim. But, although the message of Washington warned the people that the enemy *could be* in the city within a few hours, Howe, marching with his customary deliberation, gave ample time for the escape of those who had the best reason to dread capture; and it was not until the forenoon of the 26th that Cornwallis, with his Hessians and

---

* Knox's brother, William, had joined the army at this time, and was with the column until after the battle of Germantown.

English, entered the city amid the cheers of the Tories. On the 3d of October, Knox wrote to his friend Colonel Henry Jackson from "Camp at Metuchin, twenty miles from Philadelphia," as follows:

"MY DEAR HARRY,—The enemy are now encamped at Philadel. phia and its environs for about six miles. The *Delaware* frigate was given up to them in a manner scandalous to relate. The crew, it's said, after they had fired one broadside at a battery which was erecting near the city, ran her ashore, and gave her up to the Britons. The crew were principally foreigners. Our army has had several reinforcements of militia, etc., since the late action. I hope for better success in the next; and an action we shall most assuredly have before we go into winter quarters."

The British approach to Philadelphia by water was hindered by a fleet of small armed craft that hovered around the mouth of the Delaware River, just above a line of obstructions that had been drawn across the stream by the Americans, and by two forts—Fort Mifflin on an island off the Pennsylvania side of the river and Fort Mercer on New Jersey side. Howe sent down a detachment of troops to reduce these two forts, and Washington, learning by intercepted letters of this reduction of the main army of the British, resolved to attack the enemy, whose position, divided between Germantown and Philadelphia, appeared to offer an opportunity. By breaking the line of reinforcement from Philadelphia and attacking him on the flank and front, it was hoped that that part of the army quartered in Germantown could be routed before aid could arrive from Philadelphia. This well-planned assault was defeated.　The Americans moved in four columns, the main reliance being upon the two central columns, one of which was commanded by Greene and the other by Sullivan.　The movement began on the evening of the 3d of October.　The enemy were completely surprised and the Americans pressed eagerly on, Washington, Knox, and other officers of the staff riding in the rear with Lord Stirling's reserves.

Sullivan's column, which was composed of his own and Wayne's divisions, had passed the stone mansion known as the "Chew house" without noticing that a British force of about two hundred had occupied the structure, and, by barricading the lower story, had converted it into a fortress of considerable strength.　This was discovered when Stirling's reserves came up, and the British troops in the house opened fire upon them.　A consultation was held to consider the expediency of reducing the improvised fort before going on.　Knox insisted that it was against all military rule and tradition to leave a fortification in the rear, and operations against the house were begun.　But the light field-pieces and musketry of the assailants had little effect upon the solid walls of the mansion, although the scars of shot remain unto this day to testify to the severity of the fusillade.

For two hours a hot contest raged around the Chew house, and the unexpected choice of this now historic mansion as the pivotal point of the battle not only misled the troops in the advance, but it confused the line of march and detained

THE CHEW HOUSE, GERMANTOWN, PA.

Stirling's reserves who were coming up to the support of Sullivan's and Wayne's columns. Worse than this, the troops, now enveloped in the smoke of battle and a heavy fog, in the early morning light, were thrown into inextricable confusion on the left of Wayne's command. General Stephens, on the left, made the blunder of supposing the firing at the Chew house to be an attack by the British in the rear; and he accordingly changed his line of march and turning in that direction, fell upon Wayne's rear and began a fire into the American troops. This disastrous blunder lost the battle of Germantown. It was believed that the day was won for the Americans when Stephens's attack on Wayne's rear destroyed all hope of success. A court-martial showed that Stephens was drunk at the time he left his proper line of march, and he was dismissed from the service. Whether Knox's advice to attack the Chew house was sound has since been debated by competent military critics without any conclusive verdict. Washington, who was a man of independent judgment, sanctioned the attack, which was conducted under his own eyes. It may be observed that in Knox's report of the battle of Germantown, sent to General Artemas Ward, President of the Council of Massachusetts, no allusion is made to the Chew house incident. The report is herewith printed:

" Artillery Park, Perkeomy Creek,
" (27 miles from Philadelphia), October 7, 1777.
" Hon. Artemas Ward :

" Sir,—I shall endeavour to give you a short authentic account of an attack made by our army on the British army, lying at Germantown, six miles from Philadelphia, on the morning of the 4th instant.

"At six o'clock on the evening of the 3d, the army, under his Excellency General Washington, began their march in four columns on as many roads towards the enemy; the nearest column had to march fourteen, and some twenty, miles. By marching all night, the columns arrived a little after break of day (opposite) to the respective posts of the enemy assigned to them. The attack commenced by forcing their pickets, which were soon reinforced in front by all the light infantry of the line and other troops. After a smart action, these were obliged to give way, our troops pressing on with great spirit and good order.

"The different attacks being made at the same time distracted the enemy's attention so much, that after about an hour's engagement they began to give way on every part; but, most unfortunately for us, a fog which had arisen about daybreak became so excessively thick from the continued firing that it was impossible to discover an object at twenty yards' distance.

"This was the unhappy cause of our losing the victory after being in possession of it for near two hours, and having driven the enemy above two miles from the place where the engagement begun, quite through their encampment. In this unusual fog it was impossible to know how to support, or what part to push. At this instant, the enemy again rallied and obliged part of our troops to retire; and after a smart resistance, the retreat of the line became general. The enemy followed with caution, and we came off without the loss of a single piece of cannon or any thing else, except one empty ammunition waggon, the engagement from beginning to end being about two hours and forty minutes.

"Our loss in killed, wounded, and missing, is not fully ascertained, but will not exceed five hundred or six hundred. We had a very considerable number of officers of merit killed and wounded. Brigadier-General Nash, of North Carolina, mortally wounded by a cannon-ball taking off his thigh.

"The enemy's loss, we hear from pretty good authority, is very considerable; General Agnew killed, Sir William Erskine wounded. This is the first attack made during this war by the American troops on the main body of the enemy; and had it not been for the unlucky circumstance of the fog, Philadelphia would probably have been in our hands. It is matter worthy of observation that in most other countries which have been invaded one or two battles have decided their fate ; but America rises after a defeat !

"We were more numerous after the battle of Brandywine than before, and we have demonstration of being more numerous now than before the 4th. Our men are in the highest spirits, and ardently desire another trial. I know of no ill consequences that can follow the late action ; on the contrary, we have gained considerable experience, and our army have a certain proof that the British troops are vulnerable."

Washington's army fell back upon Metuchen Hill, where, about two weeks later, the inspiriting news of Burgoyne's surrender to Gates at Saratoga was received. Notwithstanding the confusion occasioned by the rivalries and jealousies among the American commanders, and the reverses with which their defensive campaign had opened, St. Leger, marching to the support of Burgoyne, had been cut off, and the battles of Bennington, Oriskany, and Stillwater rendered Burgoyne's position exceedingly critical. His final surrender on the 18th of October, 1777, was hailed by the patriotic people of the young States with rapture and hopeful enthusiasm. While this campaign was in progress, but before Burgoyne's surrender was an accomplished fact, Knox, writing to his wife, after the battle of Stillwater, or Freeman's farm, says: "Observe, my dear girl, how Providence supports us. The advantages gained by our Northern army give almost a decisive turn to the contest. For my own part, I have not yet seen so bright a dawn as the prospect, and I am as perfectly convinced in my own mind of the kindness of Providence towards us as I am of my own existence."

The British continued to batter at the forts block-
ing the entrance to the Delaware, but with very
little success. In an attack on Fort Mercer, the
Hessian colonel, Donop, and his second in command
were killed and two British ships were destroyed.
The news of Burgoyne's surrender came to raise still
higher the spirits of the Americans, who fired a joyful salute at their camp near Philadelphia. Knox,
in a letter to his wife, dated November 3d, says:

" The enemy have not yet been able to drive our galleys away, or
storm, or batter our forts with success. We have lately had a storm,
which has ruined their batteries and works erected against Fort
Mifflin. Since they had two men-of-war burnt on the 23d in the
river, and were defeated at Red Bank, they have appeared quite
silent in deeds, but not so in words. They have been very angry for
our *feux de joie*, which we have fired on the several victories over
Burgoyne, and say that by and by we shall bring ourselves into contempt with our own army for propagating such known falsehoods.
Poor fellows ! nothing but Britain must triumph."

But the attempt of the British to reduce Fort
Mifflin, made on the 10th of November, with a
formidable fleet, was successful; the garrison evacuated the fort in the night, taking refuge in Fort
Mercer, at Red Bank, on the opposite side of the
river. On the 15th, Knox, with De Kalb and St.
Clair, was sent to the relief of the beleaguered Jersey
fort with instructions to increase its defences. But
Cornwallis now advanced into New Jersey at the
head of a large force and the position at Red Bank
became untenable. It was abandoned, and the
British fleet, now that all obstructions were removed, was in full and undisputed possession of

Philadelphia. Howe vainly tried to bring on a general engagement; but Washington, secure in his entrenched camp, ten or twelve miles from Philadelphia, refused to be drawn out of his lines. Councils of war were held at Washington's headquarters to consider the expediency of attacking the enemy in the city of Philadelphia. It was proposed to attack by storming the enemy's redoubts; to throw twelve hundred troops into the city by the way of the Delaware, embarking them at Dunx's Ferry, sixteen miles above Philadelphia. These councils, held on the 26th of October and on the 3d of December, decided not to order the attack.

Knox's opinion was adverse to making the proposed assault. In his written statement, submitted in response to Washington's request, and dated at "Artillery Park, Camp Whitemarsh, 26th November, 1777," Knox, after recounting sundry reasons why the project seemed to him hopeless, considered in the light of past events, says: "My opinion is to draw our whole force together, take post at, and fortify Germantown, considering it as our winter quarters." He then advises that when the defence of the camp is amply provided for, a battle should be offered to the enemy, predicting that the superiority of the Americans would be fully evinced. He concludes: "If they should come out, fight, and defeat us, we have a secure retreat and winter quarters." To the council of December he gave these reasons for still opposing the projected attack on Philadelphia: "Our entire want of clothing; the impossibility of surprising ten thousand veteran

8

troops in a well fortified city; the impossibility of
our keeping the field to besiege their works and city
regularly, being almost totally deficient in warlike
apparatus for so arduous an enterprise; and the uncertainty of obtaining a sufficient number of militia
to warrant the enterprise." He proposed that the
army go into winter quarters with the right resting
upon Lancaster and the left at Reading, provided
sufficient cover could be there obtained; if not, then
quarters should be established near the Schuylkill,
about thirty miles from Philadelphia, huts being
constructed for the men.

Winter quarters were finally selected at Valley
Forge, somewhat nearer the city than the point in-
dicated by Knox, and the army took up its line of
march for the locality made sadly famous in American history by the subsequent sufferings of the
patriot forces. Their dreary march was undertaken
by ill-clad and barefooted men in the midst of an
inclement season. Washington's word is given for
the statement that that march of his men might
have been tracked " from White Marsh to Valley
Forge by the blood of their feet."

Knox was given leave of absence to visit his wife
in Boston, during this cessation of active operations,
and to him, on the 26th of February, 1778, General
Greene wrote from Valley Forge, giving him this
account of some of the privations of that winter:

"The army has been in great distress since you left it. The
troops are getting naked ; and they were seven days without meat,
and several days without bread. Such patience and moderation as
they manifested under their sufferings does the highest honour to the

magnanimity of the American soldiers. The seventh day they came before their superior officers, and told their sufferings in as respectful terms as if they had been petitioners for special favours. They added that it would be impossible to continue in camp any longer without support. Happily, relief arrived from the little collections I and some others had made, and prevented the army from disbanding. We are still in danger of starving. Hundreds of our horses have already starved to death. The Committee of Congress have seen all those things with their own eyes. They have been urging me for several days to accept the quartermaster-general's appointment, his Excellency also presses upon me exceedingly. I hate the place, but I hardly know what to do. I wish for your advice in the affair, but I am obliged to determine immediately."

It was during this trying and critical time for the American cause that the "Conway cabal," composed of sundry intriguers in the military service, attempted the destruction of Washington's supremacy. Gates, whose fortuitous success in the North had given him great prestige, was a leader in the opposition to Washington. Conway, whose name was given to this junta, was a soldier of fortune, sent over by Silas Deane and made Inspector-General of the army in place of the ill-fated Ducoudray. The other active members of the cabal were Mifflin and the traitorous Charles Lee, who had not then been detected in his secret correspondence with the enemy. The Continental Congress was sitting at York, Pennsylvania, and while some of its members were conspiring to remove the Commander-in-chief, that dilatory and dawdling body failed to make adequate provision for the sustenance and equipment of the dejected army at Valley Forge. The darkest days for the young republic had come.

CHAPTER VI

IN THE DARKEST DAYS OF THE WAR

1778–1781

ILITARY operations in the early part of 1778 appear to have waited on diplomacy. The long and tedious negotiations between the American envoys and the Government of France, looking to the conclusion of a treaty of amity and alliance, were brought to a crisis by the news that the redoubtable Burgoyne had surrendered his army at Saratoga. The treaty was concluded in Paris on the 6th of February and was ratified by the Continental Congress on the second of May, amid great popular rejoicings. Nowhere was the glorious news more enthusiastically celebrated than by the impoverished and suffering army in camp at Valley Forge. A day for public rejoicing was set apart in general orders, and the slender resources of the camp were taxed to their utmost to furnish means to make manifest the satisfaction with which the troops received the news of the alliance. The demonstration chiefly consisted of a general parade

of all the battalions and the firing of several salutes
of thirteen guns each.   The infantry were ordered
to keep up a running fire, and this was followed by
salutes of thirteen rounds by the artillery under the
direction of General Knox, who had returned to the
army several weeks earlier.   According to a contemporaneous account, upon a signal given, the
troops shouted at different times as follows: "Huzza!
Long live the King of France!"   "Huzza! Long
live the friendly European Powers!"   "Huzza for
the American States!"

The British Government was forced at last to
recognise the Continental Congress as a lawful body,
and commissioners to treat for terms of peace were
appointed and despatched from England.   These
officials arrived in June and their credentials were
immediately presented to that representative assembly, the Continental Congress.   The brief and
comprehensive reply to the peace commissioners
was to the effect that Congress would be satisfied
with nothing short of " an explicit acknowledgment
of the independence of these States, or the withdrawing of his [the King's] fleets and armies."   The
last attempt of the British Government to secure a
cessation of hostilities without an acknowledgment
of the independence of the new American States
had failed.

In the meantime, there were very few military
movements of importance in any part of the country,
and midsummer had arrived before these were to be
resumed.   At the Valley Forge camp were several
ladies of distinction, among them being Mrs. Martha

Washington, Lady Kitty Stirling, and the wife of General Greene. On the 20th of May, Mrs. Knox, who had been escorted from New Haven by General Benedict Arnold, arrived in the camp. She remained with the army, with which she was a great favourite, or very near its headquarters, from that time until it was disbanded at the close of the war.

Concentration of the British forces was now of more consequence than the mere occupation of territory, and orders for a return of the army to New York had arrived with the peace commissioners. The evacuation of Philadelphia was doubtless hastened by the news that a French fleet, under the command of Count D'Estaing, was momentarily expected on the coast. Sir Henry Clinton superseded Lord Howe in command of the army, which, on the 18th of June, 1778, left Philadelphia where it had been lying for eight months without having occupied any territory outside the city and its immediate environs. The army crossed the Delaware at Gloucester Point, about three miles below the city, with a baggage train that was reported to be ten miles long and which included officers' luggage and their plunder from the private houses of Philadelphia. In this plunder, it may be noted, was an assortment of books from the library of Benjamin Franklin, selected by Major John André,* who had been quartered in the house of the American patriot and philosopher, then absent in France.

As soon as Washington was informed of the evacuation of the city, he prepared to follow the trail of

* *The Many-Sided Franklin*, by Paul Leicester Ford.

the retreating army, and on the 21st his columns crossed the Delaware at Coryell's Ferry, at the point now occupied by the town of Lambertville, New Jersey. On the 28th the army struck the rear of Clinton's retreating forces and the battle of Monmouth followed. The weather was intensely hot, and officers and men on both sides suffered severely from the heat. During the trying march across the Jerseys, there were many desertions from the British columns, six or eight hundred Hessians having safely escaped from their own lines. A council of war was held at Hopewell on the 24th of June to consider the advisability of inviting from Clinton a general engagement. Six of the generals, including Charles Lee, were in favour of the enemy's being followed up and harassed on his rear and flanks by separate and cautious attacks. Six others, including Greene, Knox, and Lafayette, favoured more vigourous tactics. Next day, writing, at four o'clock in the morning, from Hopewell, Knox gave his brother, who had returned to Boston, these particulars of the situation at that time:

"The enemy evacuated Philadelphia on the 19th. Lucy and I went in, but it stunk so abominably that it was impossible to stay there, as was her first design. The enemy are now at Allen Town, about ten miles south-east of Princeton, and we are at about six miles north of Princeton, so that the two armies are now nineteen or twenty miles apart. We are now on the march towards them, and their movements this day will determine whether we shall come in close contact with each other. We have now very numerous parties harrassing and teasing them on all quarters. Desertion prevails exceedingly in their ranks, especially among the Germans. Above three hundred German and English have deserted since they left Philadelphia. Had we a sufficiency of numbers, we should be able to force them to a similar treaty with Burgoyne; but, at present, have not quite such sanguine hopes. If general actions had no other consequences than merely the killed and wounded, we should attack them in twenty-four hours. But the fate of posterity, and not the illusive brilliancy of military glory, governs our Fabian commander, the man to whom, under God, America owes her present prospects of peace and happiness."

Clinton's original intention had been to march to South Amboy, but the appearance of Washington's forces upon his left flank and rear induced him to deflect from that line, the crossing of the Raritan now becoming hazardous; he accordingly turned the head of his columns in the direction of Sandy Hook, by the way of Freehold and Monmouth. Of the battle of the 28th, Knox wrote as follows to his wife:

"June 29, NEAR MONMOUTH COURT HOUSE.

"MY DEAREST LOVE :—I wrote you some few days ago that a day or two would determine whether we should have an engagement with the Britons. Yesterday, at about nine o'clock A.M., our advanced parties, under General Lee, attacked their rear while on the march towards Shrewsbury, upon which their whole army, except the Hessians, came to the right about; and, after some fighting, obliged him to retire to the main army, which was about two miles distant. The enemy advanced with great spirit to the attack, and began a very brisk cannonade on us, who were formed to receive them.

"The cannonade lasted from about eleven until six o'clock, at which time the enemy began to retire on all quarters and left us in possession of the field. We have had several field officers killed. Colonel Ramsay, Mrs. Ramsay's husband, was taken prisoner and this morning released on his parole. I have had several officers killed and wounded. My brave lads behaved with their usual intrepidity, and the army gave the corps of artillery their full proportion of the glory of the day.

"Indeed, upon the whole, it was very splendid. The capital army of Britain defeated and obliged to retreat before the Americans, whom they despised so much! I cannot ascertain either our or the

enemy's loss, but I really think they have lost three times the number we have.   I judge from the field of battle, which, to be sure, is
a field of carnage and blood :   Three to one of the British forces lie
there.   The Britons confess they have never received so severe a
check.   The enemy took a strong post about a mile from the place
of action, to dislodge them from which, as it was dark, would cost
too many men, and by which they covered the retreat of their army.
After having been fighting all day, and one of the hottest I ever felt,
they decamped in the night and marched off with the utmost precipi-
tation, leaving a great number of their wounded, both officers and
men, in our hands.   We have sent out large bodies in pursuit, but I
believe they will not be able to come up with the main body. . . .
The number of deserters, since they left Philadelphia, must exceed
eight hundred.   The march has proved to them a most destructive
one and is very ill-calculated to give Sir H. Clinton any *éclat.*   He
may storm Fort Montgomery, but is very ill-calculated, in my
opinion, to be at the head of a large army.

   " My friend Harry [Jackson] crossed over from Philadelphia and
was in the unfortunate [*i.e.* early] part of the day.   I saw him once
on the field for a moment : He appeared much fatigued.   His
regiment had a few killed and wounded and is reported to have
behaved well."

A contemporaneous account says that soon after
the evacuation of Philadelphia, " the Honourable
Major-General Arnold took possession of Philadelphia, with Colonel Jackson's Massachusetts regiment." *   This explains Jackson's presence in the
evacuated city at that time.   It will be seen that
Knox's accounts of the battle of Monmouth were
very moderate in tone, considering the conspicuous
and gallant part which he took in that historic engagement.   Writing to his brother, July 3, 1778, he
says :

   " The enemy inclined more to their right than we expected, and

   * *Pennsylvania Evening Post,* June 20, 1778.

took the road to Sandy Hook, instead of the supposed one to South Amboy.

" A body of Jersey militia, amounting to near 2000, had endeavoured to retard them, by taking up the bridges, felling trees, and harassing their flanks and rear. Beside these, his Excellency General Washington had detached several large bodies for the same purpose, all of which, except Colonel Morgan, were, on the 28th ult., united under General Lee, who early on that morning advanced to Monmouth Court House with the intention of attacking the covering party by left flank, the main army moving on at the same time to support him, although it was some miles in the rear. The parties under General Lee, instead of finding a covering party as was expected, found their whole army or the greater part of it. After some manoeuvring, cannonading, and some other circumstances, which are not yet sufficiently explained, it was thought proper by Gen. Lee to retire until it met the main army, which it effected without much loss. The army was drawn up on advantageous ground to receive the enemy who advanced to the attack with considerable impetuosity, and began a brisk cannonade, which was returned with becoming spirit. The action of the musketry was various, and with intermissions until about six o'clock, when we pushed the enemy off the field. Their whole loss may amount to about ten or twelve hundred killed, wounded and prisoners. His Excellency, the General, has done the corps of artillery and me the honour to notice us in general orders in very pointed and flattering terms. Indeed, I was highly delighted with their coolness, bravery, and good conduct. The effects of the Battle of Monmouth will be great and lasting. It will convince the enemy and the world that nothing but a good constitution is wanting to render our army equal to any in the world."

It was at this same battle of Monmouth that Washington lost his temper and reprimanded Gen. Charles Lee in terms that have become historic. Lee, who seems to have entered into the fight with little zeal, and who had declined to agree to any concerted plan of action, preferring to be left to be governed by circumstances, so handled his men as to bring on a confused and demoralising retreat when he should have attacked the enemy with vigour as soon as he discovered that they were in motion. Whether Washington, who soon came up and took sole command of the army, really cursed Lee with sublime and righteous indignation, as tradition has told us, is not a matter of unquestioned record. Even the most rigid of moralists would have been willing to condone a more violent exhibition of wrath than that commonly credited to the usually placid Washington, under the provoking circumstances.

Dr. Thacher, in his *Military Journal*, gives this impartial and apparently dispassionate account of the affair:

" His Excellency was exceedingly mortified and astonished [at Lee's retreat] ; coming up to General Lee, and meeting part of his his corps in their flight, he with some warmth inquired the cause of his retreat, and addressed General Lee in language which implied censure. The high-spirited Lee could not brook the slightest appearance of disapprobation, and replied with an air of disrespect. He, however, requested of his Excellency fresh orders for the conduct of his corps, and these he promptly obeyed, and discovered no want of bravery in the field. But, unable to quell the rankling of a turbulent temper, he addressed, after the battle, two letters to the Commander-in-chief, containing improper and disrespectful expressions. As if in defiance of superior authority, he demanded a trial by court-martial, that he might have an opportunity of vindicating his conduct, in consequence of which his Excellency has put him under arrest to await his trial."

The result was that Lee was found guilty of disobedience of orders and misbehaviour in the face of the enemy. He was sentenced to suspension from command for one year. His military career was ended then and there.

When the battle of Monmouth was brought on, Knox in person reconnoitred in front, cheerily rallied the retreating troops (who were demoralised but not alarmed) and brought up the rear with a lively fire from a battery which had been planted during the previous night by his orders. His untiring efforts and good generalship were complimented by the Commander-in-chief, as he proudly notes in one of his letters. In general orders referring to the engagement, Washington says he " can with pleasure inform General Knox and the officers of the artillery that the enemy has done them the justice to acknowledge that no artillery could have been better served than ours." For their bravery in attacking so superior a force and securing so decided an advantage, Congress passed a vote of thanks to General Washington, his officers, and men.

Clinton's march to New York, after the battle of Monmouth, was not further disturbed. Washington followed, establishing his army at White Plains, New York, where he awaited developments. Great expectations were then entertained of the French fleet under D'Estaing, which arrived off the coast of New York in the latter part of July, 1778. It consisted of twelve ships, and carried four thousand troops. But the high hopes of the Continentals were not realised in the actions of D'Estaing. The fleet was too late to assist in the reduction of Philadelphia, the British having already evacuated that city. Instead of entering the port of New York, where a

WASHINGTON AT MONMOUTH.

FROM A DESIGN BY F. O. C. DARLEY.

considerable number of British men-of-war and
transports were assembled, D'Estaing, protesting
that he could not cross the harbour bar, sailed for
Newport, Rhode Island, where he was followed by
Howe's fleet from New York.   A misunderstanding
with General Sullivan, who was then in command at
Rhode Island, prevented that co-operation between
the French naval contingent and the land forces
which had been arranged, and both fleets put out to
sea, where they were overtaken and scattered by a
tremendous storm.   D'Estaing went to Boston,
taking his troops with him, as if his ships could not
be refitted and provisioned unless the French soldiers, so much needed by Sullivan, were on board
to witness the process.   The popular disappoint-
ment and discontent were very great.

The New England campaign was without serious
results except that the British, angered by Sullivan's
elusion of their trap to catch him, burned New Bed-
ford and Fairhaven, with all the shipping in those
parts.   Meanwhile, there was much desultory fighting in various parts of the country during the au-
tumnal months; but none of these events, although
of great importance to the people involved, was in
the least related to operations along the coast.
D'Estaing's fleet, being refitted, declined Howe's
challenge to combat and sailed for the West Indies
and left the American cause to take care of itself.

Washington still retained his position at White
Plains, keeping a wary observation on the movements of the enemy.   But there was in New York
an utter absence of all appearance of military

activity, and a strict surveillance over all channels of communication was maintained, the better to mystify and baffle the American commander. In a letter to his brother, dated at the camp in White Plains, September 14, 1778, Knox says:

"We wish to know where Lord Howe is, as it might be some clew to the designs of the enemy; though as to dangerous designs they have none, I am persuaded, nor ever had, except to themselves. It is improper for a person in my station to speak thus, were it to be divulged; but I do not believe there ever was a set of men so perfectly disqualified, by a total and profound ignorance of every thing that ought to constitute the characters of leaders of an army to conquest. I beg you not to imagine that by depreciation of their abilities I mean to exalt our own. God forbid! I shall say nothing about it but only this, that we never set ourselves up as great military men. I believe they (the enemy) are about to *quit* the continent, and perhaps *only* wait for their last orders to effect it."

Knox was ever an optimist, and to his unshaken faith in the ultimate triumph of the American cause (which he regarded as the cause of truth and righteousness), he added a hopeful spirit that never for a moment deserted him through all the dark days of the Revolution. But his belief that the silence of the British at their headquarters in New York was premonitory of their speedy departure was not to be justified by subsequent events. Weary years were to pass before Knox should lead the victorious columns of the army into the evacuated city of New York.

The year closed without any important engagements on the land; but on the sea the exploits of Paul Jones and the destructive doings of the American privateers carried panic and terror into the

commercial cities of England. The foreign commerce
of that country was paralysed by the " pirates," as
the English called these dreaded craft.   Nearly five
hundred vessels engaged in deep-sea voyages were
captured or destroyed by the Americans in the year
1777, and the admiralty courts of the New England
coast districts were crowded with proceedings for
the condemnation of English prizes brought in by
the hardy privateers fitted out in those ports.
Eighteen prizes were brought into New London in
the month of May, 1779; and the admiralty courts
for the Essex district of Massachusetts condemned
more than eight hundred prizes during 1780.

Knox and his friend Jackson were together interested in some of these privateering speculations;
but they seem to have been rather unfortunate in
such ventures.   Knox's correspondence shows that
many a vessel in which he had shares was captured
by the enemy, some of them being laden with valuable cargoes taken from the enemy's ships, and some
of them being headed off by British men-of-war just
as they were entering their home port after prosperous ventures.   In a letter to his brother dated at the
artillery camp near Pluckemin, New Jersey, at the
beginning of 1779, Knox says:

" I am sorry for the loss of the vessel you mention, but not discouraged. I hope the little vessel will at least make up for her. I
wrote for you to try something, by way of adventure in the *General
Arnold*. She is a good vessel and commander. . . . I am exceedingly anxious to effect something in these fluctuating times
which may make us lazy for life. You know my sentiments with
respect to making any thing out of the public. I abominate the
idea. I could not, at the end of the war, mix with my fellow

citizens with that conscious integrity, the felicity which I often anticipate."

There was a great scarcity of ordnance materials in camp at this time and Knox was at his wits' end to supply the deficiency. Sent on a mission of exploration to Philadelphia, in February, 1779, he wrote to his brother thus:

" We are in great want of lead. The Board of War have desired me to write to Boston to inquire what quantity can be gotten there and at the neighbouring towns, and at what price. I wish you to make the inquiry, or rather get some person to make it for you, as the gentleman speculators may suspect from your connection that you want it for the public and advance their prices in proportion. Write me the result as speedily as possible, so that I may communicate it to the board. . . . I am glad you have gotten into the old store. I thank you for the little pamphlet. The girls are the same everywhere—at least some of them : they love a red coat dearly. Arnold is going to be married to a beautiful and accomplished young lady, —a Miss Shippen, of one of the best families of this place."

Arnold's bride was Margaret Shippen, daughter of Edward Shippen, a distinguished Tory, of Philadelphia. It was this lady's correspondence with Major André, innocent enough in itself, that was subsequently believed to have opened a means of communication between the British commander and Benedict Arnold. Just here, it is interesting to recall the fact that Arnold's engagement to Miss Shippen was not his first entanglement in the meshes of a love affair. In the Knox Papers is a note from him to Mrs. Knox, dated at Watertown, Mass., March 4, 1777, enclosing a note from Arnold to " the heavenly Miss Deblois," which the writer hopes Mrs. Knox will see is forwarded to the lady

thus rapturously described.   Arnold concludes his
letter to Mrs. Knox as follows:

"I shall remain under under the most anxious suspense until I
have the favour of a line from you, who, I may judge, will from your
own experience conceive the fond anxiety, the glowing hopes and
chilling fears that alternately possess the breast of,
"Dear Madam,
"Your obd't & most Humble sev't,
"B. ARNOLD."

It was while he was in command in Philadelphia
that charges were brought against Arnold by the
State.   After some delay, he was finally arraigned
before a court-martial, and, under the sentence of
the court, he was publicly rebuked by the Commander-in-chief.   At that very time, while he was
in active communication with the enemy, having in
view a betrayal of his trusts, he had the hardihood
to allude to the charges against Adjutant-General
Reed, President of the Court (who had been accused
of an intention to desert the patriots' cause), in these
terms: " When our illustrious General was retreating through New Jersey with a handful of men, I
did not propose to my associates basely to quit the
General, and sacrifice the cause of my country to my
personal safety, by going over to the enemy and
making my peace."   The great soul of Knox could
not for a moment entertain a doubt of the loyalty
of his brother-in-arms, and, writing to William
Knox, about this time, he says: " You will see in
the papers some highly colored charges against
General Arnold by the State of Pennsylvania.   I
shall be exceedingly mistaken if one can be proven.

9

Hè has returned to Philadelphia, and will, I hope, be able to vindicate himself from the aspersions of his enemies.''

While the army was in winter quarters at Plucke-min, New Jersey, Knox endeavoured to make some humble beginning of the military academy which he insisted was absolutely needful for the proper train-ing of officers, and which subsequently took perma-nent shape in the Military Academy at West Point. A writer in the *Philadelphia Packet*, March 6, 1779, giving a description of a fête at the camp in honour of the first anniversary of the French alliance, says of Knox's artillery park, as it was called:

"A range of field-pieces, mortars, and heavy cannon make the front line of a parallelogram ; the other sides are composed of huts for the officers and privates ; there is also an academy where lectures are read on tactics and gunnery, and work huts for those employed in the laboratory, all very judiciously arranged. This military vil-lage is superior in some respects, to most of those that I had seen. Its regularity, its appearance, and the ground on which it stands, throws over it a look of enchantment, although it is no more than the work of a few weeks."

The writer says that the auditorium of the academy was fifty feet by thirty, " arched in an agreeable manner, and neatly plastered within." This was the seed from which was to spring, in years to come, the military academy which is to-day one of the finest of its kind in the world.

The fête which the writer above alludes to was rather tardily given, imperative engagements of General Washington and others of his staff having prevented the celebration of the anniversary of the

exact date of the conclusion of the treaty of alliance.
Dr. Thacher gives this account of the affair:

"The anniversary of our alliance with France was celebrated in proper style a few days since near headquarters at Pluckemin. A splendid entertainment was given by General Knox and the officers of the artillery. General Washington, and his lady, with the principal officers of the army and their ladies, and a considerable number of respectable ladies and gentlemen of the State of New Jersey, formed the brilliant assembly. About four o'clock sixteen cannon were discharged, and the company collected in a large public building [the academy hall] to partake of an elegant dinner. In the evening a very beautiful set of fireworks was exhibited, and the celebration was concluded by a splendid ball opened by his Excellency General Washington, having for his partner the lady of General Knox."

The work of Washington's army in 1779 was necessarily confined to the keeping of a watchful observation of Clinton, who rested in New York. Tories and British alike united in the proclamation in great swelling words of the impending doom of the patriot army during the coming summer. In a letter to his brother William, from Pluckemin, May 7, 1779, Knox, alluding to the enforced idleness of the American army, says: "If we are to believe Rivington's paper of May 1, we are to have bloody work this summer. They swear by monstrous big oaths that they will exterminate us this campaign. However that *may* be, we at present have but little apprehensions of it, although, from a variety of corroborating circumstances, we expect we shall have a much more active campaign than the last."

Early in June, there was every reason to suppose that Clinton would attack the important post at

West Point, his forces having advanced up the
Hudson as far as King's Ferry, thirteen miles below
West Point. The army at Pluckemin and vicinity
broke camp and marched in hot haste to Morristown,
where its heavy baggage was deposited. Knox's
headquarters were with those of the Commander-in-
chief at Middlebrook, New Jersey, from which point
he wrote as follows to his brother:

"The whole army have moved up to this place to cover the almost infinitely important posts in the highlands, which we do in so
effectual a manner that, were the enemy much stronger than they
are, I should be in no pain for the safety of the posts. The enemy
have established themselves so securely at King's Ferry that we shall
not be able to dislodge them at present. Perhaps a future and more
important operation may involve King's Ferry in its fall. The
enemy expect reinforcements, and we, with the blessing of Heaven,
expect to baffle their utmost efforts. We expect everything from
the discipline and goodness of our troops; but probably we shall
want some assistance from our brethren."

In the North, during that summer, the chief military events were expeditions into New York for the
punishment of the Six Nations. These Indians had
co-operated with the Tories and British in waging a
relentless warfare upon the citizens of the State who
were loyal to the patriot cause. The American
forces, under the command of General Sullivan,
marched with celerity, after the tedious delays of
the first start were overcome, and his punishment
of the Indians was so swift and condign that they
could never again be rallied to oppose the desolating
march of Sullivan's men.

General Benjamin Lincoln, of Massachusetts, was
entrusted with the defence of Charleston, South

Carolina, the British having developed their plan of dividing the Southern States from the Northern by the capture of Georgia, the Carolinas, and Virginia. This excellent officer, who had been described by a Tory newspaper as " one Benjamin Lincoln, late secretary to the conventions and congresses of Massachusetts Bay, and a forward person in all the rebellious proceedings of that colony," being reinforced by D'Estaing, was induced to attempt the recapture of Savannah, then held by the British under General Prevost. The expedition was a failure, and Lincoln was obliged to return to Charleston, where he was ultimately forced to surrender to Clinton, who arrived on the coast to assist in the reduction of South Carolina.

Between Knox and Lincoln there existed a deep and sincere affection which was manifested in many ways up to the day when these two men were separated by death. In a letter written by Knox to Lincoln, just after the capture of Charleston, which involved the surrender of the commanding general and his army, is this paragraph:

" The great defence made by you and your garrison in field fortifications will confer on you and them the esteem and admiration of every sensible military man. I hope and believe that Congress will most unequivocally bestow that applause which you have so richly merited. No event, except the capture of Sir H. Clinton and his army, would give me more pleasure than to see you. He is now in force at Springfield, below Morristown."

At a later period, Knox wrote this affectionate letter to Lincoln:

" The first moment I had the happiness of being acquainted with you I conceived a high degree of friendship, which uniformly has increased as I became more intimate, until the present period. I consider the confidential manner in which we have indulged as one of the happy circumstances of my life, and in all events of grief or joy there is no man from whose friendship I should more readily expect the most cordial balsam, or whose bosom would more cheerfully expand in a participation of my happiness."

It was during this summer (1779) that the Knox family were bereaved by the death of their second daughter. In the midst of his cares and anxieties, Washington found time to write to the afflicted mother a note of condolence; and an anonymous friend sent her a copy of " Elegiac Lines, Inscrib'd to Mrs. Knox, occasioned by the death of her Infant Daughter, who deceas'd near Pluckemin, N. Jersey, July 2d, 1779." From these lines, as an example of the literary taste of the time, we extract the following stanza:

" This little Cherub, like some blooming Flower,
    The soft Exotic of a happier Clime,
  Shrunk from the dawn of beauteous Childhood's hour,
    And, drooping, sought Its native Realms Sublime ! "

The winter of 1779–80 was one of great severity. The army of Washington, once more in winter quarters at Morristown, suffered from cold and hunger. The troops were insufficiently clad, and it required all the faith, patience, and fortitude for which these brave patriots had now become proverbial, to endure the privations of that inclement season. There were incursions and excursions on both sides during the winter. It was not until the middle of June that a movement from New York was observed by the watchful Americans. Washington divined that an attack was once more intended to be made upon West Point by the way of New Jersey. He made his dispositions accordingly; and the fight at Springfield, New Jersey, was the result of Greene's determined resistance to the advance of the British. It was at this encounter that Dayton's militia were inspired by the warlike example of their chaplain, Mr. James Caldwell, whose wife had been cruelly and wantonly killed in her house near Connecticut Farms. The soldiers being out of wadding, the good parson brought from the meeting-house an armful of hymn-books for this purpose, crying, " Give 'em Watts, boys ! " The enemy was checked at this point, and having burned the town, he returned to Staten Island.

An important event of that summer was the arrival at Newport of five thousand French troops under Count de Rochambeau, on the 11th of July, 1780. These were the first division of an army of twelve thousand men which Lafayette, who had returned to France for that purpose, had induced the French king to send to co-operate with the Americans. As was the case when D'Estaing arrived, the hopes of the people were now raised to an extravagant pitch of enthusiasm. It was expected that an immediate and overwhelming movement against the British would sweep them from the continent. But it was not until the 15th of the month that all the French troops were landed, and many of these were ill and were sent to hospitals for treatment. On the

25th, Rochambeau sent a messenger to the Massachusetts Council for reinforcements, an attack by Clinton and the British fleet being threatened. Weeks wore away without any capital operations, and on the 21st of September, Washington, Knox, and Lafayette went from West Point to Hartford, Conn., to meet Rochambeau and the French Admiral, de Ternay, to concert a plan of future operations. It was while returning from this conference that the three generals learned of the treason of Benedict Arnold, then in command at West Point. When Washington received and looked through the papers disclosing Arnold's treason, he exclaimed to Knox and Lafayette, as if in despair, " Whom can we trust now! "

John André, the spy, through whose activity these later negotiations between Arnold and Sir Henry Clinton had been carried on, was first taken to West Point and then to Tappan, where army headquarters were established. André was tried by a court-martial convened on the 29th of September. It is not necessary to dwell on the details of the trial and execution. The findings of the court, and the detail of officers composing it, will be found in the following extract from the record :

" The Board having considered the letter from his Excellency, General Washington, respecting Major André, Adjutant General to the British army, the confession of Major André, and the papers produced to them, report to his Excellency the Commander in Chief, the following facts, which appear to them relative to Major André. First, that he came on shore from the *Vulture*, sloop of war, in the night of the 21st of September, instant, on an interview with General Arnold, in a private and secret manner. Secondly, that he

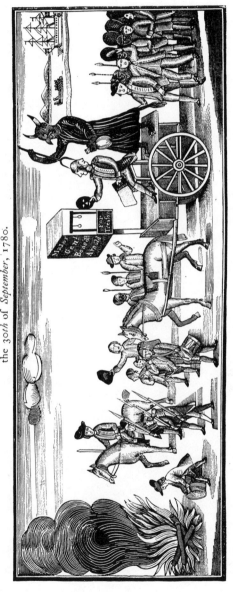

A REPRESENTATION of the FIGURES exhibited and paraded through the Streets of PHILADELPHIA, on *Saturday,* the 30th of *September,* 1780.

BENEDICT ARNOLD CARRIED IN EFFIGY.

changed his dress within our lines, and under a feigned name, and disguised habit, passed our works at Stony and Verplank's Points, in the evening of the 22d of September, instant, and was taken on the morning of the 23d of September, at Tarrytown, in a disguised habit, being then on his way to New York ; and when taken he had in his possession several papers which contained intelligence for the enemy. The Board, having maturely considered these facts, do also report to his Excellency, General Washington, that Major André, Adjutant to the British army, ought to be considered a spy from the enemy, and that agreeably to the law and usage of nations, it is their opinion that he ought to suffer death.

" (Signed)   NATHANAEL GREENE, Major General and President.
        STIRLING,   "   "
        ST. CLAIR,   "   "
        LA FAYETTE,   "   "
        R. HOWE,   "   "
        STEUBEN,   "   "
        SAMUEL H. PARSONS, Brigadier General.
        JAMES CLINTON,   "   "
        HENRY KNOX,   "   "   Artillery.
        JOHN GLOVER,   "   "
        JOHN PATERSON,   "   "
        EDWARD HAND,   "   "
        JOHN HUNTINGTON,   "   "
        JOHN STARK,   "   "
            JOHN LAWRENCE, Judge Advocate General."

André's execution was set for the first day of October, but on the arrival of a flag of truce from Sir Henry Clinton, asking for time to make further proposals for the release of the condemned man, the execution was postponed until the next day, when he was duly hanged. It was natural that Knox, as one of the general officers who composed the court-martial that sentenced André to the igno-minious but deserved death of a spy, should have found his duty on this occasion most distasteful.

Nevertheless, it was his duty, and while he recalled
with many pangs of regret the pleasant converse
which he had with the condemned man, years before, in the wilds of New York, he discharged his
task with martial implicitness.

Another winter passed without any military
operations of immediate importance being undertaken in the Northern States.   In the South, Cornwallis and Greene still struggled for the possession
of Georgia and the Carolinas.   The numerousness
of the Tories in North Carolina gave a partisan aspect to the fighting that was carried on in a desultory
manner over the eastern portion of the State.   Raids
for the capture of supplies were occasionally made
by the British into the country held by the American forces, and these forays were only slightly exceeded in importance by the expedition headed by
Benedict Arnold sent into Virginia " to steal to-
bacco " during the last days of December, 178).
The expedition landed at Westover, on the James
River, and, marching to Richmond, destroyed much
public and private property and military stores.
But although the raid was nothing more than a destructive and annoying dash into and out of a hostile
country, it excited great alarm all over the country,
and the attention of Congress and the Commander-
in-chief was arrested by its bold and successful
execution.

At this critical juncture, a serious and alarming
incident was the mutiny of the Pennsylvania line,
then stationed in winter quarters near Morristown.
About two thousand of these troops, discontented

THE CAPTURE OF ANDRÉ.

FROM A PRINT IN THE POSESSION OF DR. COUTANT.

with their destitute and impoverished condition,
resolved to mutiny against their own officers and
redress their grievances.   They had been enlisted in
a slovenly manner, their papers being drawn with
such ambiguity that it was well-nigh impossible to
decide whether they were bound for three years
only, or for the whole war.   Naturally, the troops
claimed that they were to serve for three years, and
that that term having expired, they were now free
to return home.   Many of the men were willing to
re-enlist, notwithstanding their distressed condition
in camp; but they claimed themselves entitled to
such bounties as were allowed then to recruits, under
the orders of Congress.

Some notion of the sufferings of these men, who
had been neglected by the Continental Congress, may
be gained from the following letter to William Knox,
written by General Knox, early in December, 1780:

"We depend upon the great Author of Nature to provide subsistence and clothing for us during a long and severe winter ; for the
people, whose business, according to the common course of things,
it was to provide the materials necessary, have either been unable
or neglected to do it.   The soldier, ragged almost to nakedness, has
to sit down at this period, and with an axe—perhaps his only tool,
and probably that a bad one—to make his habitation for winter.
However, this, and being punished with hunger into the bargain,
the soldiers and officers have borne with a fortitude almost super-
human.   The country must be grateful to these brave fellows.   It
is impossible to admit of the idea of an alternative."

Under such circumstances, and knowing that the
men had some show of reason for complaining that
their enlistments had been conducted with unfair-
ness and deception, the mutiny of the Pennsylvania

line does not seem wholly unreasonable. The mutineers, having provided themselves with six field-
pieces, and rejecting the advice and expostulations
of their commander, General Wayne, took up their
line of march to Philadelphia to demand of Congress
redress for their many grievances. They said that
" they had been imposed on and deceived respecting
the term of their enlistment, that they had received
no wages for more than a year, and that they were
destitute of clothing, and had often been deprived
of their rations."

This open mutiny caused great anxiety to the
Commander-in-chief, and he called a council of war
at his headquarters at New Windsor, on the west
side of the Hudson River. Sir Henry Clinton artfully endeavoured to avail himself of the revolt to
weaken the American forces. But his emissaries,
who were instructed to offer money and immunity
from military duty to such of the mutineers as were
willing to come into his lines, were repelled with
scorn and were turned over to General Wayne to
await developments. The result was that the claims
of the soldiers were found to be just and right,
and their complaints were finally met by Congress
and satisfied. Clinton's emissaries were eventually
hanged as spies. The mutiny of a part of the
Jersey line, which almost immediately followed,
did not end so happily. These troops, stationed at
Pompton, New Jersey, followed the example of the
Pennsylvanians, but more severe measures were
adopted towards them, Washington being determined to check the spirit of insubordination then

and there.   General Robert Howe, with five hundred men, was ordered to surround and capture the
mutineers and punish the ringleaders.   This was
promptly done, and three of the leaders were condemned to be shot by the mutineers.   Two of the
condemned men were instantly executed; the third
was pardoned on the spot at the intercession of his
officers.   This heroic treatment was successful, and
the troops returned to duty, much to the chagrin of
Sir Henry Clinton, whose emissaries were again sent
out with offers of aid and comfort to the mutineers,
on condition that they come over into his camp on
Staten Island.

The news of the mutiny of the Pennsylvania line
was taken to Boston by Knox, who, at the request
of Washington, had undertaken to present to the
New England States a statement of the pitiable
condition of the army.   Armed with a letter of explicit instructions from the Commander-in-chief,
Knox presented in forcible terms the woes of the
troops.   To quote his own language, he showed
" the aggravated calamities and distresses that have
resulted from the total want of pay, for nearly
twelve months, the want of clothing in a severe
season, and not unfrequently the want of provisions,"
all of which trials he declared " are beyond description."   His mission was successful to a certain extent, and the legislatures of Massachusetts and
New Hampshire voted to send at once to each enlisted man and non-commissioned officer who had
enlisted from those States " for the war " the sum
of twenty-four dollars in specie.   Relief also came

from other States, and the condition of the army, in many respects, became materially improved after this crisis had been safely passed.

Arnold's invasion of Virginia was not to be treated lightly, notwithstanding the predatory character which it had been made to assume. Washington made preparations to march to the relief of the harassed Virginians, and in February Lafayette was ordered to Chesapeake Bay to embark for the lower part of Virginia. On the sixteenth of that month Washington sent to Knox detailed instructions to procure war materials necessary for " a capital operation against New York, or against Charleston, Savannah, Penobscot, etc., in case of inability to undertake the siege of the first and principal object." Knox promptly promised to use his utmost exertions to furnish the needed supplies, but he reported the difficulties of obtaining the requisite materials, and complained of the dilatoriness of the Board of War in honouring his requisitions for these imperatively needed articles. " Powder," he said, " is an article of which we are so deficient that, when a reasonable quantity shall be appropriated for the use of the posts in the highlands (which ought and will be furnished under all circumstances), there will literally none remain."

There was evidently a clash between Clinton and Cornwallis as to the general principles on which the Southern campaign should be conducted; Clinton's notion was that the Southern States should be conquered from the southward, taking Georgia as the British base of operations. Cornwallis's plan was first to invade and hold absolute possession of Virginia. Greene and Marion gave the British troops under Rawdon and Stewart many a hard tussle during the summer. The battles of Hobkirk's Hill, the Cowpens, and Eutaw Springs, and other engagements with the enemy generally left the advantage with the Americans, and by midsummer the British forces were literally shut up in Charleston, Savannah, and Wilmington, not a handful of their men being found outside the environs of those three cities.

Proposing the complete investiture of the city of New York for his immediate objective, Washington, accompanied by Knox, went to Wethersfield, Conn., to hold a conference with Rochambeau as to the best method of employing the French fleets and the allied armies in the forthcoming operations. Knox was one of the few American generals who spoke the French language with some degree of fluency; he had studied French while engaged in the active duties of a bookseller's apprentice in the shop of the excellent Mr. Bowes, Cornhill; and he found the accomplishment of great use when he was brought into contact with the officers of our ally beyond the seas. While at Wethersfield, Knox wrote as follows, on May 20, 1781, to his brother in Boston: " I am here, my dear brother, having arrived last evening, with his Excellency, the General, and General Duportail to meet Count Rochambeau and Admiral Barras, upon some matters of great consequence. We came here last night. The French gentlemen will be here to-morrow, and we shall probably depart in two days after." But the council did not break up until five days later, for, on the 25th, Knox wrote again: " We have not finished our business until this morning. Count Rochambeau left us yesterday, and we shall set out in about one hour, and shall expect to reach New Windsor to-morrow evening."

It was probably at this conference in Wethersfield that the allied generals agreed upon the main details of the remarkable campaign which, having the siege of New York for its primary and ostensible purpose, had yet a far-reaching ulterior object which was to confound the enemy and administer to him an irretrievable defeat. Writing to Knox from army headquarters at New Windsor, under date of May 28, 1781, Washington says:

" As you are perfectly acquainted with the measures which have been concerted with the Count de Rochambeau, I have only to request that you will be pleased to make all necessary estimates of articles wanted in your department, and also to put the whole business (so far as is within your reach), in the best train of execution which our embarrassed circumstances will possibly admit. Under the present appearances of an evacuation of New York, I think it will be proper to draw the stores from the eastward rather than from the southward."

The fleet of Admiral Barras was at Newport and that of De Grasse was on the way from the West Indies and soon to be within hailing distance of the Admiral. Sir Henry Clinton, in New York, might well be bewildered when he wished to divine whether the Chesapeake, or New York Bay, was to be the objective point of the allied forces which he saw

COUNT DE GRASSE.

making preparations for a summer campaign. As far as possible, Washington strengthened Clinton's apprehensions of a siege of New York. His advance from the vicinity of West Point and similar movements on the Hudson convinced the British General that active operations against the city were imminent.

Moving in four divisions, Rochambeau's army marched from Connecticut to the Hudson in perfect order, reaching North Castle (where Washington had made his stand after the retreat from White Plains, in 1776), on the 2d, 3d, and 4th of July; and on the 6th of that month the allied armies were encamped on a line which stretched from Dobbs Ferry on the Hudson to the Bronx River.

10

CHAPTER VII

HE consummate strategy with which Washington beguiled the enemy was kept up for several weeks. The exact time when the fleet of De Grasse should be available for carrying out the details of Washington's deep-laid plan could not be definitely fixed; and upon the movements of the French ships much depended. Meanwhile, every semblance of a close siege of New York was maintained. Works were thrown up on the Jersey shore opposite the northern end of Staten Island, parties of observation were continually appearing at points near and overlooking the city of New York, and active movements were zealously practised in parts of Westchester County nearest the city. Clinton, naturally expecting a siege, which would be aided by a blockade of the harbour by the combined French fleets, withdrew from the grumbling and unwilling Cornwallis a considerable part of his forces, and it seemed as if the entire British army in Virginia might be required to defend New York against the allied forces.

It was not until the middle of August that news was brought to Washington that De Grasse would be at the mouth of the Chesapeake with his ships by the last of that month. Whatever movement was likely to be resolved upon, the army was ready for any orders. In the latter part of July, Knox wrote to his brother this characteristic letter:

" Lucy, with her sweet children, has gone up the river [the Hudson], with Mrs. Cochran* on a visit to some families. I suppose she will proceed as far as Albany ; after which, I think, she will sit down in Jersey for the remainder of the campaign. Although we are not bad in accommodating ourselves to our circumstances, yet I sensibly feel the inconveniences we labor under, to accumulate in proportion to the increase of our family. I sincerely pray God that the war may be ended this campaign, that public and private society may be restored. . . .

" The vile water-gruel governments which have taken place in most of the States are wholly disproportioned to the exigencies of the war, and are productive of sentiments unworthy an energetic republic. However, I hope we shall wade through.

" I cannot, in justice, omit paying some compliments to our State. The policy appears to be enlarged and liberal ; and the exertions greatly surpass, at this present time, any State in the union. The same tone, sentiments, and exertion, pervading all the States, would indisputably render this the last campaign.

" The enemy lately sent some ships up the river with an intent to interrupt our communication by water with West Point, but they retired yesterday without effecting any thing of consequence."

---

* Mrs. Cochran was the wife of Dr. John Cochran, of Pennsylvania, Director-General of the military hospitals of the United States. After the close of the war, he removed to New York where he practised medicine and surgery. Under Washington, he was subsequently appointed Commissioner of Loans for the State of New York.

And still the plan of campaign, the campaign on which Knox placed such high hopes, was virtually waiting on the movements of the enemy. How completely Sir Henry Clinton had been fooled by the manœuvres of Washington was not yet evident. The details of his plans could not be unfolded at present. Knox, writing from the camp near Dobbs Ferry, August 3, 1781, thus salutes his wife and attempts to parry her inquiries as to the military situation and prospects:

"Yesterday was your birthday. I cannot attempt to show you how much I was affected by it. I remembered it and humbly petitioned Heaven to grant us the happiness of continuing our union until we should have the felicity of seeing our children flourishing around us, and ourselves crowned with virtue, peace, and years, and that we both might take our flight together, secure of a happy immortality. . . . All is harmony and good fellowship between the two armies. I have no doubt, when opportunity offers, that the zeal of the French and the patriotism of the Americans will go hand in hand to glory. I cannot explain to you the exact plan of the campaign : we don't know it ourselves. You know what we wish, but we hope for more at present than we believe."

It is impossible to read without emotion letters like these, breathing alike a devout and reverent religious spirit and a sincere and exalted patriotism. Providence, in whose beneficence General Knox so implicitly trusted, had in store for him years of peace crowned with virtue, and a victorious ending of the campaign then about to be entered upon under circumstances that tried men's souls.

Some entertaining gossip regarding the French officers serving the American cause at this time is

given in this letter from William Knox to his brother
in camp :

" BOSTON, Aug. 22, 1781.

" I suppose, from necessity, you are obliged to speak much French,
which, you having long since learnt the theoretic part, I should imagine from a little practice, would come easy to you.

" If I recollect, the Compte Rochambeau does n't speak a word
of English, nor do the two brothers Viomenil, Marquis Laval, or
Compte St. Maine.   The two counts Deux Ponts, on the other
hand, speak it pretty well ; and the most amiable General Chastellux,
à merveille.   If you have opportunity I am sure must be very intimate with General C., if the two characters of the man of letters and
the polite gentleman are recommendations, I know nobody who can
be more strongly recommended.   I have reason to speak of the
civility of all the gentlemen I have named, and of many which I
have not, and who belong to that army, but more particularly of
those shown me by the Chevalier Chastellux, at whose *petits soupers*
I was invited two evenings out of the three when I was at Newport.
I mention this as being a particular mark of his attention, for the
being invited to dine is a common compliment from him to recommended strangers ; but the evening circle is always selected."

The Chevalier de Chastellux, to whom William
Knox refers in terms of admiration, was a major-
general in the army of Rochambeau and a member of
the French Academy.   After the conclusion of the
war he wrote a book descriptive of his travels in
America, in which he makes frequent mention of General Knox, for whom he appears to have conceived
a warm and ardent friendship.   In the latter part of
the preceding year he had accepted an invitation to
visit the American army headquarters at New Windsor, and in his journal he spoke of his observations
there with considerable detail.   Visiting the artillery
camp in company with General Washington, the
distinguished Frenchman was received by General

Knox at the head of his battalions. The artillery
was exhibited in fine order, each gunner at his post
and ready to fire at the word. General Knox
apologised for not firing a salute, explaining that
the troops on the Jersey side of the river had received orders to put themselves in motion, and that
an unexpected firing might mislead and alarm them.
On another occasion, Chastellux and Lafayette
visited the generals of the army at their several
headquarters, and Knox, conducting the visitors
back to Washington's headquarters, brought them
by a woodland road to his retired private residence
where Mrs. Knox and her children-were placed for
the campaign. The spot and the " real family,"
as the chevalier called it, made a vivid impression
upon the foreign visitor who makes special mention
of it in his book of travels.

After his return to France, Chastellux wrote frequently to Knox, and one of his letters, dated
March 30, 1782, gives evidence of the warmth of his
friendship. He says:

" My sentiments will always meet yours, and I hope that I shall
not be excelled in serving America and loving General Knox. Let
us be brothers in arms, and friends in time of peace. Let the alliance
between our respective countries dwell in our bosoms, where it shall
find a perfect emblem of the two powers : in mine, the seniority ; in
yours, the extent of territory.

" I depend upon your faith, and I pledge my honour that no interest in the world can prevail over the warm and firm attachment
with which I have the honour to be

" DE CHASTELLUX."

Two days before Washington heard of the destination of the French fleet, upon whose movements

so much depended, General Greene wrote to Knox from his camp on the Santee, South Carolina, in these familiar and jocular terms:

"MY DEAR FRIEND,—If accounts are true, that New York is seriously invested, you must be the hero of the day. Methinks I hear the cannon roar while I am writing. The shells and the shot fired from the besiegers and the besieged must make a terrible rattling. The splendour of such a siege will sink our puny operations into nothing. But, after you have done at New York, it is to be hoped that you will come to the southward and unfetter the poor unfortunate inhabitants of Charlestown. I should be happy to see my old friend, McDougall, in the field of speculation. How goes on his chapter of difficulties? The siege of New York, I imagine, will afford him a large collection of materials. Where is Howe,* with his nose? has he left off his port, or forgiven the boy who insulted him so grossly at Morristown? The story is told even in this country; and I declare, upon my honour, I did not bring it here.

"Where is the noble Earl [Stirling]? I hope he's had an opportunity to review the ground on Long Island; and, I presume, every officer of note in the French army has heard in detail the particulars. We have had a report here that General Howe and he had had a duel, but I do not believe it. Honest fellows! what have they to quarrel about?

"I am sending aide-de-camp after aide-de-camp to get news from the northward. I am not a little apprehensive the people on the road will think the Southern army is broken up.

"I beg you will present Mrs. Knox with my most affectionate regards and I hope you will not get in the way of a four-and-twenty pounder, but will return to her with whole bones."

The American army was set in motion on the morning of the 19th of August, with every appearance of being marched straight to New York. But the troops were at once faced westward and pressed forward in the direction of King's Ferry, on the

---

* The American Major-General Robert Howe.

Hudson River.   On the same day the French army also moved, and, by the 22d, both armies were well across the river, the Americans being headed for Springfield, New Jersey, and the French marching directly upon Trenton, with the view of crossing the Delaware at that point.   Heath was left in command on the Hudson, with three thousand men, for the defence of West Point; and it is likely that no one in the American army, save Heath and Knox, knew the direction of the masterly movement which Washington had now undertaken.

On the 2d of September the Americans were marching through Philadelphia, and the French followed on the next day.   Lafayette, who was in lower Virginia, had been instructed to prevent the retreat of Cornwallis into North Carolina, and the French fleet, after several desultory engagements with the English, was hovering off the mouth of the Chesapeake with three thousand troops on board. De Grasse's force consisted of thirty ships of the line, and he was instructed to put himself into communication with Lafayette as expeditiously as possible.

Dr. Thacher, who participated in this strategical movement, has written the following striking account of its opening·

"Our situation reminds me of some theatrical exhibition where the interest and expectations of the spectators are continually increasing, and where curiosity is wrought to the highest point.   Our destination has for some time been a matter of perplexing doubt and uncertainty ; bets have run high on one side, that we were to occupy the ground marked out on the Jersey shore, to aid in the siege of New York, and on the other, that we were stealing a march on the enemy, and actually destined to Virginia in pursuit of the army of Lord Cornwallis."

It is not likely that Benedict Arnold's town-burning expedition to Connecticut, which was started about this time, was intended to divert Washington's attention by a fire in the rear. The infamous raid which, however unjustifiable and cruel, could not add a tint to the blackness of Arnold's ill-repute, was actually planned before the news of Washington's march southward could have reached Clinton.

While the French troops were in Philadelphia, and the French officers were being entertained by the Chevalier de Lauzun, Ambassador from the French court, a message from the fleet was announced. The Chevalier, who stood at the head of his table, made the joyful statement that " thirty-six ships of the line, commanded by Monsieur le Compte de Grasse, are arrived in the Chesapeake Bay, and three thousand men have landed and opened a communication with the Marquis de la Fayette." For all practical purposes, the York peninsula was now ready for American occupation, and the doom of the army of the sullen and discontented Cornwallis was sealed. Cornwallis had appeared to find a grim pleasure in warning Clinton of the dangers of his own situation while he had ungraciously acceded to the wishes and obeyed the orders of his commanding officer.

Everywhere on the march southward the army of Washington was hailed with extravagant demonstrations of joy by the patriotic inhabitants, who seemed to see in this unexpected and formidable array the promise of a speedy deliverance of their beloved country from the heel of the invader.   General Knox is authority for the story that when passing through Pennsylvania, General Washington and his staff—General Knox and others—stopped at a farmhouse to breakfast; and when the meal was finished, and the party were waiting for their horses, the people of the neighbourhood were admitted to pay their respects to the Commander-in-chief, for whom the popular love and admiration were universal.   Among the visitors was a venerable man, evidently the patriarch of the place, who approached Washington and stood before him for a few moments, gazing in his face without speaking.   The attitude of the aged patriot was observed by all in the room in perfect silence, when, raising his hands and eyes to heaven, he exclaimed in tones of mingled pathos and veneration, " Lord, now lettest Thou Thy servant depart in peace, for mine eyes have seen Thy salvation."

On the 30th of September, the British at Yorktown were surrounded from a point on the James River above to a point below.   The French, under the command of Viomenil, were on the right; the Americans, now under the immediate command of General Benjamin Lincoln, were on the left.   Cornwallis, retired within his works, was throwing around himself a maze of redoubts, earthworks, and ditches, ineffectual for the purposes of defence.

In the Knox Papers is to be found a detailed statement of the force of artillery available for the siege

of Yorktown, furnished to the Commander-in-chief
by Knox, and dated at " Park of Artillery, 24th
August, 1781." This document shows that the
siege guns were twenty-three in number, three being
24-pounders and twenty 18-pounders, all of iron.
The brass pieces were howitzers and mortars,
twenty-one all told, and of varying calibre, mostly
10-inch bore. The field artillery numbered fifteen
brass pieces of ordnance, the largest being two 12-
pounders, and the others 6- and 3-pounders. The
French contingent in the artillery service was twenty
24- and 16-pounders and sixteen mortars and howitzers for the siege; and thirty-two large guns and
four howitzers for the field. As at the siege of
Boston, in 1775, Knox's fertility of expedient and
tireless energy were adequate to the occasion, his
power to create material apparently being implicitly
relied upon to remedy all deficiencies. Washington reported to Congress, after the siege, that
Knox's services had been of inestimable value and
that " the resources of his genius supplied the deficit
of means."

In Chastellux's *Travels in North America*, before
alluded to, the author says:

" We cannot sufficiently admire the intelligence and activity with
which he [Knox] collected from different places and transported to
the batteries more than thirty pieces of cannon and mortars of large
calibre, for the siege. . . . The artillery was always very well
served, the general incessantly directing it and often himself pointing the mortars : seldom did he leave the batteries. . . . The ·
English marvelled no less at the extraordinary progress of the
American artillery, and at the capacity and instruction of the officers.
As to General Knox, but one-half has been said in commending his

military genius. He is a man of talent, well instructed, of a buoyant disposition, ingenuous and true: it is impossible to know him without esteeming and loving him."

This cordial and apparently sincere tribute to the character of Henry Knox comes from a competent authority.

While Washington's temporary headquarters were at Williamsburg, Virginia, the Commander-in-chief, accompanied by Knox, Rochambeau, Duportail, and Chastellux went down to De Grasse's fleet, and on board the *Ville de Paris* arranged a plan of co-operation. Subsequently, expecting an attack from the British fleet, and dreading a combat inside the Capes, De Grasse announced his intention of putting to sea to meet the enemy outside. This was likely to upset the plans agreed upon, which included the cutting-off of all hope from seaward for Cornwallis, and Lafayette and Knox were sent to the French naval commander to entreat him to stay where he was; fortunately, the advice of the two generals persuaded De Grasse to remain.

General Greene, Knox's intimate and steadfast friend, still held in his camp on the Santee, wrote Knox a characteristic letter on the 29th of September, in which he says:

"Sept. 29, 1781.

"MY DEAR FRIEND,—Where you are I know not, but if you are where I wish you, it is with the General in Virginia; the prospect is so bright and the glory so great, that I want you to be there to share in them. I was in hopes you would have operated seriously against New York, which would have been still more important; but as your operations are directed another way, I take it for granted means were wanting to play the great game.

"We have been beating the bush, and the General has come to catch the bird. Never was there a more inviting object to glory. The General is a most fortunate man, and may success and laurels attend him. We have fought frequently and bled freely and little glory comes to our share. Our force has been so small that nothing capital could be effected, and our operations have been conducted under every disadvantage that could embarrass either a general or any army.

"I long to see you, and spend an evening's conversation together. Where is Mrs. Knox? and how is Lucy and my young god-son, Sir Harry? I beg you will present my kind compliments and best wishes to Mrs. Knox.

"How is my old friend, Colonel Jackson?—is he as fat as ever, and can he still eat down a plate of fish that he can't see over? God bless his fat soul with good health and good spirits to the end of the war, that we may all have a happy meeting in the North. Please to give my compliments to your brother, and tell him we are catching at smoky glory while he is wisely treasuring up solid coin."

Mrs. Washington had invited Mrs. Knox to make Mount Vernon her home for the remainder of the campaign, and about the middle of September, Mrs. Knox, leaving her young daughter in Philadelphia, went to the Washington family seat where she could be within a reasonable distance of the seat of war in Virginia. On the first day of October, Knox wrote to his wife as follows: "We came before York on the 28th [of September]; on the 29th nearly completed the investiture; but yesterday the enemy evacuated their outposts, which gives us a considerable advantage in point of time. Our prospects are good, and we shall soon hope to impress our haughty foe with a respect for continental arms."

After a vain attempt to elude the besiegers, convinced of his inability to escape or to hold out any longer, Cornwallis offered to open negotiations for a surrender; and on the 19th of October, the terms of capitulation were formally concluded. Cornwallis, chagrined and mortified, took no part in the ceremonies of the final surrender; pleading illness, he deputed General O'Hara to act in his stead. General Benjamin Lincoln, whose surrender at Charleston had been forced under aggravating circumstances, designed to humiliate the American commander, received the sword of O'Hara, but immediately returned to that officer the weapon tendered in token of the British surrender.

William Knox had hastened on to Virginia to be " in at the death " which was so confidently expected by his illustrious brother. He was now on his way to Mount Vernon to carry the great news to the ladies who there awaited with anxiety and hope tidings from their liege lords at Yorktown. Knox's letter to his wife, written on the morning of the formal surrender, is as follows:

" I have detained William until this moment that I might be the first to communicate *good news* to the charmer of my soul. A glorious moment for America ! This day Lord Cornwallis and his army march out and pile their arms in the face of our victorious army. The day before yesterday he desired commissioners might be named to treat of the surrender of his troops, the ships, and everything they possess. He at first requested that the Britons might be sent to Britain, and the Germans to Germany ; but this the General refused, and they have now agreed to surrender prisoners of war, to be kept in America until exchanged or released. They will have the same *honours* as the garrison of Charleston ; that is, they will not be permitted to unfurl their colours, *or play Yankee Doodle*. We know not yet how many they are. The General has just requested me to be at headquarters instantly, therefore. I cannot be more particular."

WEST POINT AT THE TIME OF THE REVOLUTION.

REDRAWN FROM BARBER'S "HISTORICAL COLLECTION."

As a matter of record, it is set down here that Cornwallis's entire force consisted of seven thousand men, of whom about two thousand were unfit for duty. The allied forces were about fifteen thousand men. But bad management, rather than inferiority of numbers, had brought Cornwallis to this humiliating ' pass. Washington's generalship had overwhelmed the British army in Virginia with a disaster which might have been averted, one would suppose, by a competent military strategist. Too late, on the very day of Cornwallis's surrender at Yorktown, Clinton set sail from New York, only to sail back when he learned, when off the Chesapeake, that his dilatoriness and over-caution had been the ruin of the British army in Virginia, and that Cornwallis and Cornwallis's men were prisoners of war.

Knox's account of the operations in Virginia and the final surrender of Lord Cornwallis, sent to Mr. John Jay, American Minister to the court at Madrid, is herewith appended as a valuable and entertaining contribution to the history of the time:

" CAMP BEFORE YORK, IN VIRGINIA,
" 21 Oct., 1781.

" TO JOHN JAY:

" The enemy's operations in these States, though not carried on with great armies, compared with those of 1776 and 1777, yet were so formidable as to dispel every force which the country of itself was capable of opposing. This rendered it necessary for America to march its army here, or give up the Southern States as lost. It appears, also, to have been the opinion of the French Court, as Count de Grasse gave intelligence of his intention of arriving at the Capes of Virginia. Our previous views were New York. The dispositions were made on the Hudson River for the attack of Lord Cornwallis in Virginia, and everything has succeeded equal to our sanguine wishes.

"This important affair has been effected by the most harmonious concurrence of circumstances that could possibly have happened : a fleet and troops from the West Indies, under the orders of one of the best men in the world ; an army of American and French troops, marching from the North River,—five hundred miles,—and the fleet of Count de Barras, all joining so exactly in point of time as to render what has happened almost certain.

"I shall not enter into a detail of circumstances previous to the collection of our force at Williamsburg, twelve miles distant from this place, which was made on the 27th ult. On the 28th we marched to the camp, and on the 29th and 30th we completed the investiture of York. A body of American militia, Lauzun's legion, and some marines from the fleet of Count de Grasse, at the same time formed in the vicinity of Gloucester, so as to prevent any incursions of the enemy into the country. From the 1st October to the 6th was spent in preparing our materials for the siege, bringing forward our cannon and stores, and in reconnoitring the points of attack. On the evening of the 6th we broke ground and began our first parallel within six hundred yards of the enemy's works, undiscovered.

"The first parallel, four redoubts, and all our batteries were finished by the 9th, at two o'clock P.M., when we opened our batteries and kept them playing continually. On the night of the 12th we began our second parallel, at three hundred yards' distance from the enemy. And on the night of the 14th we stormed the two redoubts which the enemy had in advance of their main works. The gallant troops of France under the orders of Baron de Viomenil, and the hardy soldiers of America under the Marquis de la Fayette, attacked separate works and carried them in an instant. This brilliant stroke was effected without any great loss on our side : the enemy lost between one and two hundred. This advantage was important, and gave us an opportunity of perfecting our second parallel, into which we took the two redoubts. On the 16th, just before day, the enemy made a sortie, and spiked up some of our cannon, but were soon repulsed and driven back to their works. The cannon were soon cleared ; and the same day our batteries in the second parallel began the fire, and continued without intermission until nine o'clock in the morning of the 17th October, ever memorable on account of the Saratoga affair, when the enemy sent a flag, offering to treat of the surrender of the posts of York and Gloucester. The firing continued until two o'clock, when commissioners on both sides met to adjust the capitulation which was not finished and signed until twelve o'clock on the 19th. Our troops took possession of two redoubts of the enemy soon after, and about two o'clock the enemy marched out and grounded their arms.

" The whole garrison are prisoners of war, and had the same honours only as were granted to our garrison at Charleston,—their colours were cased, and they were prohibited playing a French or American tune.

" The returns are not yet collected ; but including officers, sick and well, there are more than seven thousand, exclusive of seamen, who are supposed to amount to one thousand. There are near forty sail of topsail vessels in the harbour, about one-half of which the enemy sunk upon different occasions ; about two hundred pieces of cannon, nearly one-half of them brass ; a great number of arms, drums, and colours are among the trophies of this decisive stroke. The prisoners are to be sent into any part of this State, Maryland, or Pennsylvania. The consequences will be extensively beneficial. The enemy will immediately be confined to Charleston and New York and reduced to a defensive war of those two posts, for which they have not more troops in America than to form adequate garrisons."

An incident of one of the assaults alluded to by Knox in his letter to Jay is thus described by Thacher, who was present at the siege :

" During the assault, the British kept up an incessant firing of cannon and musketry from their whole line.   His Excellency, General Washington, Generals Lincoln and Knox, with their aids, having dismounted, were standing in an exposed situation waiting the result.   Colonel Cobb,* one of Washington's aids, solicitous for his safety, said to his Excellency, ' Sir, you are too much exposed here, had you not better step a little back ?'   ' Colonel Cobb,' re-plied his Excellency, ' if you are afraid, you have liberty to step back.' "

---

* David Cobb, afterwards Major-General.

11

In general orders, issued after the surrender at
Yorktown, General Washington specially complimented Knox on the skill and efficiency he had
displayed in the handling of the artillery; and he
also recommended him for promotion. Congress,
however, with its usual tardiness, did not act upon
Washington's recommendation until the following
March, when (on the 22d), Knox was promoted as
major-general, dating from the 15th of November,
1781. General Greene, from his headquarters " at
the Round O," December 10, 1781, thus congratulated his good friend Knox upon the Yorktown
victory:

" MY DEAR FRIEND,—Your favour of the 1st November has just
come to hand. Whatever sweet things may be said of me, there is
not less said of you. Colonel Lee, who lately returned from the
Northern army, says you are the genius of it, and that everything is
said of you that you can wish. I will not wound your delicacy by
repeating his remarks. Your success in Virginia is brilliant, glorious, great and important. The Commander-in-chief's head is all
covered with laurels, and yours so shaded with them that one can
hardly get sight of it.

" I long to be with you, our spirits are congenial and our principles and sentiments the same. A long distance separates, and alas!
I fear, with you, we shall not have a happy meeting for a long time
to come. But be assured my esteem and affection are neither less-
ened by time nor distance ; and I hope at some future day, when the
cannon shall cease to roar, and the olive-branch appears, we shall
experience a happy meeting. Your great success in Virginia gives
me the most flattering hopes that this winter will terminate the war.

" P.S.—Don't be surprised if you hear I attempt the siege of
Charleston ; nor must you be disappointed greatly should we fail."

MAJOR-GENERAL NATHANAEL GREENE.

FROM THE PAINTING BY COL. JOHN TRUMBULL.

CHAPTER VIII

THE END OF THE WAR

1782–1783

LTHOUGH the capture of Lord Cornwallis and his army virtually ended the war, the disbandment of the American army was long delayed thereafter. The preliminary treaty of peace was signed on the 30th of November, 1782. But negotiations for the final settlement of questions growing out of the long war dragged their slow length along for nearly one year more; and during the two years that intervened between the cessation of hostilities and the conclusion of the treaty of peace, it was necessary that the army should be left under arms. Those were sad and gloomy years for the young Republic, notwithstanding hostilities had been concluded and the long struggle for independence had so gloriously come to an end. Congress, then as ever, a meddlesome and dilatory body, failed to provide funds for the payment of an army whose continued existence under arms it zealously insisted upon. Of course, it was impossible to disband the army in the presence of an enemy, but the army—idle, unemployed, and left to brood over its neglect and its woes,—might become a danger to the country which its prowess had just delivered from the oppressor.

Meanwhile, Washington was harrassed by innumerable difficulties arising out of the complicated situation. The British military authorities, chafing under their defeat, were sullen, unyielding, and reluctant to concede even the smallest advantage to their victorious and magnanimous adversary. The exchange of prisoners which should have naturally taken place without friction, early in the truce succeeding the Yorktown surrender, was hampered by many intentional obstacles on the part of the British. General Knox and Gouverneur Morris were appointed commissioners to arrange for a general exchange of prisoners, to liquidate the expenses of their maintenance, and provide for their subsistence as long as they should be legitimately regarded as the charges of the people. One civilian, Andrew Elliot, and one military officer, General William Dalrymple, were appointed to meet the Americans. Knox had known Dalrymple in Boston, before the outbreak of the war, when that officer was in command of the 14th Regiment, H. B. M. Infantry, and it was expected that the acquaintance might facilitate the business in hand. But this reasonable expectation was not realised. Evidently acting under instructions, the British commissioners were unyielding in their demands and stubborn in their refusal to allow concessions. The sessions of the commission were held in Elizabethtown, New Jersey, and Knox, in a letter to Washington, dated at Basking Ridge, April 21, 1782, says: " We have at last left Elizabethtown. Our stay there was unreasonably protracted by frequent references to New York," where Sir Guy Carleton, who had replaced Clinton, was in command of the British forces. Knox shrewdly adds: " We have very good reason to believe that all the important propositions made by us were discussed in New York by a council of general officers. . . . Every circumstance we observed tended to convince us that we never shall obtain justice or equal treatment from the enemy but when we are in a situation to demand it." The British were not yet able to regard the Americans in any other character than that of rebels against their sovereign, the King.

In his letter acknowledging receipt of the report of Knox and Morris, Washington wrote:

" I should do injustice to my own feelings on this occasion if I did not express something beyond my bare approbation of the attention, address, and ability exhibited by you, gentlemen, in the course of this tedious and fruitless negotiation. The want of succeeding in the great object of your mission does not, however, lessen in my estimation the merit which is due to the unwearied assiduity for the public good, and the benevolent zeal to alleviate the distresses of the unfortunate, which seem to have actuated you on every occasion, and for which, I entreat, you will be pleased to accept my most cordial thanks."

In a letter from Knox to Washington giving his reasons for the failure of the Elizabethtown negotiations, he refers gratefully to his recent appointment as major-general on Washington's recommendation of the preceding year, after the Yorktown victory, and says: " I cannot express how deeply I am impressed with a sense of your kindness, and the favourable point of view in which you have regarded my feeble attempts to promote the service of my country. I shall ever retain, my dear General, a lively sense of your goodness and friendship, and shall be happy indeed if my future conduct shall meet with your approbation."

It was not without difficulty that the promotion of Knox to be a major-general was finally secured. The friends of James Clinton, of New York, and of Moultrie, of South Carolina, and McIntosh, of Georgia, insisted that those three brigadiers should be promoted at the same time; and certain members of Congress, strenuously working for their favourites, after the manner of Congressmen in all ages, refused to vote for Knox unless each of the three other brigadiers should be advanced along with him. There was a deadlock, and seven resultless ballotings were had, before some patriotic member, probably neutral in the Knox-Clinton-Moultrie-McIntosh complication, suggested that the advice of General Washington be sought. The wise General advised that the question of Knox's promotion be first considered by itself; and he took occasion to pay a strong tribute of praise of Knox's abilities and his services to his country. This counsel prevailed, and Knox was confirmed, March 22, 1781, his commission as major-general to date from November 15, 1781. This deserved promotion gave him precedence over Duportail, who had meanwhile been made a major-general, but whose commission bore a later date than that of Knox. The three aforementioned brigadiers were also promoted in regular order, their commissions being antedated by Knox's. Knox might well cherish a lively sense of the " goodness and friendship " with which Washington had attended every step of the military career which, beginning with the siege of Boston, was now so near its close.

From this time forward, Knox's headquarters were at West Point, although he was not appointed to the command of that post until the following year. The American army celebrated at West Point, on the first day of June, the birth of that hapless son of Louis XVI. who was known as the Dauphin. True to their affectionate obligation to France, the Americans united in what was styled " an elegant entertainment " in honour of the auspicious event. An immense bower was constructed on the plain at West Point, the festivities lasting through the day and evening; they were concluded by a ball at which, according to a chronicle of the time, " His Excellency General Washington was unusually cheerful. He attended the ball in the evening and with a dignified and graceful air, having Mrs. Knox for his partner, carried down a dance of twenty couple in the arbor on the green grass."

Knox, having reported upon the condition of the fortifications at West Point and its inability to stand a siege, was appointed to the command of the post, August 29, 1782; and he set himself to work, with characteristic energy, to complete and strengthen

the system of defences already planned. In his
letter of instructions, Washington, who was well
aware of Knox's familiarity with the exigencies and
needs of the situation, said: " I have so thorough
a confidence in you, and so well acquainted with
your abilities and activity, that I think it needless
to point out to you the great outlines of your duty."

Early in 1783, when the discontent of the army
had reached its height, Washington, writing to
Knox at West Point, says: " If there are any non-
commissioned officers or soldiers whose mutinous
dispositions appear to arise from their anxiety to be
discharged the Army, you have my full permission
to give them furloughs for any length of time they
wish. We are better off without them than with
them." But this was after peace had been assured,
although the final treaty had not been signed. It
was during the cheerless winter of 1782-83 that the
murmurs of the half-clad, under-fed, and long-
neglected army began to be manifested in audible
cries for immediate redress of wrongs and slights.
A calm and eminently dispassionate statement of
the grievances of the men and officers was drawn up
in December, 1783, by a committee of general officers of which Knox was chairman; the document,
which was addressed to Congress, after stating the
amounts due to the army, proposed that the half-
pay for life that had been granted to the officers
should be commuted for a specific sum, and that the
question of future pensions, arrears of pay, and
other claims of the rank and file should be at once
adjusted. The memorial was taken to Congress by

General McDougall, Colonel John Brooks, and Colonel Ogden. Immediate attention was given to the memorial, and at one time it was thought that matters were in train for a satisfactory settlement of all existing difficulties. But party feeling and the besetting sin of Congress—dilatoriness—blocked the way; nothing practical was done.

During these trying times, Knox wrote to his steadfast friend, General Lincoln, of Massachusetts, a letter which, under date of the 20th of December, 1782, gives this warning note of impending trouble:

" I am, and I believe the whole army are, perfectly in sentiment with you respecting a commutation of half-pay. The accounts up to the present period ought to be settled by somebody. The State settlement, for the reasons you have given must be preferable. The expectations of the army, from the drummer to the highest officers, are so keen for *some* pay, that I shudder at the idea of their not receiving it. The utmost sufferance upon that head has arrived. To attempt to lengthen it will undoubtedly occasion commotions. The gentlemen sent with the address have been unable to raise the money for their expenses, until yesterday. The army will have anxious moments until they shall know the result."

In a letter written to Gouverneur Morris, two months later, Knox gives his views and those of the army upon the proposition that the nation should have a strong government, since none but a strong government could be a responsible one. It was the irresponsibility of the mob of Congressmen which the army had reason to dread and distrust. Knox says, in his letter to Morris:

" The army generally have always reprobated the idea of be- ing thirteen armies. Their ardent desires have been to be one continental body looking up to one sovereign. This would have prevented much heart-burning at the partialities which have been practised by the respective States. They know of no way of bringing this about, at a period when peace appears to be in full view. Certain it is they are good patriots, and would forward any thing that would tend to produce union, and a permanent constitution ; . . . . but they must be directed in the mode by the proper authority.

"It is a favourite toast in the army, ' A hoop to the barrel,' or ' Cement to the Union.' America will have fought and bled to little purpose if the powers of government shall be insufficient to preserve the peace, and this must be the case without general funds. As the present Constitution is so defective, why do not you great men call the people together and tell them so ; that is, to have a convention of the States to form a better Constitution ? This appears to us, who have a superficial view only, to be the more efficacious remedy. Let something be done before a peace takes place, or we shall be in a worse situation than we were at the commencement of the war."

General McDougall and Colonel Ogden united in a report of their doings and of the non-doings of Congress, all of which gave a most unsatisfactory view of the situation up to the latter part of February. The report was sent to General Knox, as chairman of the committee of officers who had prepared the address carried by the three commissioners. Writing from West Point, February 21, 1783, Knox replies to McDougall:

"I received the report signed by you and Colonel Ogden, copies of which have been distributed to the different parts of the army. The business, instead of being brought to a close, seems more remote from a decision than it was before the application to Congress. The complex system of government operates most powerfully in the present instance against the army, who certainly deserve everything in the power of a grateful people to give.

"We are in an unhappy predicament indeed, not to know who are responsible to us for a settlement of accounts.

" Posterity will hardly believe that an army contended incessantly for eight years under a constant pressure of misery to establish the liberties of their country, without knowing who were to compensate them or whether they were ever to receive any reward for their services. It is high time that we should, now we have a prospect of peace, know whether the respective States or the whole, aggregately are to recognise our dues and to place them upon such principles as to promise some future benefit. Much has been said about the influ- ence of the army :—it can only exist in one point, that to be sure is a sharp point, which I hope in God will never be directed but against the enemies of the liberties of America.

" It will take much time to change or amend the present form of government : must our accounts, therefore, remain unsettled until this shall have been considered and decided upon ? I think not.

" My sentiments are exactly these. I consider the reputation of the American army as one of the most immaculate things on earth, and that we should even suffer wrongs and injuries to the utmost verge of toleration rather than sully it in the least degree. But there is a point beyond which there is no sufferance. I pray sincerely we may not pass it. I have not taken the sense of the army upon your report ; that is, I have not called any number of officers to- gether upon this subject, because, as no decision has been made, nothing they can say will, in the least, forward the matter. I ard- ently wish you may be able to fix the rate of commutation, and have a person appointed to settle the accounts of the army, and then have a reference to the respective States, to become responsible for the sums which may be found due upon both principles of accounts and commutation of half-pay.

" You will readily perceive I mean this as a private letter, nay, more, a confidential one."

Ten days later Knox writes: " The army are im- patiently waiting the result of your mission. I earnestly wish it may produce more than it at present seems to promise." One explanation of the dilatoriness of Congress at this time was the in- difference with which States regarded vacancies existing in their delegations, and the languor with which many members attended upon the sessions of the body.   Alluding to this, Knox, in his letter to McDougall says: " It is enough to sicken one to observe how light a matter many States make of their not being represented in Congress,—a good proof of the badness of the present Constitution."

On the 10th of March appeared in camp at Newburgh an incendiary document, published anonymously, which was the first of the two famous " Newburgh Addresses." The writer, who was afterwards known to be Major John Armstrong, an *aide-de-camp* on the staff of General Gates, discussed in inflammatory terms the condition of the army and the wrongs that had so long been endured by officers and men.   Referring to the late memorial to Congress, the address advised that this should be, rather, a last remonstrance before quitting the service of the Republic and retiring to some unsettled portion of the country where the army might mock when fear should again come to the young Republic. Accompanying the address was a notice calling a meeting of the general and field officers, a commissioned officer from each company and a delegate from the medical staff, to consider the inaction of Congress and the exigencies of the situation.

Washington made the call and the address the subject of general orders issued on the following day, in which he expressed his disapprobation of " such disorderly proceedings "; he also asked that the officers of the army should meet on the 15th of March, instead of on the 11th, the day set in the anonymous call. The writer of the first address, seeing that he was checkmated by Washington's calm and resolute attitude and by his invitation, attempted to cover his retreat by a second address in which he jauntily assumed that the Commander-in-chief was with him in this attempt to swerve the army from its allegiance to the only recognisable authority in the Republic.

But when the meeting took place, on the 15th of March, Washington opened the proceedings with a dignified and forcible address in which he suggested that the writer of the anonymous documents could not be a friend to the country, but, rather, an insidious foe, possibly an emissary from New York, plotting the ruin of both civil and military power of the Republic by sowing the seeds of discord. He counselled faith and patience, pointing out the fatuousness of the proposed secession of the army and urging the men to rise superior to the most complicated sufferings.

Washington's good sense and the veneration in which he was held carried the day. When he had withdrawn and Gates, as the senior major-general present, had taken the chair, Knox moved a series of resolutions thanking Washington for his wise and patriotic course and expressing unabated attachment for the Commander-in-chief. The resolutions also declared the unshaken reliance of the army on the good faith of Congress and the country, and a determination to bear with patience their grievances until, in due time, they should be redressed. Congress, alarmed by these significant and impressive proceedings, once more took up the subject of the army's wrongs and agreed to grant the provisions asked for in the memorial. While the commissioners from the army were yet in Philadelphia, urging upon the attention of Congress the imminence of the impending crisis, but before the meeting at which Washington's address was made, Knox wrote to General McDougall, vehemently imploring him to bring before the dawdling Congressmen the magnitude of the ills which their inaction invited. He says: " Endeavour, my dear friend, once more to convince the obdurate of the awful evils which may arise from postponing a decision on the subjects of our address."

On the 16th of March, after the crisis at Newburgh had passed, Knox wrote to his friend, General Benjamin Lincoln, enclosing a transcript of the proceedings of the meeting of the 15th, and adding: " The occasion, though intended for opposite purposes, has been one of the happiest circumstances of the war, and will set the military character of America in a high point of view. If the people have the most latent spark of gratitude, this generous proceeding of the army must call it forth. For these reasons, I think the proceedings ought to be published. Can you not have this done immediately ? If so, forward some hundred copies to the army. The General's address is a masterly performance."

It was about this time that Knox conceived the happy idea of organising a society to perpetuate the friendships formed by the officers of the army and to provide for their indigent widows and surviving children; each officer, on joining the society, was

HEADQUARTERS OF MAJOR-GENERAL KNOX AT VAIL'S GATE, NEWBURGH, N. Y.

to contribute to its fund one month's pay. In the Knox Papers is to be found a document, endorsed in Knox's handwriting, ' Rough draft of a society to be formed by the American officers, and to be called the Cincinnati." The paper is dated " West Point, 15 April, 1783." The preamble, which is couched in the somewhat inflated language of the time, reads as follows:

" Whereas it has pleased the Supreme Governor of the Universe in the disposition of human affairs, to cause the separation of the Colonies of North America from the domination of Great Britain, and, after a bloody conflict of eight years, to establish them free, independent and sovereign States connected by alliances founded upon reciprocal advantages with some of the Great Princes and Powers of the Earth—To perpetuate therefore as well the remembrance of this great event as the mutual friendships which have been formed under the pressure of common danger, and in numerous instances cemented by the blood of the parties—The officers of the American Army do hereby in the most solemn manner associate, constitute and combine themselves into one Society of Friends, to endure while they shall endure, or any of their oldest male posterity who may be judged worthy of becoming its supporters and members."

It was further declared that as " these officers were originally taken from the citizens of America, with high veneration for the character of the illustrious Quinctius Cincinnatus, and being resolved to follow his example by returning to their citizenship, they think they may with propriety denominate themselves ' The Cincinnati.' " Knox's plan was complete, even down to the smallest details of the society's seal, badge, etc. It was further recommended that the Count de Rochambeau be asked to furnish the names of such foreign officers as were eligible to election to membership in the society.

This project was hailed with enthusiasm by officers of the army, and with derision and contempt by many who were not entitled to membership in the fraternity. The provision to make the society self-perpetuating by the election of eldest sons to succeed their parents was greeted with the most acrid criticism. This clause, it was urged, was intended to create a new order of nobility, and whereas the law of primogeniture had always been highly offensive to every true son of liberty, it was now proposed to link the illustrious name of Washington to an insidious attempt to set up such a method of regulating succession in this Republic. Among the civilians who scouted the project were the two Adamses, John and Samuel, and Benjamin Franklin; this venerable cynic assailed the scheme with his own peculiar sarcasm, deriding the institution in every particular. During the turmoil caused by the publication of Knox's scheme, that redoubtable general, not in the least dismayed by the clamour, wrote to Washington thus: " The Cincinnati appears, however groundlessly, to be an object of jealousy. The idea is that it has been created by a foreign influence, in order to change our form of government.''

In spite of this wordy and unreasonable opposition, the officers of the army went forward with the formation of the society, an eminently practical and patriotic institution whose existence unto this day testifies to its vital energy and to the wisdom of its founders, whose illustrious example still serves to keep alive the fires of patriotism that burn throughout the great Republic. The first president of the order was George Washington; its first secretary was Henry Knox, who became vice-president in 1805. Knox was also chosen vice-president of the Massachusetts branch of the society in 1783.

On the 26th of August, 1783, Knox was left in command of the army with instructions from Washington to proceed with the difficult and delicate duty of disbanding it. Late in the following October (the definitive treaty of peace having arrived), preparations for a popular celebration of the great event were begun; but Washington, in a letter to Knox, dated October 23d, suggested that it would be better to omit the celebration until the city of New York should be evacuated by the British, when all who would might join and could find ample accommodations in that city. At the same time, Washington directed Knox to be prepared for an early occupation of New York with his troops, and requested him to confer with Governor Clinton, of New York, as to the necessary arrangements to be made for entering and taking possession. Governor Clinton was ill and unable to take any part in the preliminary arrangements, and Knox, acting upon the instructions received from the Commander-in-chief, wrote to Sir Guy Carleton, asking him to give him (Knox) five or six days' notice of the embarkation of the first of his troops.

On the 12th of November, Carleton wrote from New York to Washington and to Knox announcing his intention of " relinquishing the posts at King's Bridge and as far as McGowan's Pass, inclusive, on this island on the 21st instant; to resign possession

12

of Herrick's and Hampstead with all the eastward
to Long Island, on the same day; and, if possible,
to give up this city with Brooklyn on the day following, and Paulus Hook, Denny's and Staten Island
as soon after as may be practicable." The British
General at the same time stipulated that in case any
repairs should be needed by his ships, before sail-
ing, " free and uninterrupted use of the Ship Yard "
should be had for that purpose.

On the 25th of November, 1783, the British finally
and definitively evacuated the city. On the same
day, Knox, at the head of his troops, took military
possession. But this was a military precaution, not
a formal ceremony. Having disposed such guards
as were necessary to preserve order, a more imposing ceremonial was observed. A contemporaneous
account says * :

" The British army evacuated New York, and the American troops,
under General Knox, took possession of the city. Soon after, General Washington and Governor Clinton, with their suite, made their
public entry into the city on horseback, followed by the lieutenant-
governor and the members of the council, for the temporary government of the southern district, four abreast. General Knox and the
officers of the army, eight abreast ; citizens on horseback, eight
abreast ; the speaker of the assembly and citizens on foot, eight
abreast."

The final act of the military drama was closed;
but a more touching and affecting scene occurred
on Tuesday, December 4th, when Washington took
final leave of his brothers in arms at Fraunce's Tav-
ern. The occasion when these men who had suffered

* Thacher's *Military Journal.*

together and had fought for many years parted from
each other and from their beloved commander, was
one of historic impressiveness. Washington took
no pains to conceal the emotions that shook his
frame. Raising a glass of wine, he said: " With a
heart full of love and gratitude, I now take leave of
you. I most devoutly wish that your latter days
may be as prosperous and happy as your former
ones have been glorious and honourable." Having
drank, he added, " I cannot come to each of you to
take my leave, but shall be obliged to you, if each
of you will come and take me by the hand." With
manly tears coursing down his face, Washington
turned to Knox, who stood nearest him, grasped his
hand and kissed him with sincere affection. In the
same manner he took leave of each succeeding
officer. The simple ceremonial was concluded in
solemn silence, not a word being spoken to interrupt the gravity of the scene. When all was done,
the great commander left the room, walked to
Whitehall, where he entered a barge, and so was
rowed to Paulus Hook. Having embarked, he
turned to the illustrious company on the water's
edge, took off his hat and waved a last, silent farewell.

CHAPTER IX

A TRYING INTERREGNUM

1783–1788

N his return to West Point, after the American occupation of New York had been formally and smoothly conducted, Knox was given an official vote of thanks for the attention to the rights of the citizens of the State and the preservation of peace and good order maintained by General Knox and his associates in arms. Governor Clinton, in transmitting the resolution to General Knox, took occasion to add a few words of his own, warmly commending the services of the army.

The West Point command was now the most important of any in the country; not only was the commanding officer charged with the delicate and responsible duty of reducing the numerical strength of the army as rapidly as was practicable, but the defences of the post must not be neglected, arms and military equipments were to be collected there, and visits to the outlying posts of the command were frequently necessary. The small pay of a

WASHINGTON'S FAREWELL TO HIS OFFICERS.

FROM THE PAINTING BY ALONZO CHAPPEL.

major-general was hardly adequate to bear the expenses entailed upon commandant of the post, and Knox accordingly wrote to Washington, reminding him that it was customary to make a special allowance to a major-general commanding in a separate department; but this allowance had been suspended before Knox was assigned to the post; and he begged the Commander-in-chief to communicate the facts to Congress. Knox was known to be the embodiment of hospitality, and at no time during the war did he find the emoluments of his military rank and station sufficient to meet his expenses.

It was not an unusual condition of things, therefore, that surrounded him at this time, when he wrote: "That the unavoidable expenses arising from the command of this post and its dependencies have greatly exceeded any emoluments of office arising from my rank in the army; and that, in order to support my station with some propriety, so as not to reflect disgrace upon the public rank I sustain, I have been obliged to make use of my private resources to a considerable amount." This reasonable statement was approved by Congress, and the additional allowance permitted under such circumstances (ninety dollars per month) was granted him, the extra sum being included in his allowance dating from September 1, 1782.

There was much private and public discussion now going on over what was called the Peace Establishment. Congress was disposed to be economical in making any military dispositions for the future. The voluminous correspondence of Washington and

Knox contains many references to this absorbing topic, both of the distinguished writers being of the opinion that the hostile attitude of the Indians on the north-western frontier, and the mischief-making tactics of the British in the frontier posts would seem to require the maintenance of at least a skeleton army.   There were not wanting those who advocated the immediate and complete disbandment of the entire force, leaving not one man to mount guard in the so-called Peace Establishment.

One scheme for the defence of the Western frontier was the organisation of a new state westward of the Ohio, where much land would be taken up by officers and discharged soldiers under the land-warrants to which they were entitled for military services. Writing on this subject, in September, 1783, Knox says to Washington: '' I am daily solicited for information respecting the progress of the officers' petition for a new State westward of the Ohio. . . . Were the prayer of the petition to be granted, the officers in a very few years would make the finest settlement on the frontiers, and form a strong barrier against the barbarians.''

Knox's active mind, ever revolving projects for the better defence of his country and for the enhancement of the dignity of the new Republic, was also busy with schemes for the efficient maintenance of so much of an army as might be allowed under the Peace Establishment policy of a frugal Congress. At this time, the Constitution of the United States not having been adopted, the general care of the army was vested in a Secretary at War, and General

Benjamin Lincoln filled the office. Lincoln did not desire to remain in office, and it was well known that Washington's choice for his successor, if, indeed, a successor were to be allowed, was the well-beloved Knox; and that officer, in the same letter, from which quotation has just been made, says:

> " I have had it in contemplation for a long time past, to mention to your Excellency the idea of a *master general* of ordnance. But I hesitated, and finally declined it in my last opinion to you upon a Peace Establishment, lest it might be concluded that I was endeavouring to create a post for myself. But the resignation of the minister of war eventual upon the definitive treaty of peace, and his opinion that no successor will be appointed, joined to the necessity of having some person responsible to Congress, seem to combine to render such an officer peculiarly necessary, who should principally reside near Congress to execute orders as they thould think proper for the dignity and security of the republic. It is a well-known fact that so complex and extensive a business as the formation of an ordnance and its numerous dependencies, the manufacture of small arms and accoutrements, must be the work of much time, and can only be effectually prepared in time of profound peace."

Knox frankly adds that his own desire is for a private life, and on this he has formed his plans and expectations. But if any office " should be formed upon the broad scale of national policy," he would give the plan his assistance if he were thought worthy.

These considerations, then so novel, and to many persons so unwelcome, are of interest to us when we come to the study of the rise and growth of what are now known as the executive departments of the National Government. There was no department of the navy; the postal service was so inconsiderable that its chief officer was a functionary of humble rank; and the financial interests of the young nation were in the hands of a so-called Financier—an officer unknown to the present generation, and then held immediately amenable to Congress.

General Lincoln's resignation was offered in October, 1783, and Washington wrote to Knox as follows:

" ROCKY HILL, 2d Nov. 1783.

" General Lincoln's resignation has been offered, and accepted by Congress. . . . I have conversed with several members of Congress upon the propriety, in time of peace, of uniting the offices of Secretary at War and Master of Ordnance in one person, and letting him have command of the troops in the Peace Establishment, not as an appendage of right,—for that I think would be wrong,—but by separate appointment at the discretion of Congress. Those I have spoken to on the subject seem to approve the idea, which, if adopted, would make a handsome appointment. I will converse with others on this head, and let you know the result. My wish to serve you in it you need not doubt, being with much truth

" Your most affectionate
" GEORGE WASHINGTON."

There was considerable correspondence between Knox and Washington on this subject, and in a letter dated January 3, 1784, Knox informs Washington that he has very nearly wound up his military work at West Point, and is ready to leave. Referring once more to the familiar topic, he says:

" I believe I did not mention to your Excellency my ideas of the pay of the offices that might be associated ; viz., the duties of Secretary at War, Master of Ordnance, and the charge or command of any troops that might be retained in service. It appears to me, and I hope that I fairly estimate the expenses and trouble, that the pay and emoluments of a major-general in a separate department free of any encumbrances would not be an unreasonable appointment. Should Congress think proper to honour me with an offer of these offices associated together, I should be willing to accept them upon the above terms ; but I should do injustice to myself and family to accept of any employment which would not prevent my involving myself."

This question of compensation for the discharge of official duties in the much-talked-of Peace Establishment, as we shall see, was continually coming up at this time, and under the Constitution, to vex the souls of the statesmen of the period.

Thus Washington, writing to Knox from Rocky Hill under date of October 23, 1783, refers to the debates in Congress on the Peace Establishment, and says:

" By what I can learn, there is a great diversity of sentiment among the Members of Congress respecting the Peace Establishment ; and that great opposition will be given to the measure whenever it is brought forward. It may be well, therefore, for you to consider, whether upon the footing and with the emoluments agreed upon by the Committee, the office of Secretary at War (which I presume will very soon be acted upon) would meet your views. If it should, and you will let me know by return of the Post, I will mention your name to those gentlemen of my acquaintance in Congress as I have already done, and shall be happy if any endeavours of mine can serve you. Gen'l Lincoln is of opinion that a capable & confidential assistant may be had for, say between 500 and 1000 dollars ; but when to this, travelling expenses, wood, paper, candles, &c., are added, *I* should think it would sink pretty deep into the residue ; *He* conceives otherwise, unless the Secretary, whoever he may be, chuses to travel with a retinue & incur more expenses than is necessary."

This characteristically Washingtonian letter is concluded in the following manner:

" My best wishes attend Mrs. Knox, and I am, with the greatest truth & friendship,

> " Dear Sir, Y'r most obed't and
> " affectionate serv't
> " GEORGE WASHINGTON."

Later, on the same day, Washington writes to Knox to say that he has now learned that the salary of the Secretary of War is to be $3500 per year, the Secretary to keep a clerk, or assistant, and bear all incidental expenses of travel, wood, lights, etc., and to visit the magazines, military stores, etc.

Virtually, there was now almost no army, but the young Republic was in possession of a large supply of arms, ammunition, and military stores at West Point and Pittsburgh; for the care of these no adequate provision had been made. Knox's work was done when the army was dissolved, and the popular prejudice against the maintenance of even the semblance of a military establishment prevented the taking of any steps to perpetuate the functions of general officers. Writing from West Point to the President of Congress, January 3, 1784, Knox informs that functionary that, under the directions of the Commander-in-chief, several lines of troops have been dissolved; but one regiment, commanded by Brigadier-General Henry Jackson, is still on duty, together with 120 men in the artillery, their terms of enlistment not having expired. As there were at that time about 500 men in what was left of Jackson's regiment, the standing army of the United States then consisted of less than 700 men. Of this force Knox reports that he has detached some to guard the military stores at Springfield, Mass.; others are ordered to duty in New York, under the directon of Governor Clinton, and still others are sent to Fort Schuyler and the lake posts.

Knox then enumerates the stores of arms and munitions of war deposited at West Point, and indulges in this excusable flight of patriotic rhetoric: " I hope it will not be thought presumptuous or impertinent to indulge the rapture which fills my mind upon so interesting a contrast, so honourable and so highly flattering to my country—especially when so great a part of the cannon are trophies, wrested by the hand of virtue from the arm outstretched to oppress it."

Having concluded his labours at West Point, Knox departed for Boston to await the development of events. He took up his residence in the ancient village of Dorchester, now a part of the modern city. Before leaving the military post which he had filled with so much energy and ability, he addressed a letter to Washington, in which he announces his intention to depart for New England, having sent his wife and family before him. He concludes: " I should do violence to the dictates of my heart were I to suppress its sensations of affection and gratitude to you for the innumerable instances of your kindness and attention to me. And, although I can find no words equal to their warmth, I may venture to assert that they will remain indelibly fixed. I devoutly pray the Supreme Being to continue to afford you his especial protection."

On his part, Washington, having now established himself in his seat at Mount Vernon, wrote with much warmth and affection to his old companion in arms, and congratulating himself on the calm and tranquillity of his present station. In a letter dated at Mount Vernon, February 20, 1784, Washington, after referring to past events, says to Knox:

" I feel now, however, as I conceive a wearied traveller must do, who, after treading many a painful step with a heavy burthen on his shoulders, is eased of the latter, having reached the haven to which the former were directed ; and from his own housetop is looking back, and tracing with an eager eye the meanders by which he escaped the quicksands and the mines which lay in his way ; and into which none but the all-powerful Guide and Dispenser of human events could have prevented his falling."

In the summer of this year, Knox was appointed by the General Court of Massachusetts to serve on a commission to treat with the Penobscot Indians and induce them to relinquish a part of their lands on the Penobscot River, District of Maine, that region still being the territory of Massachusetts. There were about one hundred families of these people, and it was desired that they move up the river, ceding to the State, for a consideration, so much of their lands as lay below the head of tide-water. After a speech by Knox in which he presented the white man's view of the case with his customary affability and force, a reply was made by the chief, Orono, whom Knox describes as " one of the old chiefs, half-Indian and half-French of the Castine breed." The Baron de St. Castine, a soldier of fortune who established himself near the mouth of the Penobscot, early in the seventeenth century, gave his name and lineage to some of the aboriginal tribesmen of the region. It was in vain that the old chief pleaded, "The Almighty placed us on the land, and it is ours." The white man's imperious necessities prevailed and the Penobscots retired up the river.

Knox and his associates, General Lincoln and Mr. George Partridge, were also instructed by the General Court to examine into the charge that the people of Nova Scotia had trespassed upon American territory, and to settle the eastern boundary line, there being a sharp dispute as to which was the true river St. Croix, designated in the treaty of peace as the line of demarcation between Maine and the British possession on the east. The report of the commissioners was made in August, but it was not until later that the much-vexed boundary question was finally settled.

During these and later years, Knox maintained a regular correspondence with the foreign officers who had aided in the war of the Revolution, and who, from their homes on the other side of the Atlantic, regarded with unabated interest the gradual development of the young Republic and with steadfast affection their American companions in arms. Lafayette appears to have entertained for Knox and Greene an almost romantic affection. With both of them he kept up a vigorous and intimate correspondence, and he eventually adopted into his own family the son of General Greene. Writing to Knox, from Paris, in January, 1784, Lafayette says:

" It has been to me a great happiness to hear from you, and while
we are separated, I beg you will let me enjoy it as often as possible.
You know my tender affection for you, my dear Knox, is engraved
in my heart, and I shall keep it as long as I live. From the beginning of our great Revolution, which has been the beginning of our
acquaintance, we have been actuated by the same principles, impressed with the same ideas, attached to the same friends, and have
warmly loved and confidentially intrusted each other. The remembrance of all this is dear to my heart ; and from every motive of
tenderness and regard, I set the greater value by the happiness of
your possession as a bosom friend. I have been much employed in
rendering America what service I could in the affairs of her commerce. What I can do must be entirely done before the spring,
when I intend embarking for my beloved shores of Liberty. My
delays in Europe are owing to motives of American public service.
. . . Dunkirk, L'Orient, Bayonne, and Marseilles have been
declared free ports of America."

Lafayette's plans for visiting the United States
were finally carried out, and he was received with
great enthusiasm upon these shores. In October of
that year, he went to Boston, and was met at Watertown by a large party of officers of the late Revolutionary army, headed by General Knox, and the
illustrious company sat down to a handsome repast
which had been provided for the occasion. On the
following day, these officers waited upon Lafayette
in a more formal manner, presenting to him an address of welcome and congratulation, written by
Knox, to which the distinguished visitor made a
suitable reply. A few days later, the citizens of
Boston tendered Lafayette a public banquet in
historic Faneuil Hall; among the many distinguished
persons present were seventy-five officers of the late
Continental army.

Washington, at this time, was living at Mount

Vernon in as complete seclusion as was possible under the circumstances. But his frequent and intimate letters to Knox show that he was often inundated with company and that he was always burdened with a vast correspondence growing out of his long service at the head of the military affairs of the country. In a letter to Knox, dated at Mount Vernon, January 5, 1785, Washington recites some of his difficulties and burdens, referring especially to his correspondence, which, he says, " would require the pen of a historian to satisfy," so numerous were the inquiries proposed to him; and he adds:

" This, my dear sir, is a friendly communication. I give it in testimony of my unreservedness with you & not for the purpose of discouraging your letters ; for, be assured that, to correspond with those I love is among my highest gratifications, and I persuade myself you will not doubt my sincerity, when I assure you I place you among the foremost of this class. Letters of friendship require no study, the communications are easy, and allowances are expected and made."

After much discussion, Congress decided to continue the office of Secretary of War, combining in the duties of the place all those which had been before specified as legitimately belonging to separate offices. The salary, out of which the incumbent was to provide for the pay of a clerk, or assistant, was fixed at $2450, and on the 8th of March, 1785, Congress proceeded to elect Knox to fill the office thus continued. It will be noticed that the settlement of the pay and emoluments of the place was in the nature of a compromise, the sum mentioned by Washington in his letter to Knox, dated October 23, 1783, being reduced to $2450, while the incidental expenses of the office, on which so much stress was laid by the Commander-in-chief, were to be liquidated at public cost. Knox accepted the place, writing to Mr. Charles Thomson, Secretary of Congress, to say that he hoped to have leave of absence to allow him to settle some of his private affairs. He adds: " I have a perfect reliance upon a candid interpretation of my actions, and I shall hope that application to business and propriety of intention, may in a degree, excuse a deficiency of talents."

Still residing in Boston, Knox wrote to Washington, on the 24th of March, in these terms:

"You may probably have heard that Congress have been pleased to appoint me Secretary at War. I have accepted the appointment, and shall expect to be in New York [then the seat of the National Government] about the 15th of next month. From the habits imbibed during the war, and from the opinion of my friends that I should make but an indifferent trader, I thought, upon mature consideration, that it was well to accept it, although the salary would be but a slender support. I have dependence upon an unwieldy estate of Mrs. Knox's family, and upon the public certificates given for my services ; but neither of these is productive, and require a course of years to render them so. In the meantime, my expenses are considerable, and require some funds for their supply. Congress have rendered the powers and duties of the office respectable ; and the circumstances of my appointment, without solicitation on my part, were flattering, nine States out of eleven voting for me. I do not expect to move my family to New York until June next."

Washington, doubtless, was sincerely gratified by Knox's appointment, and when, some time later, he wrote to the newly chosen Secretary to congratulate him on his advancement, he said, " Withou' a compliment, I think a better choice could not have been made."

A period of political chaos and confusion now intervened, and the small powers of the National
Government were taxed to their utmost to maintain
for itself even a semblance of respect from the individual States. Congress was frequently obliged
to suspend its sessions on account of their being no
quorum present. The States, jealous of each other,
were united only in their dread of the centralised
government which they thought they saw emerging
from the jarring elements that composed the Congress of Delegates. The western counties of Pennsylvania were in a chronic condition of unrest and
defiance of the General Government, and the western
counties of North Carolina set up an independent
government which was styled the State of Frank-
land; and similar claims for independent statehood
were set forth by that part of Virginia which afterwards became the State of Kentucky. The people
of the District of Maine also clamoured for a separation from Massachusetts and a State government
of their own.

The most acute stage of these internal troubles
was reached in Massachusetts when, in the autumn
of 1786, a party of malcontents, headed by one
Daniel Shays, formerly a captain in the Continental
army, openly took the field against all constituted
authority. The complaint of these men was that
the taxes were oppressive, that the rich were becoming richer, and the poor, poorer; in short, their ful-
minations were almost identical with those of the
so-called Populists of a later period in American
history. Knox, writing to Washington from New

13

York, under date of the 23d of October, 1786, gives this vivid and accurate picture of the commotion in New England:

"I have lately been far eastward of Boston on private business, and was no sooner returned here than the commotions in Massachusetts hurried me back to Boston on a public account.

"Our political machine, composed of thirteen independent sovereignties, have been perpetually operating against each other and against the federal head ever since the peace. The powers of Congress are totally inadequate to preserve the balance between the respective States, and oblige them to do those things which are essential for their own welfare or for the general good. The frame of mind in the local legislatures seems to be exerted to prevent the federal constitution from having any good effect. The machine works inversely to the public good in all its parts: not only is State against State, and all against the federal head, but the States within themselves possess the name only without having the essential concomitant of government, the power of preserving the peace, the protection of the liberty and property of the citizens. On the very first impression of faction and licentiousness, the fine theoretic government óf Massachusetts has given way, and its laws are trampled under foot. Men at a distance, who have admired our systems of government unfounded in nature, are apt to accuse the rulers, and say that taxes have been assessed too high and collected too rigidly. This is a deception equal to any that has been hitherto entertained. That taxes may be the ostensible cause is true, but that they are the true cause is as far remote from truth as light from darkness. The people who are the insurgents have never paid any or but very little taxes. But they see the weakness of government: they feel at once their own poverty compared with the opulent, and their own force, and they are determined to make use of the latter in order to remedy the former.

"Their creed is, that the property of the United States has been protected from the confiscations of Britain by the joint exertions of all, and therefore ought to be the common property of all; and he that attempts opposition to this creed is an enemy to equality and justice, and ought to be swept from the face of the earth. In a word, they are determined to annihilate all debts public and private, and have agrarian laws, which are easily effected by the means of unfunded paper money, which shall be a tender in all cases whatever. The numbers of these people may amount, in Massachusetts, to one-fifth part of several populous counties ; and to them may be added the people of similar sentiments from the States of Rhode Island, Connecticut and New Hampshire, so as to constitute a body of twelve or fifteen thousand desperate and unprincipled men.   They are chiefly of the young and active part of the community, more easily collected than kept together afterwards.   But they will probably commit overt acts of treason, which will compel them to embody for their own safety.   Once embodied, they will be constrained to sub-mit to discipline for the same reason.

" Having proceeded to this length, for which they are now ripe, we shall have a formidable rebellion against reason, the principle of all government, and against the very name of liberty.

"This dreadful situation, for which our government have made no adequate provision, has alarmed every man of principle and property in New England.   They start as from a dream, and ask what can have been the cause of our delusion ?   What is to give us security against the violence of lawless men ?   Our government must be braced, changed, or altered to secure our lives and property.   We imagined that the mildness of our government and the wishes of the people were so correspondent that we were not as other nations, requiring brutal force to support the laws.

" But we find that we are men,—actual men, possessing all the turbulent passions belonging to that animal, and that we must have a government proper and adequate for him.

" The people of Massachusetts, for instance, are far advanced in this doctrine, and the men of property and the men of station and principle there are determined to endeavour to establish and protect them in their lawful pursuits ; and what will be efficient in all cases of internal commotions or foreign invasions, they mean that liberty shall form the basis,—liberty resulting from an equal and firm administration of law.

" They wish for a general government of unity, as they see that the local legislatures must naturally and necessarily tend to retard the general government.   We have arrived at that point of time in which we are forced to see our own humiliation, as a nation, and that a progression in this line cannot be productive of happiness, private or public.   Something is wanting and something must be done, or we shall be involved in all the horror of failure, and civil war without a prospect of its termination. Every friend to the liberty of his country is bound to reflect, and step forward to prevent the dreadful consequences which shall result from a government of events. Unless this is done, we shall be liable to be ruled by an arbitrary and capricious armed tyranny, whose word and will must be law.

" The Indians on our frontiers are giving indisputable evidence of their hostile intentions. Congress, anxiously desirous of meeting the evils on the frontiers, have unanimously agreed to augment the troops now in service to a legionary corps of 2,040 men. This measure is important, and will tend to strengthen the principles of government, if necessary, as well as to defend the frontiers. I mention the idea of strengthening government as confidential. But the State of Massachusetts requires the greatest asssistance, and Congress are fully impressed with the importance of supporting her with great exertion."

The legionary troops mentioned in this letter as likely to be raised under the authority of Congress, nominally for the defence of the north-western frontier, were not needed in Massachusetts; nor was the feeble attempt to disguise the real purpose of this move successful. The insurgents marched around the country, threatening the courts and defying the State authorities. An attack on the United States arsenal at Springfield was meditated, and Secretary Knox was applied to by the law-abiding citizens of Massachusetts to permit the use of the national arms for general defence. He replied that the arms could be taken only for the defence of the armory, and should be returned as soon as danger of an attack was passed. The prompt measures of Governor Bowdoin, and of General Lincoln, then commanding the State militia, put an end to the rebellion. Lincoln

chased the insurgents from Springfield to Peter-
sham, where after an ineffectual attempt to rally
his followers, Shays was finally compelled to
give up his hare-brained scheme, and his little
force melted away, Shays finding it convenient to
protest that he never meant anything serious by
his demonstration.

Great was the relief felt throughout the country
when it was announced that the Shays rebellion
had finally been suppressed. At this distance of
time, when the affair has assumed the dimensions
of a mere incident, generally esteemed of light account to the State, it is difficult to understand the
sense of depression that exercised the patriots of
those days, when, pending the formation of a strong
and respectable central government, a handful of
malcontents actually raised the standard of revolt
and defied all government. No man was more
sensibly lifted from this state of depression than
Washington, who had regarded the incident with
feelings of lively apprehension. Writing to Knox
from Mount Vernon, February 25, 1787, Washington expressed his gratitude for letters keeping him
informed concerning the progress of events in Massachusetts and the final quelling of the revolt. Of
Knox's letters he says:

" They were indeed exceedingly satisfactory, and relieving to my
mind, which had been filled with great & anxious uneasiness for the
issue of General Lincoln's operations and the dignity of government. On the happy termination of this insurrection I sincerely
congratulate you ; hoping that good may result from the cloud of
evils which threatened not only the hemisphere of Massachusetts,
but, by spreading its baneful influence, the tranquility of the Union."

It will be recollected that Knox, writing to Gouverneur Morris, in February, 1783, at the time when the imbecility and sluggishness of the Continental Congress threatened to alienate the entire army, argued in favour of a convention to frame a new constitution. " As the present Constitution is so defective," he wrote, " why do not you great men call the people together and tell them so; that is, have a convention of the States to form a better Constitution." And Alexander Hamilton, who had before this advocated a national convention for that very purpose, now proposed the assembling of such a convention to meet in Philadelphia in May, 1787, " to take into consideration the situation of the United States, to devise such further provision as shall appear to them necessary to render the Constitution adequate to the exigencies of the Union, and to report such an act for that purpose to the United States in Congress assembled, as, when agreed to by them, and afterwards confirmed by the Legislature of every State, will effectually provide for the same."

Hamilton's proposition was offered to a convention which had assembled at Alexandria, Virginia, for a purely commercial purpose—the regulation of the navigation of the Potomac and the Chesapeake; but it took shape with readiness and promise of success. Writing to his old friend, General Lincoln, February 14, 1787, Knox, after congratulating him on the efficiency and spirit with which he had quelled the Shays rebellion, says:

" The convention proposed by the commercial convention last September, to meet in Philadelphia in May next, engrosses a great portion of the attention of men of reflection. Some are for it, and some are against it ; but the preponderance of opinion is for it. None of the New England States have yet chosen, and it appears quite problematical whether any will choose unless Massachusetts. The convention will be at liberty to consider more diffusively the defects of the present system than Congress can, who are the executors of a certain system. If what they should think proper to propose, after mature deliberation, should require the assent of the people of the respective States, which is supposed necessary in an original compact, the convention would recommend to the respective legislatures to call State conventions for the sole purpose of choosing delegates to represent them in a continental convention, in order to consider and finally decide on a general constitution, and to publish the same for observance. If a differently constructed republican government should be the object, the shortest road to it will be found in the convention. I hope, therefore, that Massachusetts will choose, and that you, Mr. [Rufus] King, and Mr. [Stephen] Higginson should be three of the delegates."

To Mr. Higginson, Knox wrote about the same time a long letter to the same purport, in which he thus shrewdly outlined the work of the proposed national convention :

" Should the convention agree on some continental constitution, and propose the great outlines, either through Congress, or directly to their constituents, the respective legislatures, with the request that State conventions might be assembled for the sole purpose of choosing delegates to a continental convention in order to consider and decide upon a general government, and to publish it for general observance, in the same manner as Congress formed and decided upon the articles of confederation and perpetual union, would not this, to all intents and purposes, be a government derived from the people, and assented to by them as much as they assented to the confederation ? If it be not the best mode, is it not the best which is practicable ? If so, one would conclude that it ought to be embraced."

During this formative period, Washington requested the opinions of several of his intimate friends and old companions relative to a plan of a general government. Knox wrote a modest and manly letter in which he advised that it were "prudent to form the plan of a new house before we pull down the old one"; and he proceeded to write of a plan for a federal government, "instead of an association of governments." He adds:

"Were it possible to effect a general government of this kind, it might be constituted of an Assembly, or Lower House, chosen for one, two, or three years; a Senate, chosen for five, six, or seven years; and the executive, under the title of Governor-General, chosen by the Assembly and Senate for a term of seven years, but liable to an impeachment by the Lower House and triable by the Senate; a Judiciary, to be appointed by the Governor-General during good behaviour, but impeachable by the Lower House and triable by the Senate; the laws passed by the general government to be obeyed by the local governments, and, if necessary, to be enforced by a body of armed men, to be kept for the purposes which should be designated; all national objects to be designed and executed by the general government without any reference to the local governments. This rude sketch is considered as the government of the l ast possible powers to preserve the confederated governments. To attempt to establish less will be to hazard the existence of republicanism, and to subject us either to a division of the European powers, or to a despotism arising from high-handed commotions."

The impartial reader cannot fail to be struck by the closeness with which Knox's crude plan for a general government projects the lines on which the Federal Constitution was finally moulded. If it varied in some particulars, it is not for us to say that the variance was not better for the country, or that some of the ills that now afflict us might not have been avoided by a closer adherence to the scheme so aptly sketched by this master mind while all plans for a general government were as yet *in nubibus.*

A little later than this, Washington wrote to Knox (the Continental convention being determined upon), asking his friend's advice as to whether he (Washington) should attend that convention. In his reply, dated at New York, 19 March, 1787, Knox warmly advises his old chief to go to the convention. He says:

"I imagine that your own satisfaction or chagrin, and that of your friends, will depend entirely upon the result of the Convention. For I take it for granted that, however reluctantly you may acquiesce, you will be constrained to accept the president's chair. Hence the proceedings of the Convention will more immediately be appropriated to you than to any other person. . . . I am persuaded that your name has had already great influence to induce the States to come into the measure ; that your attendance will be grateful, and your non-attendance chagrining ; that your presence would confer on the assembly a national complexion, and that it would more than any other circumstance induce a compliance to the propositions of the Convention."

The Constitutional Convention met in Independence Hall, Philadelphia, May 14, 1787, with George Washington, a delegate from Virginia, in the chair of presiding officer. Knox was overjoyed at the happy turn which affairs had taken; and, writing to Rufus King, one of the Massachusetts delegates, on the 15th of July, he says: "I am happy the convention continue together without agitating the idea of adjournment. If their attempts should prove inadequate to effect capital alterations, yet experience will be gained, which may serve important purposes on another occasion." The doctrine

of State Rights, in its most virulent form, had
vexed the souls of other patriots than Henry Knox;
and the sturdy general, accustomed to the use of
vigorous language when vigour was apparently
needed, indulged in this burst of righteous wrath.
" The State systems are the accursed thing which
will prevent our being a nation. The democracy
might be managed, nay, it would remedy itself after
being sufficiently fermented; but the vile State governments are sources of pollution, which will con-
taminate the American name perhaps for ages.
Machines that must produce ill, but cannot produce
good, smite them in the name of God and the
people." We may better understand the vehem-
ence of Knox, in denouncing the State governments
of his time, if we recall the fact that the return of
the power originally issuing from the people was
then being demanded by them individually, and
that the extreme logic of this sort of local sovereignty
was accepted by the States, many of which insisted
that the confederation was, and should continue to
be, a voluntary association of nations, each of which
was virtually independent of every other.

While the Constitutional Convention was in
session in Philadelphia there were occasional re-
cesses of that august body. Washington was invited by Knox to take advantage of one of these
adjournments to visit New York and meet some of
his old friends with whom he had been associated
during the war. Replying to this invitation, Washington takes occasion also to offer to the Knox
family his condolences on the loss which they had

lately sustained by the death of one of their children. Referring to the proposed visit to New York, he says:

"I should have had great pleasure in a visit to New York during the adjournment of the Convention ; but, not foreseeing the precise period at which it would take place, or the length of it ; I had, previously thereto, put my carriage into the hands of a workman to repair, and had not the means of going. I condole very sincerely with Mrs. Knox and yourself on your late misfortune ; but am sure, however severe the trial, each of you have fortitude to meet it. Nature, no doubt, must feel severely before calm resignation can overcome it. I offer my best respects to Mrs. Knox, and every good wish for the family—With great regard and unfeigned aff'n,

"I am yours,
"GEORGE WASHINGTON."

On the 17th of September, 1787, the Federal Constitution, finally agreed upon by the convention sitting in Philadelphia, was signed by the delegates, three only (from Virginia and Massachusetts) withholding their signatures. The instrument was now submitted to Congress, and that body submitted it to the States, its ratification by nine of said States being necessary to give it vitality. The story of the devices and the arguments needed to reach the desired end in the several States cannot be told here. But, in passing, we may take note of the discussion that at once arose among the people when they began to scrutinise the new Constitution in all its bearings upon the problem of future government. General Knox, in a letter to Lafayette, dated October 24, 1787, gives a very good view of the attitude of the public mind at that time. Prefacing his statement with the remark that that attitude is one of "anxious attention," he says:

"The discussions are commenced in the newspapers and pamphlets, with all the freedom and liberty which characterise a people who are searching, by their own experience, after a form of government most productive of happiness. . . . The transition from wishing an event, to believing that it will happen, is easy indeed. I therefore am led to a strong persuasion that the proposed government will be generally or universally adopted in the course of twelve or fifteen months."

Knox did not, in this instance, exhibit that oversanguine disposition with which his friends had usually credited him. The ninth State to ratify the new Constitution was New Hampshire, and that event occurred on the 21st of June, 1788, only eight months after Knox had written to Lafayette that the desired result would be reached in twelve or fifteen months.

Knox was naturally interested in the contest going on in his own State of Massachusetts over the proposition to ratify the Constitution, and in a letter to Washington, dated at New York, January 14, 1788, he summed up the situation in Massachusetts very admirably and in concise terms. He said that there were three parties in the State: the first being made up of men engaged in commercial pursuits, to whom were added the clergy, the lawyers, the judiciary, and the officers of the late army; the strength of this party he estimated at three-sevenths of the entire population. This party, he said, was "for the most vigorous government." The second party was in the eastern part of the State and in the District of Maine; the members of this party were hoping for the erection of their section into a new State, and they were waiting to see if the new Constitution would facilitate, or hinder, their great project. Their faction was about two-sevenths of the whole population. The third party was made up of " the insurgents and their favourers, the great majority of whom are for an annihilation of debts, public and private, and therefore cannot approve the new Constitution. This party may not be less than two-sevenths of the State." He predicted that the first and second parties would unite and that the Constitution would be adopted, notwithstanding the bitter opposition of Samuel Adams.

Massachusetts ratified the Constitution on February 6th, and one element of the strength of the Federalists in the Convention was the adhesion of John Hancock, who, after much coquetry and elusion on his part, finally gave his support to the cause. A letter from Rufus King to General Knox, written a few days before the final vote in convention, gives a clue to the motives that induced Hancock to pledge himself at that late hour. After announcing that Hancock had committed himself, King says:

" The final question will probably be taken in five or six days. You will be astonished, when you see the list of names, that such a union of men has taken place on this question. Hancock will hereafter receive the universal support of Bowdoin's friends, and we tell him that if Virginia does not unite, which is problematical, that he is considered as the only fair candidate for President.

Hancock's vanity was flattered by the prospect thus held out to him by the artful friends of the Constitution. But Virginia, then holding off its ratification of the great instrument, finally did ratify, and George Washington, rather than John Hancock, became " the only fair candidate for President."

In a letter written to Lafayette, in April of that year, Knox, after reciting the history of the adoption of the Constitution, up to that date, expresses himself in such vigorous and energetic language as he was wont to employ when writing to an intimate friend concerning any matter in which he was deeply interested.   He says: " As to Rhode Island, no little State of Greece ever exhibited greater turpitude than she does.   Paper money and Tender Law engross her attention entirely; this is, in other words, plundering the orphan and widow by virtue of laws."

Passing to matters of more immediate personal interest, to Lafayette Knox says:

" Mrs. Greene [widow of General Nathanael Greene] and her little family you so kindly inquire after, are seated at Wethersfield, in Connecticut, under the auspices of our friend, Colonel Wadsworth. Mrs. Greene is most honourably and industriously employed in the education of her children.   Colonel Wadsworth is anxious George should be sent to France, to which Mrs. Greene consents.   It is possible the young gentleman may be addressed to your care in the course of one or two packets hence."

About the middle of the following month, Knox again wrote to Lafayette notifying him that the lad, whose full name was George Washington Greene, had been sent to Paris in charge of " Mr. Barlow, of Connecticut, author of the poem entitled the ' Vision of Columbus,' " a gentleman whom he specially recommended to the kindness of the distinguished Frenchman.   As for young George, his friend and guardian suggested to Lafayette, who was now to have charge of his education, that " The classics and modern languages, as being the work of memory, will probably constitute his first studies, together with learning the necessary personal exercises to form his manners. Mathematics, geography, astronomy, and the art of drawing will follow, of course." Knox further says that the lad's disposition is good and that, with proper education, he promises to be " an honour to the memory of his father, and the pride of his mother and other friends." The " Mr. Barlow, of Connecticut," mentioned in this letter, it is hardly necessary to explain, was the redoubtable Joel Barlow, whose ponderous epic, " The Columbiad," and mock-heroic poem, " The Hasty Pudding," were the pride of our forefathers.

One year later than this, Knox wrote the following wise and affectionate letter to the son of his dear old friend:

" MY DEAR WASHINGTON :

" The only news we have had of you is from M. St. John de Crèvecœur's son, who is in your academy. His report of you, on a very short acquaintance, is much in your favour.

" I flatter myself that you will most industriously make yourself master of the several objects that shall be assigned to you.

" You will recollect that you are the son of General Greene, who, by the force of his own talents, became so dear and so important to his country ; that you are to qualify yourself to support his name and to become the protector of your family.

" You will entertain the most respectful affection for the Marquis de la Fayette and implicitly obey all his directions,—propriety, gratitude, and a regard for your own happiness require the most perfect attention to this hint.

"As I beg leave to consider myself in the light of your dearest friend, I shall hope to receive letters from you occasionally and that you will make me the channel of communication to your other friends.

"Your honoured mother has gone to Charleston, South Carolina, at which place she arrived safely in the month of May last. Previously to her departure, she placed your sister at Bethlehem, in Pennsylvania, for her education. Your brother Nathanael is at Lebanon, in Connecticut, under the care of Colonel Wadsworth.

"I am, my dear Washington,
"Your affectionate friend,
"H. KNOX."

Knox had a paternal interest in the lad's prosperity and progress as this admirable letter shows. When young Greene had sailed for France, Knox wrote to Washington (who also had a lively interest in the lad's career) to inform him of the departure of the ship bearing the youngster and his fortunes to Europe. He added: "It is proposed that he return in about six years. Indeed, this will be long enough, lest he should receive habits inconsistent with those necessary to be practised in this country. He is a lively boy, and with a good education, he will probably be an honour to the name of his father, and the pride of his friends."

But alas for the vanity of human expectations! Young Greene remained in France until the great upheaval that overthrew the throne of the Bourbons and set up the Reign of Terror. Returning to the United States, in 1794, at the earnest solicitation of his mother, he joined her at Savannah, and was accidentally drowned in the Savannah River not long after his arrival, thus ending a career which, under the affectionate direction of Washington,

Lafayette, and Knox, promised so much for his family and for his country.

Lafayette also had a son named for Washington — George Washington Lafayette. During the troublous times of the French Revolution, the family of Lafayette were proscribed, and the young man, aided by some of his American friends in Paris, escaped on board a vessel bound to America. Reaching Boston in September, 1795, he promptly reported to General Knox, whose house appears to have been the refuge of many a distressed foreigner. Knox wrote to Washington: " The son of M. de Lafayette is here, accompanied by an amiable Frenchman as tutor. Young Lafayette goes by the name of Motier, concealing his real name, lest some injury should arise to his mother, or to a young Mr. Russell, of this town, now in France, who assisted in his escape. Your namesake is a lovely young man, of excellent morals and conduct." In due course of time, the youngster was sent by Knox to Mount Vernon, and his name is not further mentioned in the Knox memoirs.

Knox's letters contain many examples of the friendly and confiding manner with which he always addressed his more intimate friends. Thus, to select almost at random one of these pleasant communications, a letter written to the Rev. David Mc-Clure, one of his old-time playmates, and later the pastor of a parish in Connecticut, he says:

" Our situations, however, have been widely different. You have been deeply exploring the natural and moral world, in order to impress on the minds of your fellow-mortals their relative connection

14

with the great scale of intelligent being : leading them by all the
powers of persuasion to happiness and humble adoration of the Supreme Head of the universe ; while I have been too much entangled
with the little things of a little globe.   But, as it is part of my belief
that we are responsible only for the light we possess, I hope we have
both acted our parts in such a manner as that a reflection on the
past will give us more pleasure than pain, and that we shall possess
a well-grounded hope of a happy immortality."

CHAPTER X

T HE momentous events of the adoption of the Constitution, the election of the first President, the formation of the new Government, and the selection of the seat of that Government were accomplished without disorder but not without much debate and some confusion. The adoption of the Constitution, attended as it was with acrimonious discussion, gave occasion for the organisation of two distinct parties—Federalists and Anti-Federalists. In the course of time, those who were opposed to the new Constitution, or to some of its provisions, found it expedient to adopt a more individual title than Anti-Federalist; but as the chief " plank " of their political platform was that which separated them from the supporters of the new scheme of fundamental law, they were still proud to be known as opponents of " the Gilded Trap," as some of them called the Constitution.

Knox, as we have seen, was a furious Federalist,

and when President Washington formed his Cabinet,
it was natural that the man who was his first and
only choice for Secretary of War under the elder
dispensation of the Confederation should be gladly
invited to continue in that office under the Constitutional Government of the Republic.   The Cabinet
was so framed as to preserve a judicious balance between the two parties.   Hamilton, another ardent
Federalist, was appointed Secretary of the Treasury.
Jefferson, an Anti-Federalist, then on his way home
from France, was Secretary for Foreign Affairs,
as his office was then styled.   Congress had authorised only three executive departments, but an At-
torney General was imperatively needed for the
guidance of the Chief Magistrate and his Cabinet
in matters of law, and Edmund Randolph, of
Virginia, who had refused to vote for the adoption
of the Constitution, was appointed to that post.
The postal service of the new Republic was weak
and feeble, and the office of Postmaster-General
was considered of so little importance that Samuel
Osgood, of Massachusetts, who discharged the simple duties of that office, was not regarded as a
member of the Cabinet.

The powers and functions of the War Department
were important, though the army of the United
States at that time did not number more than seven
hundred men.   There were at least the beginnings
of a navy, and the management of that branch of
the public service was lodged in the hands of the
Secretary of War.   He also was charged with the
care of Indian affairs and with the distribution of

MAJOR-GENERAL HENRY KNOX.

FROM THE PAINTING BY EDWARD SAVAGE.

the so-called bounty lands among the soldiers who
were entitled thereto.

Under the Confederation the Secretary of War
was entrusted with large executive powers in military matters, and it may be understood that the
first President assumed that those powers were continued under the Constitution.   But a conflict very
soon arose between Knox and the Secretary of the
Treasury, neither of whom was disposed to minimise
the importance of his office.   Secretary Hamilton
thought that the purchase of military stores and
supplies was one of the functions of the Treasury
Department.   Secretary Knox differed with him,
insisting that the War Department should not only
control the distribution but the purchase of these
materials for military purposes.   Hamilton persuaded Congress to enact a law authorising his department to purchase all supplies for the use of the
War Department in all of its branches.   This
anomalous condition of affairs, with some changes,
continued until 1799, when repeated untoward incidents provoked Congress to rescind the action by
which the Treasury Department was charged with
the duty of purveying for the War Department, and
that responsibility was laid upon the Secretary of
War, where it has ever since remained, nominally if
not in fact.

Knox was a persistent advocate of a national
militia system, and the plans which he had submitted to Congress, during the war of the Revolution, were revised and urged by him as Secretary of
War during his first year in office.   Those plans

contemplated what was known as the legionary formation in which all citizens of the United States between the ages of eighteen and sixty years were to be enrolled. The legions were to be sub-divided into three classes—" the Advanced Corps," " the Main Corps," and the " Reserves." Each subdivision was to consist of 2880 non-commissioned officers and privates and 153 commissioned officers; each legion being commanded by a major-general. To the average American citizen this system seemed drastic and costly. There was also abroad, both during and after the prosecution of the war for independence, a dread of a standing army, to which an institution like a national militia appeared to be a plausible introduction. General Benjamin Lincoln, of Massachusetts, Knox's lifelong and well-beloved friend, while he cordially approved of Knox's scheme, warned him that it would be unpopular. Massachusetts, he was confident, would not adopt it. He wrote to say this emphatically to the Secretary, and he explained: " The expense, pay of officers, no pay of men, the burden on masters, calling on the youth indiscriminately, disfranchisement for a time in certain cases, officers excluded from actual service, subjection to a draft for a service of three years, etc., will be magnified here and damn the bill." The bill, accordingly, was damned, notwithstanding it had the support of Washington, who favoured it with frankness if not with active zeal. A plan embodying less energy and less burdensomeness was subsequently adopted by Congress.

Knox, like many another later statesman, " took care of his friends." General Lincoln had fallen upon evil times, and, in a pathetic letter to Knox, he had explained his financial embarrassments, which were then so common among the patriotic men who had spent years of unprofitable service in the Revolutionary army, and asking his friend's aid in securing for him the office of United States Marshal for Massachusetts. We may suppose that Knox's efforts brought Lincoln a better place, that of Collector of the Customs. In a letter from Knox to Lincoln, dated August, 1790, the Secretary said: " Although I do not conceive the office of Collector of the Port of Boston adequate to the merits of my friend, yet, as it is the best thing that can be offered at present, I sincerely congratulate you on the appointment."

Subsequently, when Congress authorised the building of six frigates, the work of supervising the construction of the *Constitution*, laid down at Boston, was entrusted to Knox's old friend, Colonel Harry Jackson, who was Navy Agent at that port.

Knox considered it his duty, as it undoubtedly was his pleasure, to maintain his social standing and office with all the state that was attainable at that time. His establishment was costly, if we regard costs from the point of view of an official with a meagre salary. In his papers is to be found a memorandum giving an estimate of his annual expenses about this time. This curious document, which is headed " Knox, Mrs. Knox, his brother William, four or five children, two female servants, one girl without wages, and two German boys, indented servants," may give some idea of the scale and cost of living in those days.   The family food is estimated to cost one pound, " York currency," per day.   The house rent, stable, and taxes are put in at two hundred and fifteen pounds a year.   The item of wine is set down at one hundred pounds a year, and there is a charge of twenty-four extra dinners per year, at five pounds each.   " Clothing for self and family " is set down at one hundred pounds, and the next largest item is for " Contingencies, including charities, subscriptions, etc.," for which eighty pounds are set apart.

The Knox family first established their home in New York in the house of " Lady Anne Poettnitz," and there is extant a lease between the Secretary of War and Stephen Sayre, agent of said Lady Anne, of premises " situated in the bowery lane."   Later in their residence at the temporary capital the family lived in a house on Broadway.   Knox kept two horses, and the rent of a stable, wages of groom, and so on, were no inconsiderable item of his expenditures.   His salary at that time was £980 per annum; his total expenses were £1314 16s., leaving a deficit balance of £334 16s. on the wrong side of the ledger.   In the careful and neat penmanship of Secretary Knox is still preserved an annual statement of the total expenses of the War Department, which in these later and more extravagant times, seem ludicrously small.   Thus, in the statement for the year 1793, the total annual expenses of the department are set down at $7550, of which the

Secretary's salary, $3000, is the largest item; the other salaries are $500, each, except that of Frederick Sprigg, messenger, who is given one-half that amount for his annual stipend.   At an earlier period, when Knox was first inducted into office under the Constitution, five persons drew pay in the department, and the total sum paid on account of salaries, including the salary of the Secretary, was about nine hundred dollars per quarter.

Some of the smaller incidental expenses that are set down in the accounts of the Secretary, while living in New York, give us a notion of the customs and fashions of the time.   Mrs. Knox's dresses are duly charged in the accounts, but are not described in so minute a manner as to interest the women of these days.   There is a receipted bill to Knox of one Anthony Latour, hair-dresser, for three months' hair-dressing at twenty shillings per month, and in the same account is a charge of two yards of ribbon for the tying of the Secretary's queue, and two pounds of powder for the decoration of his *chevelure*. Later in the same year, Latour gives place to J. M. Land, who charges ninepence for each hair-dressing, and who brings in a bill for one pot of pomatum and four pounds of powder consumed in the ornamenting of the Secretary's hair.

The hair-dressing fashions of the time were extravagant in some respects, but the ladies evidently bore off the palm, as they do now, for elaborateness. Dr. Manasseh Cutler, the agent of the Ohio Land Company of Massachusetts, an organisation in which Knox was a stockholder, sets down in his journal an

account of his dining at the house of Secretary
Knox, on which occasion several notables were
present.   The repast, he says, was " served in high
style, much to the French taste," perhaps out of
compliment to the Marquis Lotbinière, who was one
of the guests.   Mrs. Knox, he says, was " very
gross," meaning large in person; but her manners,
he adds, were easy and agreeable.   Her manner of
dressing her hair, which was very likely the work of
Monsieur Anthony Latour excites the worthy Doc-
tor's attention and disgust.   He says:

"She seems to mimic the military style, which to me is very dis-
gusting in a female.   Her hair in front is craped at least a foot
high, much in the form of a churn bottom upward, and topped
off with a wire skeleton in the same form, covered with black
gauze, which hangs in streamers down her back.   Her hair behind is a large braid, and confined with a monstrous crooked
comb."

If we were dependent upon Dr. Cutler's account
alone for this glimpse of the strange fashions of
that time, we might suppose Mrs. Knox to have
been the only " female " who dressed her hair in
this preposterous style.   But art has handed down to
us the portraits of numerous women of fashion who,
in those far-off days, employed an expert hair-
dresser to build just such fantastic structures upon
their heads.

General Knox and his wife were both conspicuous
in court society at this time, partly on account of
their generous size, and partly on account of their
official station.   It is said that Mrs. Washington
rather shrank from the discharge of such public

social duties as would naturally devolve upon " the first lady of the land," and that Mrs. Knox was by no means averse to taking the lead in all semi-official matters.   John Adams's married daughter, Mrs. William S. Smith, who visited New York during the residence there of the Knox family, wrote thus to her mother: " General and Mrs. Knox have been very attentive to us.   Mrs. Knox is much altered from the character she used to have. She is neat in her dress, attentive to her family, and very fond of her children.   But her size is enormous: I am frightened when I look at her; I verily believe that her waist is as large as three of yours at least. The general is not half so fat as he was."   Knox's weight at this time was about two hundred and eighty pounds, and his height was a trifle over six feet.

In his *The Republican Court*, Rufus W. Griswold says that Mrs. Knox had been one of the heroines of the Revolution and that she was nearly as well known in the camp as her husband.   Of her position in New York at the time of which we are writing, Griswold says:

" She and her husband were, perhaps, the largest couple in the city, and both were favourites, he for really brilliant convers-ation and unfailing good humour, and she as a lively and meddle-some but amiable leader of society, without whose co-operation it was believed by many besides herself that nothing could be properly done in the drawing-room or the ball-room, or any place indeed where fashionable men and women sought enjoyment."

In New York, as elsewhere, Knox proffered a gen-erous and elegant hospitality that far exceeded in cost the moderate estimate he made for it in the memorandum above quoted. Dr. Manasseh Cutler says in his diary that he dined at Knox's table with forty-four other gentlemen, and that the entertainment " was in the style of a prince." Baron Steuben was one of the guests, and every gentleman at the table, except the diarist, was a member of the Society of the Cincinnati, and each wore his appropriate badge.

But the active temperament of Knox did not waste his energies in social functions, however gracious a figure he may have been in these during his term of office. The watchful eyes of the Anti-Federalists were upon every movement of the political leaders of the Administration, and every semblance of the assumption of regal airs and manners was eagerly pounced upon by these carping critics as evidence of the ambitious and soaring aims of Washington and his associates in the Federal Government. The relations of the President to the Congress, the style of addressing the Chief Magistrate, and the rules of etiquette which should regulate the intercourse of President and Cabinet with the Congress were all matters of deep concern; before they were settled, the heartburnings and the bitterness engendered on both sides were exceedingly trying to the temper of moderate and large-minded men.

Thus the verbal communications of the President to the Senate were for a long time subject to the sharpest criticism from the men who were watchful for invasions of their prerogatives and powers. That staunch old Anti-Federalist Senator from Pennsylvania, William Maclay, has left on record in his journals many lively pictures of tilts between the Executive and the Senate during this formative period, when the machinery of the Republic was slowly " finding itself " and settling to its work. Washington read his messages in person, and when matters of importance were to be brought before the Senate by the Executive, the President drove down to the temporary capitol and discoursed to that body, accompanied by such members of his Cabinet as were immediately and officially interested in the propositions to be presented. As may be readily supposed, these visits were anticipated by the members of the opposition with suspicion and aversion. Secretary Knox was actively engaged in promoting the negotiation of treaties of amity between the Federal Government and the Indian tribes, then slowly coming into the relationship of wards of the young nation. On one occasion, when President Washington sought the advice and consent of the Senate concerning one of these treaties, he went to the Senate by appointment, taking the Secretary of War with him. The appearance of Knox seems to have excited the ire of the Anti-Federalists, one of whom, Maclay, says that it was apparent that Washington wished " to tread on the necks of the Senate," and that " he sat there, with his Secretary of War, to support his opinions and overawe the timid and neutral part of the Senate." Up to that time, no member of the Cabinet had made an oral communication to either branch of Congress, but

Knox, in answer to a question from a Senator, who desired to know when General Lincoln could be brought thither, answered " Not till Saturday next." Maclay italicises this four-word reply; and, so far as history has recorded the doings of those days, this was the first, last, and only time when a member of the Cabinet personally addressed that august body, the United States Senate.

Maclay, who speaks of the " sullen dignity " of the Father of his Country, the " silly laugh " of John Adams, and the " bacchanalian figure " of Secretary Knox, was subsequently able to record the gradual cessation of these personal visits of the President and his advisers; and " the shamefacedness," which the diarist complains kept everybody silent in the presence of the President, had no excuse for continuance in the Senate.

It was the custom for the members of the Cabinet to give the President their views in writing when his messages were to contain reference to matters within the purview of their respective departments. Thus Knox's humane and temperate views as to the policy to be pursued towards the Indian tribes are to be found among the papers of Washington and of Knox. In minutes for the President's message to Congress, in October, 1791, the Secretary advocated that segregation of the Indian lands which, in these later days, has engaged the attention of American statesmen. He also recommended an impartial administration of justice towards the Indians, and argued that generous treatment of them and condign punishment of lawless men who infringed upon the rights of these people would win the allegiance of the wards of the nation and secure lasting peace with them. The generous side of Knox's nature is apparent in his observation: " A system producing the free operation of the mild principles of religion and benevolence towards an unenlightened race of men would be at once economical and highly honourable to the national character."

In August, 1790, a deputation of the Creek Indians were induced to visit the capital, and Knox, as sole commissioner of the United States, negotiated with them a treaty by which extensive tracts of land, claimed by Georgia, were relinquished to that State. The Creeks, by their incursions into Georgia and East Tennessee, had caused great and continual uneasiness to the white people. On behalf of their nation, Alexander McGillivray and twenty-three other chiefs now promised to maintain a policy of peace and amity for all time to come. McGillivray, by way of reward for his services, was commissioned a brigadier-general in the army of the United States. One of the defences of East Tennessee in those troublous times was Fort Knox, named in honour of the Secretary of War. The fortification has long since disappeared from the face of the earth, but Knoxville remains to perpetuate the name of the illustrious man who did so much to pacify the red men who once roved those regions.

The first act of the Governor (William Blount) and judges of " the territory south of the river Ohio," now Tennessee, was the establishment, in June, 1792, of Knox County. The patriotism of the commissioners gave the names of Washington, Jefferson, Sullivan, Greene, Knox, Monroe, Sevier, Hamilton, and other military heroes and statesmen, to the early framed counties of the territory, and Knoxville became the capital of the young State.

General Knox was an early and strenuous advocate of the building of a navy. His mind reached forward to the growing necessities and the looming prosperity of the young Republic. He also zealously advocated the construction of a chain of fortifications for the better defence of our extensive seaboard against attacks from without. The timid and the conservative held their breath with awe at the disclosure of the far-reaching and costly plans of the Secretary of War. The Cabinet was divided in opinion on the subject, and it is worthy of remark that Jefferson, the malignant Anti-Federalist, was Knox's supporter in his strenuous exertions to carry his measures.

But the poverty of the treasury and the fixed popular prejudice against everything resembling extensive military preparations and operations defeated Knox's patriotic plans, for a time. The depredations of the Algerine pirates, the enslavement of American citizens by these cruel barbarians, and their threatened destruction of American commerce in the Mediterranean (under the unfriendly aid of Great Britain), moved Congress to speedy action. In response to Washington's message of March 3, 1794, Congress authorised the construction, or purchase, of six frigates, or of a naval force which should not be less than that number of frigates, no vessel to be equipped with less than thirty-two guns. The long-continued depredations of the pirates of northern Africa enforced at last the passionate arguments of the Secretary of War. The famous names of the *Constitution*, the *President*, the *United States*, the *Chesapeake*, the *Constellation*, and the *Congress* made up the list of these first frigates ordered by Congress to be built. Under Knox's administration their keels were laid; under the management of his successor, Timothy Pickering, they were largely constructed, and they were completed and launched during the tenure of office of Secretary of War McHenry. The system of coast and harbour defences was authorised by Congress about this time, and the forts and batteries so ardently asked for by Secretary Knox were in a condition of tolerable efficiency when the Republic of the United States was called upon to defend itself against Great Britain, in 1812.

Meanwhile (in 1791), after much wrangling and log-rolling, the seat of the National Government was removed from New York to Philadelphia. Knox, whose stay in the Cabinet was not to be much longer continued, for a time occupied a house belonging to John Adams, and in a letter from the Secretary to the Vice-President, written in June of the year of removal, Knox takes occasion to thank Adams for the use of the house, situated on Bush Hill, in what were then the suburbs of Philadelphia. " While the inhabitants of this city," says the Secretary, " are gasping for breath like a hunted hare, we experience in the hall at Bush Hill a delightful and animating breeze—a little heated, however."

Near the close of Knox's term of office, the country was vexed and harassed by the episode of Citizen Genet, the feather-headed French Envoy who strove to embroil the United States with Great Britain by lending money and furnishing to France other means of making war. One of his attempts upon the Secretary of War was made with the intention of securing from Knox an underhanded and secret use of some of the resources of his department in the prosecution of his belligerent designs against Great Britain. It was in vain that the arguments of Genet were forced upon the immovable Secretary. Knox made a minute of the conversation which he had had with Genet, and this he showed to the President.

The conversation took place, according to the date of the memorandum, June 7, 1793. Genet said that French ships had appeared off Martinique and Guadaloupe, in need of arms and ammunition, and that if the War Department of the United States would furnish these to the vessels, Genet would guarantee that the cost of the same should be deducted from the debt due from the United States to France. There were long arguments on both sides of this strange proposition, but Knox's final reply was to the effect that such a transaction would be a violation of neutrality to which Great Britain would enter objections. He also insisted that the President had not the power to order such a transaction.

On the back of the memorandum which sets forth

Genet's arguments and Knox's replies, is endorsed
in Knox's handwriting, " Read to the President of
the U. S. the before recited conversation, in the
presence of the Secretary of the Treasury." The
President approved the reasons that had been given
to M. Genet for Knox's refusal to comply with his
requests; and the endorsement further specifies that
Washington emphatically approved Knox's asser-
tion that the President had no authority to direct
the Secretary of War to do the things requested of
him by Genet; and that such acts would be a clear
violation of the neutrality so lately proclaimed by
the United States, apropos of the hostilities pending
between France and Great Britain. In due season,
Monsieur Genet ran his erratic course, and, after
sowing seeds of discord which long after bore a
plentiful crop, he departed in disgrace from our
shores.

The last year of Knox's administration of the
War Department was marked by another unhappy
complication. The three western counties of Pennsylvania rose in rebellion against certain acts of Congress providing for the imposition and collection of
taxes on whiskey. The so-called Whiskey Insurrection was a forcible attempt to resist the execution of a law of Congress. The distillers and their
sympathisers protested that the tax was excessive,
and that the provision requiring them to cross the
mountains and pay that tax, or otherwise answer for
non-compliance with the provisions of the law, was
an insufferable hardship. Congress endeavoured to
ameliorate the burden of the law so far as it related

to the collection of taxes and the compulsory journey of non-paying distillers from one end of the State
to the other; but there still remained the obnoxious
provision which gave to the Federal courts, and not
to State courts, sole jurisdiction of all excise cases.

The malcontents armed themselves, defied the law
and the Federal Government, and drove its officers
and outspoken supporters across the mountains.
Assembling on Braddock's Field, the insurrectionists organised themselves into an armed mob and
swore to accomplish dreadful things. Through the
War Department the President·called upon the
States of Virginia, Maryland, Pennsylvania, and
New Jersey for troops to assist in the suppression
of the rebellion. The militia called out by proclamation were to number 12,950. Another proclamation by the President warned the rebels to
desist and disperse. Washington took the field in
person, and he gave audience to a commission from
the insurrectionists who endeavoured to stay the
progress of the troops and secure from the President
the promise of a let-alone policy. It was in vain;
the troops marched on, and, although bloodshed,
riot, and incendiarism were rife in the disaffected
counties, that march of the volunteer militia so dismayed the rebels that the insurrection was over in
sixty days, and Washington returned to the national
capital. Only two of the malcontents were convicted of treason; and these were subsequently
pardoned by President Washington. The response
of the States to the call for troops was prompt and
cordial. The " invasion " of Pennsylvania by armed

men from Virginia, Maryland, and New Jersey, to enforce the laws of the United States, was the first instance of its kind in history; and the first forcible attempt to resist the authority of the officers of the Republic ended in defeat and confusion.

Events like these, we may be certain, did not lessen Knox's official energy, nor yet turn away his thoughts from his plan for retiring to private life. He found real pleasure in the activities of his station, and his desire to serve his country was always keen and unselfish. But he had long before determined to return to a private station and devote some portion of his abundant energies to making such provision for his young and growing family as was due to them. His expenses in public life far exceeded the income from his official emoluments, and the needs of a large landed estate which belonged to his wife required his personal supervision. He was now forty-four years of age, and he had spent nearly all of his years of manhood in the service of his country. Two years before, that is to say, in 1792, he had written to his daughter Lucy to say that the objects of life did not longer appear to him as they did when he was in the heyday of his youth.

" All my life," he said, " I have been pursuing illusive bubbles which burst on being grasped, and 't is high time I should quit public life and attend to the solid interests of my family, so that they may not be left dependent upon the cold hand of charity ; and in order to retire with reputation, it is indispensably necessary that I should not afford subject for calumny to feed upon, by neglecting for a moment the services belonging to my station. I wish for ease, but in order to enjoy it, I must make some exertions for pecuniary objects."

It is likely that the death of his well-beloved friend, General Nathanael Greene, who left a family insufficiently provided for, after a career of the most honourable and patriotic service, had made some impression on the observant mind of Knox. He could no longer, in time of peace, neglect the interests of his family. President Washington, from time to time, had persuaded Knox to remain with him longer, urging him to stay at least until the end of the presidential term. But Knox finally wrote the following letter to his illustrious chief:

"PHILADELPHIA, 28 Dec., 1794.

"SIR :—In pursuance of the verbal communications heretofore submitted, it is with the utmost respect that I beg leave officially to request you will please to consider that, after the last day of the present month and year, my services as Secretary for the Department of War will cease.

"I have endeavoured to place the business of the department in such a train that my successor may without much difficulty commence the duties of his station. Any explanations or assistance which he may require shall be cordially afforded by me.

"After having served my country nearly twenty years, the greatest portion of which under your immediate auspices, it is with extreme reluctance I find myself constrained to withdraw from so honourable a situation.

"But the indispensable claims of a wife and a growing and numerous family of children, whose sole hopes of comfortable competence rest upon my life and exertions, will no longer permit me to neglect duties so sacred.

"But, in whatever situation I shall be, I shall recollect your confidence and kindness with all the fervour and purity of affection of which a grateful heart can be susceptible."

WASHINGTON TO KNOX.

"PHILADELPHIA, Dec. 30, 1794.

"SIR,—The considerations which you have often suggested to me, and are repeated in your letter of the 28th inst., as requiring your departure from your present office, are such as to preclude the possibility of my urging your continuance in it.

" This being the case, I can only wish that it was otherwise. I cannot suffer you, however, to close your public service without uniting, with the satisfaction which must arise in your own mind from a conscious rectitude, my most perfect persuasion that you have deserved well of your country. My personal knowledge of your exertions, while it authorises me to hold this language, justifies the sincere friendship which I have ever borne for you, and which will accompany you in every situation of life. Being with affectionate regard,

" Always yours,
" GEO. WASHINGTON."

CHAPTER XI

THE RETURN OF CINCINNATUS

1795–1800

HE ex-Secretary of War left Philadelphia on the 1st of June, 1795, for his estates in the district of Maine. Tarrying for a while in his native town of Boston, he was invited to a public banquet in his honour, and when he reached Thomaston, Maine, where he had fixed his future place of residence, he was given a grand welcome and reception, in which the people of the region joined to greet with great warmth the famous general and statesman, their fellow-townsman. A local historian * says:

" The year 1795 is a memorable epoch in the history of this town and the adjacent country ; made so in consequence of the resignation of Maj.-Gen. Henry Knox, as Secretary of War under Washington, and his removal to Thomaston. . . . Wherever Washington fought, Knox was by his side ; and there can be no higher testimony to his merits than that, during a war of so long continuance, he uniformly retained his confidence and esteem. This confidence, before their separation, had ripened into friendship which was kept up by

---

* Cyrus Eaton, author of *History of Thomaston*, etc.

"MONTPELIER," THE HOME OF GENERAL KNOX, THOMASTON, MAINE.

FROM AN OIL PAINTING.

a frequent and affectionate correspondence till discontinued by the death of Washington."

Knox had previously ordered the building of an elegant mansion on his estate, and he now took possession of the domicile, furnished it in a manner sumptuous for those primitive days in primitive Maine, and went heartily to work clearing up the title and improving the vast tract of land to which he had come into possession. Unto this day there are extant many legends of the splendour of " Montpelier," as Knox dubbed his fine house; and the original cost of the building was variously reputed to be anywhere between twenty-five thousand dollars and fifty thousand dollars. As a matter of fact, Knox's own private accounts show that the house cost about fifteen thousand dollars. It was built at the head of St. George's River, a small stream emptying into Penobscot Bay. The situation was one of great beauty and picturesqueness, the site of the mansion being elevated and surrounded with native forest trees. In the rear of the building, which was largely constructed of brick, stone, and timber from the Knox estate, were a number of outbuildings, stables, and cook-houses, after the ample and generous style of the best Virginia homesteads; these were arranged in the form of a crescent, and a covered way from a section of these provided means for communication with the mansion in all manner of weather. The house long remained, after the death of its builder, one of the sights of the region. It is pleasant to remember that in these quiet and picturesque shades the

war-worn veteran passed the last and happiest years
of his busy life.

But the General's repose was by no means undis-
turbed by cares and vexations. The tract of land
now in possession of Knox was known as the Waldo
patent, and to it Knox added by purchase many
thousand acres. The domain (some thirty miles
square) lay between the Penobscot and Kennebec
rivers, and included the greater part of what is now
the territory of Knox, Waldo, Penobscot, and Lincoln counties. The Waldo patent was originally
issued to General Samuel Waldo, the maternal
grandfather of Mrs. Henry Knox. This soldier was
appointed a brigadier-general by William Shirley,
Governor of the Province of Massachusetts Bay, in
1744. He was in command of the forces raised in
the province for the reduction of Louisburg, and
when that important fortified post surrendered to
the British colonial arms, he continued to garrison
Louisburg until relieved by the regular troops.
" All of which was greatly to the detriment of his
private fortune," says General William Pepperell,
acting Governor of Massachusetts, in a certificate
attached to Waldo's petition to the King of England, praying for a grant of wild land by way of
compensation for his services. Before the grant
could be issued and confirmed, General Waldo died,
and his heirs, Samuel Waldo, Francis Waldo, Isaac
Winslow and Lucy Waldo (his wife), Thomas
Flucker and Hannah Waldo (his wife), all of Boston, petitioned the King for confirmation of the
royal grant. This secured, the so-called Waldo

patent became the property of the heirs; and eventually the share of the Flucker family, and then the entire tract, came into possession of Lucy Flucker Knox and her husband, partly by inheritance and partly by purchase.

Knox was also one of the members of the speculative organisation known as the Eastern Land Associates, Henry Jackson, Royal Flint, and other friends of the General being united with him in the purchase of a tract of wild land bought of the Commonwealth of Massachusetts, in 1792, and bounded on the south by lands which they had previously purchased; on the west by a line six miles from the east branch of the Penobscot River; on the east by the Schoodic River; north by the Canada line. For this immense tract the purchasers were to pay the Commonwealth twenty-five cents an acre, of which gross sum $5000 was to be paid within thirty days, and the remainder in payments of $30,000 per annum; bonds and securities were given by the buyers for the faithful performance of this contract.

Speculation in the wild lands of Maine was then rife, and extravagant stories of the hidden wealth of the region had induced many settlers and purchasers to take up as many acres as they could secure " by hook or by crook." When Knox acquired his first interest in the Waldo patent he sent thither one Monsieur Monvel, " a judicious young French gentleman who had been educated in the Royal Academy at Paris," to explore the region to discover its wealth in ores and minerals. It does

not appear that he found anything more valuable
than excellent beds of limestone, a product of which
the proprietor made use when he established himself
on his purchase.

Knox was greatly bothered by the incursions of
squatters upon his land, and as many of these were
Revolutionary veterans who had " located " their
claims under bounty-land warrants upon the Waldo
patent, in possible ignorance of their trespassing on
private property, the embarrassments of the general
were doubled. By his firmness and gentleness, as
well as by his generous treatment of the interlopers,
he secured most of them in their holdings without
serious damage to himself. A more difficult class
to deal with were the lawless invaders who squatted
upon his lands, shot at the surveyors sent to run
boundary lines, and generally carried themselves in
an exasperating and unfriendly manner towards the
rightful proprietor. Vilifying attacks were made
upon Knox in the public prints, and at least one of
these attained the dignity of a published pamphlet
entitled *The Unmasked Nabob of Hancock County.*
Hancock County, whose western boundary is the
Penobscot River, then extended over what is now
a part of Waldo and Penobscot counties, on the
west bank of that stream.

Another prolific source of difficulty was the defini-
tion of boundary lines where islands were concerned.
The Waldo patent gave to the grantee all islands
within a certain distance of the mainland; but where
a part of the island was without that limit and a part
within it, litigation arose, as in the case of Long

Island, Penobscot Bay, a part of which lay within the line of the patent; and a similar embarrassment arose where the title to Brigadier's Island conflicted with that of the actual settlers.   In the case of the Long Islanders, the General Court of Massachusetts enacted a law to quiet title by impartial appraisement, and purchase by the settlers; and Knox bought outright the holdings of the men on Brigadier's Island.

It is not surprising that General Knox, with these vexatious and expensive lawsuits on his hands added to the burdens which he had assumed in his vast purchases, became embarrassed in his financial arrangements.   As early as 1792, when he was deep in his land speculations, he had recourse to his steadfast friend, Mr. William Duer, with whom his transactions in that year amounted to more than $29,000.   Duer was a staunch Federalist, a man of wealth, and the writer of at least three papers in *The Federalist;* he was a friend beloved by both Knox and Hamilton.   Another of Knox's comrades who was involved in his disastrous speculations was Colonel " Harry " Jackson, who, with General Benjamin Lincoln, endorsed heavily the notes of Knox. These men, however, were amply secured by bonds and mortgages, and they were eventually able to make good their temporary losses.   In the Knox Papers is to be found a memorandum of notes and bonds given by the General to Lincoln, June 17, 1797, the gross sum being $56,000.

While Knox was building his house in Thomaston, he wrote an entertaining letter to his friend

Jackson in which he described the budding magnificence of the mansion. Then, passing to the consideration of the habits of one of Jackson's sons, whose education had been entrusted to him, Knox says:

> "I have considered your son as very extravagant in the article of clothing, and without the least economy as it respects them, and unless he is put under some control (*he has no idea of the value of money*), his expenses would exceed all bounds. . . . I have no doubt but his expense for clothing is more than the sum of any lad at the academy at the same time."

This glimpse of the extravagance and prodigality of a lad in private school, given by the pen of his much-vexed guardian, is ended by the further remark of Knox that he has "directed that the lad's expenditures be checked by the preceptor," which, he thinks, "Master Harry will find irksome."

Some years later, writing to his friend, Joseph Peirce, of Boston, Knox casually touches upon his troubles with another lad for whose well-being he has become responsible. This youngster appears to have been one of several of his wife's nephews who had returned from England to America. Knox apologises for troubling his friend "with the young Fluckers so much"; but he sends him Thomas of that ilk with the request that Mr. Peirce shall, if possible, aid him in securing for the lad an appointment as midshipman on the frigate *Constitution*. If successful in this, young Flucker will need suitable clothing, a uniform, a hanger, or short sword, and other things. Knox plaintively adds, "I don't know what to do with him if he fails of the

MAJOR-GENERAL BENJAMIN LINCOLN.

appointment."¹ Unfortunately, history does not record the ultimate fate of young Flucker and his brothers.

Knox's industrial occupations and enterprises, like everything that he undertook, were on a very large scale. Lumber, lime, bricks, fish, and other products were the objects of his untiring and energetic industry. Of saw-mills he had no less than five, and minute reports of their output, " from fish-time until the water failed," are given in his papers. His private list of workmen employed on the estate—labourers, quarrymen, brickmakers, carpenters, coopers, blacksmiths, farmers, gardeners, and millwrights—shows a total of 103 men. The pay-roll is not to be found; but we notice that during one year, 1798, there were killed on the estate beeves which yielded over 15,000 pounds of beef, 900 pounds of tallow, and 2500 hides. The sustenance of an army of workmen and an unceasing stream of visitors required, it was said, the slaughter of one beeve and twenty sheep each week, to say nothing of the fish, fowls, game, and other lesser articles of food that were daily consumed at Montpelier. Local tradition, which still lingers lovingly over the fleeting splendours of the Knox mansion, further sets forth the fact that one hundred beds were made every day in that hospitable abode. Abating much from these extravagant legends, it is evident that the Knox establishment, with its adjuncts of ship-building, brick-making, quarrying, and farming, must have been a costly experiment in the hands of our generous and expansive Cincinnatus. In the course of time the experiment succeeded; but at its earliest stages, it nearly bankrupted General Knox and many of his friends.

A pioneer, to a certain extent, in the wilds of Maine, Knox was the first to introduce many features of social life that were novel in those parts. His wife's piano was the first brought into the region. His library, which was the second largest in Maine, comprised nearly sixteen hundred volumes, of which about one-fourth were in the French language. His entertainments were on a scale as much larger as his Thomaston house exceeded in size the humbler domicile which he occupied in " the bowery lane," New York. At his house-warming, on Independence Day, 1795, five hundred people came in answer to a general and generous invitation for all the inhabitants of the locality to be the guests of General and Mrs. Knox. The entire Tarratine clan of the Penobscot Indians were his guests for days and weeks, and after feasts of beef, pork, corn, and bread had exhausted the General's larder, if not his patience, it was needful for him to say to the chief, " Now we have had a good visit, and you had better go home."

Knox sedulously searched for the best forest trees indigenous to Maine for the embellishment of his grounds. Brigadier's Island, which he bought of the men who had squatted there on his own property, he utilised as a fancy stock farm for the breeding of imported cattle. His superintendent was Captain Thomas Vose, formerly commanding in the Continental artillery, and highly esteemed by General

Knox. Captain Vose eventually became a partner with General Knox in the extensive trading and manufacturing business in which he was engaged. In a letter, a model of its kind, written to this good man by his employer, in September, 1794, Knox says:

" Having with great satisfaction viewed the progress of the building of my house under your direction, aided by the industry and exertion of Messrs. Simpson & Hersy, and Messrs. Dunton and Cushing [architects], I conceive it a matter of duty to thank you particularly for your care and attention in the arduous task imposed upon you, and to express to them my approbation of their conduct ; for your time and trouble in this business, I shall be desirous of making you satisfactory compensation."

Among the visitors who were lodged under the ample roof of the retired soldier and statesman were many distinguished men from beyond the seas. Talleyrand, Louis Philippe, the Count de Beaumetz, the Duke de Liancourt Rochefoucauld, and Alexander Baring, afterwards Lord Ashburton, were of these famous men. The Duke de Liancourt was an unfortunate *émigré* whose poverty was so dire that he was forced to accept from his friend Knox sundry much-needed replenishments of his personal wardrobe. It is related of him that he once said to a sympathising American companion, " I have three dukedoms on my head, and not one whole coat on my back! "

During the acrimonious dispute which engaged the attention of the United States and France, in 1797, the Duke de Liancourt wrote to Knox a kindly letter in which he told the General of rumours

16

affecting Knox's attitude towards France. In his reply, Knox said:

" Under every vicissitude of human affairs I shall love and esteem you as a brother. You are not truly informed of my having a hatred for the French nation. Their great qualities of gallantry and magnanimity are above, far above, my eulogy. But as it relates to this country, they are acting under a mistaken impression of our being attached to the British nation. I hope time and better information will lessen the resentment of France against this country ; it cannot be for their happiness or ours that we should quarrel."

During the latter years of his life, and while he was engaged in the multifarious occupations of farmer, manufacturer, and stock-raiser, General Knox found time to take a hand in public affairs and to review some of the matters which had come under his observation during his term of official life. Thus he was appointed on the commission to ascertain the true situation of the river St. Croix, which, under existing treaties, was the eastern boundary of the United States. In 1801 he was chosen a member of the General Court of Massachusetts, and in 1804 he was appointed one of the Governor's Council and was often consulted by Strong, the Chief Executive of the Commonwealth.

National commerce also became the object of his solicitude, and he busied himself with an elaborate compilation of returns showing that the tonnage of vessels employed in trade between Great Britain and the United States, before the Revolutionary War, amounted to 65,058, or 497 vessels. Of these, 165 vessels, of 21,686 tons, were the property of the

colonists. After the war was over, the General
found that 261 vessels were engaged in the same
trade, with a tonnage of 52,595, of which 163 vessels, of 26,564 tonnage, were the property of American owners. The project of a canal across Cape Cod,
to connect the waters of Buzzard's Bay and Barn-
stable Bay, also gave him a topic for discussion and
careful estimates of the costs. It was estimated
that the total cost, including piers, bridges, etc.,
would be £70,707 10s. In his papers also are found
minute plans of a harbour-defence craft, or floating
battery, submitted to his inspection and afterwards
examined and commented upon by him in his retirement.

In 1787 his attention was attracted to the increasing demand for copper, and he was one of a company
organised for the purpose of mining for that metal.
The company of which he was a member contracted
with the Government of the United States for the
delivery to the agents of said Government of stipulated amounts of copper, which was to be coined
under certain conditions. The copious memoranda,
which are in Knox's handwriting, do not show that
operations under the contract ever amounted to
anything.

His charities were extensive, and, although he
was at times cramped in his vast financial operations, he was ever liberal with his contributions.
He was by profession a Unitarian, but he gave
generously to a church building in Thomaston
which was to be occupied by any denomination of
Christians who might choose to take it for occasional

use in the fitful religious ministrations of those days when sparse settlements and imperfect means of communication prevented regular " stated worship." He gave to that church a Bible and a bell. In his papers is found a bill from Paul Revere for the casting of said bell, which weighed 683 lbs. and cost 85 pounds, 7 shillings, and 6 pence. For the engraving of a motto on the same the charge was fifteen shillings. Some years after Knox's death, the bell was cracked, and it was sent to Boston to be recast. It still bears the name of Paul Revere, still swings in the steeple where it has hung for so many years; but the legend selected by Knox was omitted in the recasting, and we are left without any hint of its pertinence. Among the General's papers is one, evidently written by him at the request of some of his friends, entitled " The Duties of a Christian Minister," in which the deportment, personal character, and parochial functions, rather than the pulpit exercises of the minister, are descanted upon by the writer.

He also drew up and headed with fifty dollars a subscription for the relief of the " four amiable daughters of the Compte de Grasse, in recognition of the services of De Grasse at Yorktown," etc., these ladies being then in the West Indies where they were in great financial straits. Knox was a subscriber to the publications of Noah Webster; and to the extent of his ability he was a patron of the fine arts. He drew a bill for Congress to authorise the purchase of certain paintings by John Trumbull, of Connecticut, " illustrative of the late important revolution which secured the independence of the United States." The preamble to the bill declared that "the encouragement of the arts and sciences has been justly esteemed honourable and worthy of the wisest and most enlightened nations"; and the Secretary of the Treasury was to be authorised to purchase said paintings and control the engraving of the same. The scheme fell through on account of the discovery of the inability of the Government to house them in any gallery or other public place. But Congress, in 1816, did order the purchase of four paintings at $8000 each. These were *The Signing of the Declaration of Independence, The Surrender of Lord Cornwallis at Yorktown, The Surrender of Burgoyne,* and *Washington Resigning his Commission to Congress.* In the Knox Papers is a receipt for three guineas, paid by the General for two prints executed in London by Anthony C. Poggie, engraver, from Trumbull's paintings representing the death of Montgomery and the battle of Bunker Hill, and dated November 10, 1788. John Trumbull and Anthony C. Poggie united in signing this receipt.

During this period, so filled with miscellaneous activities and cares, General Knox maintained an active correspondence with all the leading spirits of the American Revolution, whether living in this country or in Europe. The letters of Washington to Knox are characterised by the same affectionateness and intimacy that always constituted the chief charm of the correspondence of these two great men. When Washington, on the eve of his departure from the national capital, in 1797, reviewed his closing years of administration, he wrote to Knox, who had recently suffered bereavements by deaths, the following interesting letter:

"PHILADELPHIA, March 2, 1797.

"MY DEAR SIR:

"Among the last acts of my political life, and before I go hence into retirement *profound*, will be the acknowledgement of your kind and affectionate letter from Boston, dated the 25th of January.

"From the friendship I have always borne you, and from the interest I have ever taken in your prosperity & happiness, I participated in the sorrows which I know you must have felt for your heavy losses. But it is not for man to scan the wisdom of Providence. The best he can do, is to submit to its decrees. Reason, Religion, & Philosophy teaches us to do this, but 't is time alone that can ameliorate the pangs of humanity & soften its woes.

"To the wearied traveller who sees a resting-place and is bending his body to lean thereon, I now compare myself ; but to be suffered to do *this* in peace is, I perceive, too much to be endured by *some*. To misrepresent my motives ; to reprobate my politics ; and to weaken the confidence which has been reposed in my administration are objects which cannot be relinquished by those who will be satisfied with nothing short of a change in our political System. The consolation, however, which results from conscious rectitude, and the approving voice of my Country, unequivocally expressed by its Representatives, deprives their sting of its poison, and places in the same point of view both the weakness and the malignity of their efforts.

"Although the prospect of retirement is most grateful to my soul, and I have not a wish to mix again in the great world or to partake of its politics, yet, I am not without my regrets at parting with (perhaps never more to meet), the few intimates whom I love,—among those be assured you are one.

"The account given by Mr. Bingham,* and others, of your agreeable situation at St. George's gave me infinite pleasure ; and no one

---

* Senator Wm. Bingham of Pennsylvania, an intimate friend of Knox's.

wishes more sincerely than I do that they may increase with your years. The remainder of my life (which in the course of nature cannot be long), will be occupied in rural amusements, and though I shall seclude myself from the noisy and bustling crowd, none more than myself would be regaled by the company of those I esteem, at Mount Vernon, more than 20 miles from which, after I arrive there, it is not likely I shall ever be."

After describing the events which are to take place during the following week, when he is to give formal farewell of the diplomatic corps, the heads of the departments, etc., Washington says he will witness the inauguration of his successor, Mr. John Adams, and then take his leave. He thus concludes:

" Mrs. Washington unites with me in every good wish for you, Mrs. Knox, and family ; and with truth, I am yours always and affectionately, GEO. WASHINGTON."

Twelve children were born to General and Mrs. Knox. Of these, nine died in infancy or at an early age. One son, Harry Jackson, lived to maturity and was married, but died without issue, so that the name of Knox disappeared from his direct line of descent. Two daughters, Lucy Flucker and Caroline, survived their parents. Lucy, the eldest, born in 1776, married Mr. Ebenezer Thatcher ; and Caroline married first, James Swan, of Dorchester, Mass., and, second, John Holmes, of Alfred, Maine, who was the first United States Senator elected from that State. Harry Jackson Knox was nominated a midshipman in the United States navy, during his father's lifetime, but failed of confirmation by the Senate. He did, however, subsequently enter the navy, and his after-life was eccentric and

not altogether creditable to the illustrious name he
bore. In his last years, he became deeply religious,
and he regarded with remorse his misuse of time and
his failure to sustain the dignity of the Knox family.
In token of this repentance, he directed that he
should be buried in the Thomaston burying-ground
in a grave of great depth, and that no memorial
should mark his last resting-place. This request
was carried out, and only an iron fence denotes the
spot where he was entombed.

The *Columbia Centinel*, of April 27, 1796, noting
the death of two of the Knox children, who were
taken on the same day, says: " Seven healthy,
blooming children have been torn almost as suddenly from the same fond parents, who, with lacer-
ated hearts, hang over the bed of another child,
labouring under the same disease." The fatal dis-
temper which wrought so much grief in the Knox
household was then known as " putrid sore throat ";
and is now better known and more successfully
treated as diphtheria. The same newspaper, subsequently chronicling the death of the child who
was ill when her brother and sister were taken away,
said: " To support the death of so lovely a child,
added to the loss of eight others, requires the combined efforts of Reason, Philosophy, and Religion;
for she possessed all the amiable qualities of the head
and heart, to promise the highest satisfaction and
comfort to her friends and parents." In the *Centinel*, a few days later, appears a tender and sympa-
thetic elegiac poem, inscribed *Aux manes de Julia
Knox* from the pen of " A Scientific Foreigner."

Among the numerous correspondents of General Knox none was more intimate and confiding than John Adams, the second President of the United States. We have seen how confidential was this statesman in his communications with Knox, during the Revolutionary period. This intimacy was maintained as long as the two men lived. A letter from Adams to Knox, written just after the President's inauguration, is an amusing example of what one of his biographers * calls his " truculent letters about men." Knox had written to Adams congratulating him on his success in the recent presidential election. Adams, in his reply, acknowledges that he would have been mortified if he had been defeated. " But," he adds, " to see such a character as Jefferson, and much more such an unknown Being as Pinckney, brought over my head and trampling on the Bellies of hundreds of other Men infinitely his Superiors in Talents, Services, and Reputation, filled me with apprehension for the Safety of us all. . . . We should have been set afloat and landed the Lord knows where." † His reference to Jefferson as " the first Prince of the Country and the Heir Apparent to the Sovereign Authority " is a caustic comment, and a prophecy to be later fulfilled. The times have not greatly changed since John Adams told Henry Knox that " To a Frenchman the most important man in the world is himself, and the most important Nation is France. He thinks France ought to govern all Nations,

---

* Rev. Theodore Parker.

† See Appendix.

and that he ought to govern France." No
wonder that Adams, at the close of this entertaining epistle, cautions Knox that " This is all in
confidence."

But, notwithstanding Adams's aversion to Pinckney, when war with France seemed inevitable, in
1798, he found it necessary * to appoint this " unknown Being " to a major-generalship in the provisional army then raised. Washington was appointed
lieutenant-general, and Alexander Hamilton, C.
C. Pinckney, and Henry Knox major-generals, in
the order thus given. How far Knox's old friend,
President Adams, was influenced by others in the
choice which placed him third in the list, cannot
now be ascertained. But Knox, naturally enough,
was mortified and indignant that he should be
placed after those who had been his juniors in rank
during the late war. Pinckney, on the other hand,
had outranked Hamilton during that war, having
been made a brigadier by brevet just before its
close, whereas Hamilton had never been ranked
higher than lieutenant-colonel. As Pinckney was
then absent in Europe, he was absolved from all
suspicion of having influenced the strange choice of
Adams. And when he heard that Knox was wrath-
ful at Pinckney's being second to his own third, he
offered to give place to him; but Knox's continued

---

* Harrison Gray Otis, who was a Member of Congress at this
time, says in his reminiscences : " Mr. Adams, however, did not
conceal his preference for Knox, nor his chagrin at being overruled;
and he imputed this, not to the decided predilection of Washington,
but to a cabal of his cabinet ministers,"

indignation subsequently induced Pinckney to withdraw even that offer.

Washington had made his own acceptance of the lieutenant-generalship conditional on his being first consulted in the choice of staff and general officers. It is not certain that he was so consulted in this instance. Knox wrote to Washington protesting against a reversal of the order of precedence, and Washington's reply to his former chief of artillery was conciliatory and explanatory, the explanation being that the army as now organised was not in any way to be regarded as having any connection with the old army; rank was to be determined by present needs, not by past arrangements. Knox's letter was sent to Hamilton by Washington, and Hamilton manifested a disposition to place upon others the responsibility for this unfortunate complication. As Washington had delicately intimated that he was unwilling to wound the feelings of Knox, Hamilton wrote to the latter as follows:

" My judgment tells me that I ought to be silent on a certain subject, but my heart advises otherwise, and my heart has always been the master of my judgment. Believe me, I have felt much pain at the idea that any circumstance personal to me should have deprived the public of your services or occasioned you the smallest dissatisfaction. Be persuaded, also, that the views of others, not my own, have given shape to what has taken place, and that there has been a serious struggle between my respect and esteem for you and the impression of duty. This sounds, I know, like affectation, but it is, nevertheless, the truth."

The upshot of the matter was that although Hamilton reluctantly offered to leave the arrangements wholly in the hands of Washington, Pinckney's withdrawal of his offer to go below Knox induced that war-worn veteran to persist in declining any place in the provisional army; Adams's Cabinet insisted that Pinckney should outrank Hamilton, and it was not until Washington intimated that a failure to place Hamilton above Pinckney would be regarded by himself as a breach of an existing agreement, that Hamilton's preference was acquiesced in by the President's advisors. Knox still remained the Cincinnatus of his fields, devoting his energies to redeeming them from debt. In a letter to Washington, in 1799, he said: "I am here [at Thomaston], and should be more happy in my pursuits than I have ever been, were some embarrassments entirely dissipated. But this will require time. My estate, with indulgence, is competent, and greatly more, to the discharge of every cent I owe. . . . I pray that your days on earth may be days of felicity, without clouds, sickness, or sorrow."

This letter was dated December 22d, eight days after the illustrious Washington had breathed his last. But the slowness with which the mails were then carried about the country had kept Knox in ignorance of the event that deprived the young Republic of the advice and counsel of Washington. Three months later, writing to his old friend, General David Cobb,* who, at one time, had been a

---

* David Cobb was a member of the Massachusetts Provincial Congress, 1775 ; 2d Lieutenant-Colonel in the Massachusetts Regular Militia from May to December, 1775 ; Lieutenant-Colonel in 16th

member of his military family, he expressed himself
as entirely reconciled to the dignified exit of their
former chieftain. He said of Washington : " He
exhibited a most glorious setting sun; and the
people of the United States have exhibited human
nature in its brilliant attitudes by their gratitude.
His death and the testimonials of respect will be an
excellent stimulus to future patriotism." Knox
was by no means thus self-contained when the
tidings of the tragical death of his much-loved
Hamilton came to him, in July, 1804. The bluff
man of war broke out into a most violent and un-
controllable agony of grief and tears.

General Cobb, like several others of the Revolutionary worthies, sought to recover his wasted
fortunes by taking up his residence in the promising
land of the District of Maine. In a letter to Knox,
to which the above quotation was written in reply,
Cobb referred to his downcast condition of mind ;
whereupon Knox says :

" You mention that your spirits are not good. For God's sake
bear up against the devil of Gloom. Put yourself in motion. Visit

---

Massachusetts Continental Infantry ; Lieutenant-Colonel in Col.
Harry Jackson's regiment, from Jan. 12, 1777, to Dec. 31, 1780 ;
Lieutenant-Colonel 9th Massachusetts Continental Infantry, 1781 ;
Aide to General Washington from 1781 to 1783 ; Lieutenant-Colonel
commanding 5th Regular Massachusetts Line, 1783 ; Brevet-Briga-
dier-General, Sept. 30, 1783 ; and served to the close of the war.
He was later chosen to fill two terms of Lieutenant-Governor of
Massachusetts, and then two terms in the National Congress from
the Bristol district of that State. He was serving as judge at Taun-
ton during the Shays rebellion and made for himself a name in the
judicial resistance to the mob.

even me if you can find nothing better.   Get Willich, a new author on diet and regimen ; but above all, get—on horseback.

"I shall have bright days yet.   My daughter had been there [in Boston] for two months.   She returned with me.   Mrs. K. and Caroline stayed at home, which is to me, after all, the most agreeable place, provided I had you and a few other friends near me.

"Bonaparte, what a glorious fellow ! how completely he has averted the monster anarchy and mad democracy !   I hope in God that no fanatic will assassinate him, which is to be dreaded."

This letter, it should be said, was written in March, 1800, while Napoleon Bonaparte was yet First Consul, and nine months before the attempt was made to kill him with an infernal machine.

CHAPTER XII

A BUSY LIFE ENDED

1806

E have seen how the advent of General Knox into the community where he had fixed his residence was regarded as an event of moment. The natural expectations of the people of Thomaston were not disappointed. The dominating personality of the retired soldier and statesman very soon exerted a pervasive influence in every activity of the country, whether social, industrial, political, or religious. His was a commanding figure, and the ample generosity of his house set the pace, as it were, for those whose social life even distantly imitated his own. His multifarious enterprises gave employment to a host of men, quickened the pulses of trade and commerce, and stimulated the productive energies of a considerable stretch of sea-coast. His positive opinions and zealous public spirit gave him a preponderating influence in the politics of the time; and in all matters pertaining to the maintenance of religious ordinances and beneficent organisations, Knox's hand and Knox's name were always foremost. The death of such a man meant the withdrawal of an energising force from the concerns of a thrifty and growing community.

The end of his useful career, which came to his neighbours and fellow-citizens like a sudden calamity, fell on the 25th of October, 1806. The General inadvertently swallowed a small fragment of chicken bone, which, lodging in the intestinal system, caused mortification and death. In the midst of his mature years, his strenuous labours were abruptly discontinued; the inventive brain and diligent hand rested from their labours.

General Knox's funeral took place on the 28th of the month, and was celebrated with military honours. After services in the mansion, a long procession, headed by an artillery company, a company of cavalry, and one of infantry, escorted the remains of the veteran soldier to the tomb which had been constructed under the General's favourite oak tree, on his own domain. There were the usual military exercises at the grave—volleys of musketry and lowering of standards. The concourse of sincerely mourning citizens was very large, and the journals of the day published in various parts of New England, vied with each other in paying tributes of honour and respect to the hero, who, after years of arduous service " in the imminent deadly breach " and in the tented field, rested tranquilly in the sylvan shade of his beloved Montpelier. Later changes in the management and ownership of the estate necessitated frequent removals of this burial-place,

THE GRAVE OF HENRY KNOX AT THOMASTON, MAINE.

and the last removal left the grave of the General in the cemetery which he had, in his lifetime, given to the town of Thomaston. A severely plain shaft of limestone is placed over the grave with this inscription:

THE TOMB

OF

MAJOR-GENERAL

HENRY KNOX,

WHO DIED OCT. 25TH, 1806,

AGED 56 YEARS.

" 'T is Fate's decree ; Farewell, thy just renown,
The Hero's honour, and the good Man's crown."

On the south side of the same column are carved the names of Mrs. Lucy Knox, widow, who died in 1824, and Caroline Holmes (daughter of General Knox and wife of Hon. John Holmes), who died in 1851. The graves of Senator Holmes and General Knox's second son are within the same enclosure. Senator Holmes's grave is unmarked. In one of the public squares of Alfred, Maine, in which town the Senator spent the best years of his life, is a monument to his memory.

The General's will had for its preamble the following unique sentence, in which the testator, after the fashion of those times, declared his religious belief:

" Know all men by these presents that I, Henry Knox of Thomaston, county of Lincoln, Mass., but at this time [November 26, 1802] doing business in Boston, do hereby make and ordain this to be my

17

last will and testament. First, I think it proper to express my unshaken opinion in the immortality of my soul, or mind, and to dedi-
cate and devote the same to the Supreme Head of the Universe ;
to that great and tremendous Jehovah who created the universal
frame of nature, worlds and systems of worlds in numbers infinite,
and who has given intellectual existence to his rational beings of
each globe, who are perpetually migrating and ascending in the scale
of mind according to certain principles always founded on the great
basis of morality and virtue ; to this sublime and awful Being do I
resign my spirit, with unlimited confidence in his mercy and protection."

Then follow directions for the final disposition of
the estate and personal effects, an inventory of which
showed a valuation (apart from all real estate except
that immediately around the mansion) of $100,000.
The house and furniture, some of which latter was
very elegant, were valued at $42,656; and the real
estate of Montpelier, with carriages, horses, etc.,
were appraised at $33,000. In the inventory were
seven carriages, fifteen horses, and a number of
sleighs, harnesses, and other adjuncts of a large
riding and driving establishment. The General's
scale of living, as has been said, was generous. In
his account books are to be found entries of madeira
imported from Funchal for his own use, and of rum
and spruce beer for the consumption of his workmen.
In those days it was customary for employers to
make provision for the refreshment of their employed
as well as for their payment in wages.

At the death of Mrs. Holmes, in 1851, the only
immediate descendant of the general was Mrs. Lucy
Knox Thatcher, then a widow. With her daughter,
Mrs. Hyde, she resided, until her death in 1854, in

the old mansion from which all its former glories and spirit had fled. A local historian says that up to that time

" enough remained to show that the house had been the home of opulence and taste. The papering, of antique style, resembling tapestry, with figures dressed in ancient costumes, was in good pre- servation on the wide halls and staircases ; the general's secretary, mirror-fronted, with gilded handles and decorated richly with inlaid work, and a large bookcase in the same style, both said to have been brought from the Tuileries of Paris ; the state bed with its silken damask draperies ; the old-fashioned, well-worn sideboards and large round table ; oval mirrors curiously bordered ; Mrs. Knox's own toilet glass, an admirable portrait of Knox [by Gilbert Stuart] and another of Thomas Flucker [by John Singleton Copley], were still there."

But the ultimate division of these effects made ne- cessary a sale by which all the handsome and curious articles were dispersed. Stuart's portrait finally became the property of the city of Boston; that of Knox's father-in-law, Secretary Thomas Flucker, adorns the walls of the art museum of Bowdoin College. Some of the objects of art and curiosity, whose very mention would make a modern col- lector's mouth water, still remain in the hands of Maine people who revere the name of Knox and cherish fondly the memory of his deeds.

The contemporaries of Knox, some of them illus- trious and still famous, unite in according to him talents of a high order and a character of marked attractiveness and versatility. The Marquis de Chastellux, whose book on the United States has been already mentioned, says of him: " To praise him for his military talents alone would be to de- prive him of half the eulogium he merits; a man of understanding, gay, sincere, and honest—it is impossible to know without esteeming him, or to see without loving him,—thus have the English without intention added to the ornaments of the human race, by awakening talents where they least wished or expected.'' Dr. Thacher, in his *Military Journal*, says that Lord Moira, afterwards Marquis of Hastings, the accomplished British officer who, as General Rawdon, defeated Greene at Hobkirk's Hill, praised in high terms the military talents of General Knox. Chief-Justice Marshall, in his biography of Washington, says of Knox:

" Throughout the contest of the Revolution, this officer continued at the head of the American artillery, and from being a colonel, had been promoted to the rank of major-general. In this important station he preserved a high military character, and on the resignation of General Lincoln, had been appointed Secretary of War. To his great services and to unquestionable integrity, he was admitted to unite a sound understanding; and the public judgment as well as that of the chief magistrate, pronounced him in all respects competent to the station he filled. The President was highly gratified in believing that his public duty comported with his private inclination, in nominating General Knox to the office that had been conferred upon him under the former government."

Dr. Thacher, who knew Knox well, says:

" Long will he be remembered as the ornament of every circle in which he moved, as the amiable and enlightened companion, the generous friend, the man of feeling and benevolence ;—his conversation was animated and cheerful, and he imparted an interest to every subject that he touched. In his gayest moments he never lost sight of dignity ;—he invited confidence, but repelled familiarity. His imagination was brilliant, his conceptions lofty, and no man ever possessed the power of embodying his thoughts in more vigorous language ; when ardently engaged, they were peculiarly bold

THOMAS FLUCKER.

FROM THE PAINTING BY JOHN SINGLETON COPLEY, IN THE ART COLLECTION IN
BOWDOIN COLLEGE.

and original, and you irresistibly felt in his society that his intellect
was not of the ordinary class. Yet no man was more unassuming, none
more delicately alive to the feelings of others. He had the peculiar
talent of rendering all who were with him happy in themselves ; and
no one ever more feelingly enjoyed the happiness of those around
him. Philanthropy filled his heart ; in his benevolence there was no
reserve—it was as diffusive as the globe, as extensive as the family
of man."

A more elaborate pen picture of Knox is given by
William Sullivan in his *Familiar Letters on Public
Characters and Events from 1783 to 1815*. The
writer says:

" He was a large, full man, above the middle stature ; his lower
limbs inclined a very little outward, so that in walking his feet were
nearly parallel. His hair was short in front, standing up and pow-
dered and queued. His forehead was low ; his face, large and full
below ; his eyes, rather small, grey and brilliant. The expression
of his face was altogether a very fine one.

" When moving along the street, he had an air of grandeur and
self-complacency, but it wounded no man's self-love. He carried
a large cane but not to aid his steps ; and sometimes, when he happened to stop and engage in conversation with his accustomed ardour, his cane was used to flourish with, to aid his eloquence. He
was usually dressed in black. In the summer he commonly carried
a light silk hat in his hand while walking in the shade. When engaged in conversation, he used to wind and unwind the black silk
handkerchief which he wore wrapped around his mutilated hand,
but not so as to show its disfigurement.

" When thinking, he looked like one of his own heavy pieces,
which would surely do execution when discharged ; when speaking,
his face had a noble expression, and was capable of displaying the
most benignant feeling. This was the true character of his heart.
His voice was strong and no one could hear it without feeling that
it had been accustomed to command. The mind of Knox was
powerful, rapid and decisive, and he could employ it continuously
and effectively. His natural propensity was highly social, and no
man better enjoyed a hearty laugh.

" He had a brilliant imagination, and no less brilliant modes of expression. His conception of the power and glory of the Creator of the universe were of an exalted character. The immortality of the soul was not with him a matter of induction, but a sentiment or a fact, no more to be questioned than his own earthly existence. He said that he had through life left his bed at dawn, and had always been a cheerful and happy man."

Cyrus Eaton, in his *History of Thomaston*, speaks of Knox as " The leading man of the parish, the benefactor of the town, the life of the business community, the friend of virtue, his country, and the human race." Among other anecdotes narrated of Knox, Eaton gives one which evinces the keen perception of the General. In his day, it was customary for the legal voters of a parish to be assessed for the costs of the preaching of the gospel in the parish church, with certain exemptions. General Knox was one of the members of the committee on the supplying of the pulpit, and being suspicious of the sincerity of a preacher, the Rev. W. H. H. Chealy, he ventured to advise against his permanent settlement. Knox thought that the clergyman had too much to say about himself and his own achievements, and he added: " Even Cicero could never speak of himself without appearing ridiculous." Open accusations being brought against Mr. Chealy, General Knox declared that " the minister of Thomaston must be, like Cæsar's wife, not only pure, but unsuspected." The reverend gentleman was subsequently discharged; and he justified some of the suspicions entertained of him by going into the business of rumselling in Boston.

The General was accustomed to use very forcible language on occasion. It is related of him

that, having a dispute with a man who had as
he thought, made an overcharge of four shillings
and sixpence in his bill, the General stoutly declared that this small amount was in excess of
the honest charge ; whereupon the man offered
to make oath that the invoice was true. Knox,
drawing himself up to the full of his imposing
height, said, in solemn tones, " Well, if you are
willing to risk your immortal soul for four and sixpence, do it, in the name of God! " The man
quailed before that awful voice and fled precipitately
from the presence.

The Rev. Thurston Whiting, who for a time supplied the Thomaston pulpit, was, for some reason,
an object of aversion to Mrs. Knox. On one occasion, the parson being invited to the General's house
to dine, Mrs. Knox preceded the company to the
dining-room and seated herself at the table. It was
the custom of the time to say grace standing, and
the General said, " Rise, my dear, and the parson
will ask a blessing." Mrs. Knox made no motion,
and the General repeated the remark; and still the
lady, smiling, kept her seat; whereupon General
Knox, " with something of that stentorian voice
that rose above the tempest at the battle of Trenton," said, " Rise—my—dear—the parson is going
to ask a blessing! " The lady, still smiling, remained
unmoved, and the parson invoked the blessing without more being said or done.

Harrison Gray Otis, who was associated with
Knox while the General was Secretary of War and
Otis was a member of Congress, says:

"As Knox's matrimonial connection was a love-match, and both parties possessed great good sense and were proud of each other, it was understood by their friends that their mutual attachment had never waned. It was, however, well-known that they frequently differed in opinion upon the current trifles of the day, and that the *iræ amantium*, though always followed by the *integratio amoris*, were not infrequent, and that in those petty skirmishes our friend showed his generalship by a skilful retreat. On one occasion, at a very large dinner-party at their own house, the cloths having been removed, the general ordered the servants to take away the woollen cover, which Madam, in an audible voice, prohibited. He then instantly, addressing the whole circle, observed: 'This subject of the undercloth is the only one on which Mrs. Knox and I have differed since our marriage.' The archness and good humour of this appeal to the company were irresistible, and produced, as was intended, a general merriment."

An old resident of Thomaston has related how, when he was a lad, he was loitering about the Knox mansion while a great festivity was in progress within. To give pleasure to the large company assembled, General Knox had ordered from his stables a number of saddle-horses for a ride through the grounds and park. Among the animals thus saddled and brought to the house was Mrs. Knox's favourite horse, and, in the presence of the assembled company, the lady turned to the General and asked why her horse had been brought up. He replied that it was brought for the use of one of the guests. To the mortification of the General, she protested against the use of her horse by anybody but herself; and she did not propose to ride. Calling to the groom, the General said, "John, put Mrs. Knox's horse in the stable, and do not take it out again until God Almighty, or Mrs. Knox, tells you to."

The General's full habit has already been noted, and it is recorded * of him that his weight, in 1783, was the greatest of eleven distinguished officers of the army, being 280 pounds, Washington's weight being set down at 209 pounds. With a Captain Sargent, he was selected to present the hard case of the starving and naked men at Valley Forge to the attention of a committee of Congress. One of the Congressmen, willing to show his wit and sarcasm, said that he had never seen a fatter man than General Knox nor a better dressed man than his associate. Knox managed to keep his temper and remained silent, but his subordinate retorted : " The corps, out of respect to Congress, and themselves, have sent as their representatives the only man who had an ounce of superfluous flesh on his body and the only other who possessed a complete suit of clothes.''

It is evident that the sanguine temperament of General Knox was the cause of the misfortunes that clouded his later years. Harrison Gray Otis, in his reminiscences of him, says:

" When this great and good man left the Federal cabinet, he became a victim to anticipation. Coming into possession of large tracts of land in Maine, he expected to accelerate, and to realise in a few years, not merely the growth and prosperity which Maine has now attained, but the high destination to which she may probably arrive in another half-century. His own palace raised in the woods was a beau ideal only of the ' castles in the air ' which floated in his ardent imagination ; and his projects of improvement and civilisation were worthy of Peter the Great, and would have required no inconsiderable portion of Peter's resources to be carried into effect. He

* Winthrop Sargent's *Life of Major John André.*

regarded his lime-kilns as mines of gold, and his standing timber as if cut and dried in the markets of Boston."

This foible in the character of the great man was overlooked by the people who were his fellow-townsmen and his most intimate friends and neighbours. His genius will be respected by future generations of patriotic Americans; his example as a lover of his country — able, incorruptible, and devoted — may well be commended to the emulation of those who, though they may not be so richly endowed as he, may desire to live so that they shall serve well the land that bore them.

Henry Knox deserved the eulogium with which a local bard, during his lifetime, apostrophised him:

> " Raised by thy toils the brazen bulwark stands,
> Thy care creates it, and thy voice commands ;—
> Yet as the truly brave are truly kind,
> And mildest manners mark the noblest mind,
> ' So, while a country's wrongs thy spirit fires
> And patriot ardour every deed inspires,
> Not more in arms revered than loved by fame
> For every worth the social virtues claim,—
> In war, the terror of the blazing line,
> In peace, the soul of gentleness is thine."

APPENDIX

CAMP NEAR SCHUYLKILL, 13th Sept., 1777.

SIR:

I do myself the honour to transmit to you an account of an action which happened between the American and the British troops, the 11th instant, on the heights of Brandywine.

Brandywine is a creek which empties itself into the Delaware, near Wilmington, about thirty miles from Philadelphia. On the 9th instant our army took post about eleven miles up this creek, having it in front at a place called Chad's Ford, that being the most probable route by which the enemy would endeavour to pass to Philadelphia. The enemy on the 10th advanced to Kennet Square, within three miles of our advanced parties, and at eight o'clock in the morning of the 11th a considerable body of their army appeared opposite to us. Immediately a heavy cannonade commenced, and lasted with spirit for above two hours, and more or less the whole day. Our advanced light corps, under General Maxwell, engaged the advanced parties of the enemy on the other side of the creek with success, having twice repulsed them, and entirely dispersed a body of three

267

hundred Hessians. This light corps was engaged with their advanced parties almost through the day. At the same time this body advanced opposite to our army, another large column, consisting of the British and Hessian grenadiers, light infantry, and some brigades, took a circuitous route of six miles to our right, and crossed the creeks at the forks of Brandywine. His Excellency, General Washington, notwithstanding his utmost exertions to obtain intelligence, had very contradictory accounts of the numbers and destination of this column until it had crossed the creek six miles to our right. He immediately ordered General Sullivan's, Lord Stirling's, and General Stephen's divisions to advance and attack them. This was about three o'clock P.M. These divisions, having advanced about three miles, fell in with the enemy, who were also advancing. Both sides pushed for a hill situated in the middle.

The contest became exceedingly severe, and lasted without intermission for an hour and a half, when our troops began to give way, having, many of them, expended all their cartridges.

His Excellency, who in the beginning of this action galloped to the right, ordered Greene's division and Nash's brigade from the left; but, the distance being so great, the other divisions had retreated before they arrived. However, they formed and were of the utmost service in covering the retreat of the other divisions, particularly Weedon's brigade of Greene's division, which behaved to admiration in an excessive hot fire, checked the British grenadiers, and finally, after dark, came off in great order.

While this scene was acting on the right, the enemy opened a battery on the left of seven pieces of cannon opposite to one of ours of the same number. General

Wayne, with a division of the Pennsylvania troops, having Maxwell's light corps on his left, and Nash's brigade (which was afterward drawn off to support the right wing) on his right, formed the left wing. The enemy's batteries and ours kept up an incessant cannonade, and formed such a column of smoke that the British troops passed the creek unperceived on the right of the battery, on the ground which was left unoccupied by the withdrawal of Nash's brigade.

A very severe action immediately commenced between General Wayne and the enemy, who had now got possession of a height opposite to him. They made several efforts to pass the low grounds between them, and were as frequently repulsed. Night coming on, his Excellency, the General, gave orders for a retreat, which was regularly effected without the least attempt of the enemy to pursue. Our troops that night retired to Chester, and will now take post in such a manner as best to cover Philadelphia.

It is difficult at present to ascertain our loss; but, from the most particular inquiry I have been able to make, it will not exceed seven hundred or eight hundred killed, wounded, and missing, and ten field-pieces.

KNOX'S DRAFT OF AN ADDRESS TO WASHINGTON, IN REPLY TO THE GENERAL'S FAREWELL ADDRESS TO THE ARMY

All the officers of the part of the army remaining on the banks of the Hudson have received your Excellency's Serious and Farewell Address to the Armies of the United States. We beg your acceptance of our unfeigned thanks for the communication and your affectionate professions of inviolable attachment and friendship. If

your attempts to insure them the just, the promised rewards of their long, severe, and dangerous services have
failed of success, we believe it has arisen from causes
not in your Excellency's power to control.   With extreme
regret do we reflect on the occasion which called for such
endeavours.   But, while we thank your Excellency for
these exertions in favour of the troops you have so successfully commanded, we pray it may be believed that in
this sentiment our own particular interests have but a
secondary place; and that even the ultimate ingratitude
of the people (were that possible) would not shake the
patriotism of those who suffer by it.   Still with pleasing
wonder and grateful joy shall we contemplate the glorious
conclusion of our labours.   To that merit in the Revolution, which, under the auspices of Heaven, the army
have displayed, posterity will do justice: and the sons
will blush whose fathers were their foes.   Most gladly
would we cast a veil on every act that sullies the reputation of our country.   Never should the page of history
be stained with its dishonour, even from our memories
should the idea be erased.   We lament the opposition
to those salutary measures which the wisdom of the
Union has planned,—measures which alone can recover
and fix on a permanent basis the credit of the States,—
measures which are essential to the justice, the honour,
and interest of the nation.   While she was giving the
noblest proofs of magnanimity, with conscious pride we
saw her growing fame; and, regardless of present sufferings, we looked forward to the end of our toils and
dangers, to brighter scenes in prospect.   There we beheld the Genius of our country dignified by sovereignty
and independence, supported by justice, and adorned
with every liberal virtue.   There we saw patient Hus-
bandry fearless extend her cultured fields, and animated

Commerce spread her sails to every wind that blows. There we beheld fair Science lift her head, with all the arts attending in her train. There, blest with Freedom, we saw the human mind expand; and, throwing aside the restraints which confined us to the narrow bounds of country, it embraced the World. Such were our fond hopes; and with such delightful prospects did they present us. Nor are we disappointed. Those animating prospects are now changed and changing to realities; and actively to have contributed to their production is our pride, our glory. But Justice alone can give them Stability. In that Justice we still believe. Still we hope that the prejudices of the misinformed will be removed, and the arts of false and selfish popularity, addressed to the feelings of avarice, defeated, or in the worst event, the world, we hope, will mark the just distinction. We trust the disingenuousness of a few will not sully the reputation, the honour, the dignity of the great and respectable majority of the States.

We are happy in the opportunity just presented of congratulating your Excellency on the certain conclusion of the definitive treaty of Peace. Relieved at length from long suspense, our warmest wish is to return to the bosom of our country, to resume the character of citizens; and it will be our highest ambition to become useful ones.

To your Excellency, this great event must be peculiarly pleasing; for while at the head of her armies, urged by patriot virtues and magnanimity, you steadily persevered, under the pressure of every possible difficulty and discouragement, in the pursuit of the great objects of the war,—the freedom and safety of your country,—your heart panted for the tranquil enjoyments of peace. We cordially rejoice with you that the period of indulging

them has arrived so soon. In contemplating the bless-
ings of liberty and independence, the rich prize of eight
years' hardy adventure, past sufferings will be forgotten;
or, if remembered, the recollection will serve to heighten
the relish of present happiness. We sincerely pray God
this happiness may long be yours; and that when you
quit the stage of human life you may receive from the
Unerring Judge the rewards of valour exerted to save the
oppressed, of patriotism and disinterested virtue.

EXTRACTS FROM KNOX'S LETTERS TO WASHING-
TON RESPECTING THE FORMATION OF THE
FEDERAL GOVERNMENT

BOSTON, 31st Jan., 1785.

Your remarks on the present situation of our country
are indeed too just. The different States have not only
different views of the same subject, but some of them
have views that sooner or later must involve the country
in all the horrors of civil war. If there is any good
policy which pervades generally our public measures, it
is too mysterious to be comprehended by people out of
the cabinet. A neglect in every State of those principles
which lead to union and national greatness, an adoption
of local in preference to general measures, appear to
actuate the greater part of the State politicians. We are
entirely destitute of those traits which should stamp us
one nation, and the Constitution of Congress does not
promise any capital alteration for the better. Great
measures will not be carried in Congress so much by the
propriety, utility, and necessity of the thing, but as a
matter of compromise for something else, which may be
evil itself, or have a tendency to evil. This perhaps is

not so much the fault of the members as a defect of the confederation.   Every State considers its representative in Congress not so much the legislator of the whole Union as its own immediate agent or ambassador to negotiate, and to endeavour to create in Congress as great an influence as possible to favour particular views, etc.   With a Constitution productive of such disposi- tions, is it possible that the Americans can ever rival the Roman name ?   The operation of opening the navigation of the rivers so as to communicate with the Western States is truly noble; and, if successful, of which I hope there is no doubt, it must be followed by the most ex- tensively beneficial consequences, which will increase in exact proportion to the increase of the population of the country.   I am pleased that you interest yourself so much in this great work.

You are so good as to ask whether General Lincoln and myself had an agreeable tour to the eastward, and whether the State societies are making moves towards obtaining charters.   We went to the eastern line of this State, and found that the British had made excessive en- croachments on our territories.   There are three rivers in the Bay of Passamaquoddy, to which the British have within twenty years past, with a view to confound the business, given the name of St. Croix.   But the ancient St. Croix is the eastern river.   The British have settled and built a considerable town called St. Andrews on the middle river, which has always sustained among the people in that country the Indian name Schudac.   The proper St. Croix and the Schudac are only nine miles distant at their mouths.   They run into the country about sixty miles, and they diverge from each other so much, that although at their mouths they are only nine miles apart, yet at their sources they are one hundred

18

miles distant from each other; and it is from the source
the north line to the mountains is to begin. The mountains are distant from the source about eighty or one
hundred miles; so that the difference to this State is one
hundred miles square above the heads of the rivers,
and the land between the rivers, which must be sixty
by fifty miles square. Our Legislature have transmitted
the report we made on this business to Congress and the
Governor of Nova Scotia. The matter has been involved
designedly by the British in such a manner that it can
now be settled only by commissioners mutually appointed for that purpose. I have seen a letter from Mr.
John Adams, dated last October, which mentions that
the river meant by the treaty of peace was decidedly
the river next to St. John's River westward; and there
are plenty of proofs that the ancient St. Croix was next
to St. John's. I have been particular in this narration,
that you may know the precise state of this affair, which
it is probable will sooner or later occasion much conversation.

As to the Cincinnati, the objections against it are apparently removed. But I believe none have yet applied
for charters. In this State it is pretty evident from communicating with the members of the Legislature that we
should not succeed. However, we shall attempt it previous to our next meeting in July.

PLAN FOR A GENERAL GOVERNMENT

NEW YORK, 14th Jan., 1787.

Notwithstanding the contrary opinions respecting the
proposed Convention, were I to presume to give my own
judgment it would be in favour of the Convention, and
I sincerely hope that it may be generally attended. In

my former letters I mentioned that men of reflection and principles were tired of the imbecilities of the present government, but I did not point out any substitute. It would be prudent to form the plan of a new house before we pull down the old one. The subject has not been sufficiently discussed as yet in public to decide precisely on the form of the edifice. It is out of all question that the foundation must be of republican principles, but so modified and wrought together that whatever shall be erected thereon should be durable and efficient. I speak entirely of the federal government, or, which would be better, one government instead of an association of governments. Were it possible to effect a general government of this kind, it might be constituted of an Assembly or Lower House, chosen for one, two, or three years; a Senate, chosen for five, six, or seven years; and the Executive, under the title of Governor-General, chosen by the Assembly and Senate for the term of seven years, but liable to an impeachment of the Lower House and triable by the Senate; a Judiciary, to be appointed by the Governor-General during good behaviour, but impeachable by the Lower House and triable by Senate; the laws passed by the general government to be obeyed by the local governments, and, if necessary, to be enforced by a body of armed men, to be kept for the purposes which should be designated; all national objects to be designed and executed by the general government without any reference to the local governments. This rude sketch is considered as the government of the least possible powers to preserve the confederated governments. To attempt to establish less will be to hazard the existence of republicanism, and to subject us either to a division of the European powers, or to a despotism arising from high-handed commotions.

I have thus, my dear sir, obeyed what seemed to be your desire, and given you the ideas which have presented themselves from reflection, and the opinion of others. May Heaven direct us to the best means for the dignity and happiness of the United States.

JOHN ADAMS TO GENERAL KNOX

[This letter was written by President Adams in reply to one from Knox, in which the General had congratulated Adams on his elevation to the presidency, and, in order to remove the possibility of war with France, then imminent, had made several suggestions, one of which was the appointment of Jefferson as special envoy to the French Republic.]

PHILADELPHIA, March 30, 1797.

DEAR SIR:

I have received with much pleasure your favour of the 19th. If I should meet with any " Roses " in my path, I shall thank you for your congratulations, and also when I set my foot on " thorns," as I certainly shall, I will thank you equally for your condolence. But when you assure me that you " feel confidence in the Safety of our political bark," you give me much comfort, and I pray you may not be disappointed.

It is a delicate thing for me to speak of the late election. To myself personally, my " elevation " might be a matter of indifference or rather of aversion. Had Mr. Jay, or some others, been in question, it might have less mortified my vanity, and infinitely less alarmed my apprehensions for the Public. But to see such a character as Jefferson, and much more such an unknown Being as Pinckney, brought over my head and trampling on the

Bellies of hundreds of other Men infinitely his Superiors
in Talents, Services, and Reputation, filled me with apprehensions for the safety of us all. It demonstrated
to me that, if the Project succeeded, our Constitution
could not last four years; we should have been set afloat
and landed the Lord knows where.

That must be a Sordid People indeed, a People destitute of a sense of honour, Equity, and Character, that
could submit to be governed, and see hundreds of its
most meritorious Public Men, governed by a Pinckney
under an elective Government. Hereditary Government, when it imposes young, new, inexperienced Men
upon the Public, has its Compensations and equivalents;
but elective Governments have none. I mean by this
no disrespect to Mr. Pinckney. I believe him a worthy
Man. I speak only by comparison with others.

I have it much at heart to settle all disputes with
France, and nothing shall be wanting on my Part to accomplish it, except a violation of our faith and a Sacrifice
of our Honour. But, old as I am, war is even to me less
dreadful than Iniquity or deserved disgrace. Nothing
can be done of much moment in the way of even negotiation without the Senate, and nothing else without
Congress.

Your Project has been long ago considered and determined upon. Mr. Jefferson would not go. His reasons
are obvious. He has a station assigned him here, by the
Nation, which he has no right to quit, nor have I any
right to call him from. I may hereafter communicate to
you what I have never communicated to any other, what
has passed upon that subject. The Circumstance of
Rank is too much. We shall never be respected in
Europe while we confound Ranks in this manner in
their Eyes. The Chief Justice was too much to send

to England. I have Plans in Contemplation that I dare say will satisfy you, when they come to be developed. I regret the time that must be lost before the Senate and Representatives can assemble.

If we wish not to be degraded in the Eyes of Foreigners, we must not degrade ourselves. What would have been thought in Europe, if the King of France had sent Monsieur, his Eldest Brother, as an Envoy? What of the King of England, if he had sent the Prince of Wales? Mr. Jefferson, in essence, is in the same situation. He is the first Prince of the Country, and the Heir Apparent to the Sovereign Authority, *quoad hoc*. His consideration in France is nothing. They consider nobody but themselves. Their apparent respect and real Contempt for all Men, and all Nations but Frenchmen are proverbial among themselves. They think it is in their power to give Characters and destroy Characters as they please, and they have no other rule but to give Reputations to their Tools, and to destroy the reputations of all who will not be their tools. Their efforts to "popularise" Jefferson and "depopularise" Washington are all upon this Principle. To a Frenchman the most important Man in the world is himself, and the most important Nation is France. He thinks France ought to govern all Nations, and that he ought to govern France. Every Man and Nation that agrees to this, he is willing to popularise. Every Man and Nation that disputes or doubts it, he will depopularise if he can.

This is in all confidence from, Sir, your most
humble servant,

JOHN ADAMS.

GENERAL KNOX.

INDEX

A

Adams, John, at Lexington, 29; letter to Knox, 35; ditto concerning army promotions, 61; peace commissioner, 64; ditto concerning his own election to presidency, 249 and Appendix; appoints Hamilton and Pinckney over Knox, 250
Alexandria, Va., convention at, 198
Algerine piracies, 224
André, John, meets Knox, 41; his plunder from Franklin's library, 118; his trial and execution, 136–137
Armstrong, Major John, author of Newburgh addresses, 172
Arnold, Benedict, at Valley Forge, 117; at Philadelphia, 121; marriage, and a previous courtship, 128–129; charges against, 129; his treason, 136; tobacco-stealing expedition in Virginia, 138; burns Connecticut towns, 153
Artillery company, Paddock's, in Boston, 19
Ashburton, Lord, 241

B

Barlow, Joel, 207
Barras, Admiral, 144

Beaumetz, Count, 241
Bonaparte, Napoleon, 254
Boston, "Massacre," 7, 8; Knox's bookstore in, 9; Port Bill, 15; American siege of, 31, 37 *et seq.*; Howe's evacuation of, 46; Knox returns to, 187; General Lincoln Collector of, 215
Bounty-jumpers in American army, 94
Brandywine, battle of, 103
Brigadier's Island, Me., 240
Brooks, John, 169
Bunker Hill, battle of, 31
Burbeck, William, 51
Burgoyne's surrender at Saratoga, 111
Burr, Aaron, on Putnam's staff, 55; aids Knox in retreat from New York, 67
Bushnell's torpedo, 68

C

Cabinet, Washington's first, 211–212
Caldwell, Rev. James, 135
Canal, the Cape Cod, 243
Carleton, Sir Guy, 177
Castine, the Baron de St., 188
Chealy, Rev. W. H. H., 262
Chew house, siege of, 108
Cincinnati, Society of, 175 *et seq.*

279

Clinton, General and Governor, 54 ; prepares for evacuation of New York by British, 177 ; thanks Knox, 180

Clinton, Sir Henry, supersedes Lord Howe, 118 ; withdraws troops from Cornwallis, 146

Cobb, Gen. David, at Yorktown, 158; Knox's letter to, 252–253

Cochran, Mrs. John, 147

Concord and Lexington, beginning of troubles at, 29, 30

Congress, soldiers' memorial to, 168 ; ratifies new Constitution, 203 ; authorises building of six frigates, 215, 224

Constitutional convention at Philadelphia, 202, 203

Constitution finally ratified, 204

"Conway cabal," the, 115

Copper, Knox's, mining scheme, 243

Cornwallis, Lord, goes up the Hudson, 75 ; at Trenton, 77 ; enters Philadelphia, 107 ; returns to New Jersey, 112 ; clash between him and Clinton, 142 ; opens negotiations, and surrender at Yorktown, 158 *et seq.*

Cutler, Dr. Manasseh, 217

D

Dauphin, birthday of the, celebrated, 167

Deane, Silas, his mission to France, 90

D'Estaing, Count, arrives with French fleet, 124–125

De Grasse, 144 ; his fleet in Chesapeake Bay, 153 ; penury of his daughters, 244

De Kalb, Baron, joins American army, 102

Ducoudray, ready to supersede Knox, 91 ; subsequent career, 93

Dudley, Dorothy, letter describing American generals, 37

E

Eastern Land Association, 235

Eaton, Cyrus, historian of Thomaston, Me., 232, 262

Exchange of prisoners, difficulties of, 164

F

Falmouth, the burning of, 44

Flucker, Miss Lucy, customer at Knox's store, 12 ; marriage to Knox, 22, 24

Flucker, Secretary Thomas, 12, 46 ; younger member of his family, 238 ; portrait of, by Copley, 259

France, aids American patriots, 90 ; treaty with (1778), 116 ; French troops in Philadelphia, 153

Franklin, Benj., peace commissioner, 64

G

Gage, General, threatens to seize arms of Boston militia, 20 ; sends military force to Concord, 29 ; his angry proclamation, 33

Gates, Gen. Horatio, appointed brigadier-general, 32 ; arrogates separate command, 77 ; victory at Saratoga, 111 ; presides at Newburgh meeting, 175

Genet, Citizen, his intrigues in America, 226 *et seq.*

Germantown, battle of, 108 ; Knox's description of, 109 *et seq.*

Greene, Geo. Washington, 206

Greene, Nathanael, General, appointed brigadier, 32 ; letters to Knox concerning capture of Fort Washington, 73 ; with

Greene, Nathanael— *Continued.*
Knox in New Jersey, 88 ; his
letters to Knox from South
Carolina, 151, 156, 162
Gridley, Richard, artilleryman,
34

H

Hale, Nathan, executed as a
spy, 69
Hamilton, Alexander, aide to
Washington, 54 ; warns Philadelphia of approach of British, 106 ; proposes national
convention, 198 ; Secretary of
the Treasury, 212 ; military
rank over Knox, 250–251
Hancock, with Adams at Lexington, 29 ; supports the new
Constitution, 105
Harlem Heights, Washington's
headquarters at, 69
Heath, William, General, 32 ;
his brigadiers, 49
Higginson, Stephen, 199
Howe, British admiral, 55
Howe, General, and Lord, in
command at Boston, 44 ;
evacuates Boston, 46 ; arrives off New York, 55 ; sends
embassy to Washington, 58–
59 ; moves against Americans
on Harlem Heights, 71 ; is-
sues proclamation of amnesty,
76 ; his operations in New Jersey as described by Knox, 97
et seq.; withdraws to New
York, 101 ; sails for Philadelphia, 102 ; superseded by Clinton, 118
Howe, General Robert, American, 141

I

Indians, Penobscot, Knox's errand to, 188 ; Knox's policy
towards, 222 ; Penobscots'
visit to Montpelier, 240

J

Jackson, Col. Harry, General
Knox's friend, 97 ; in Phila-
delphia, 121 ; left late in his
command, 186 ; Navy Agent
at Boston, 215 ; member of
Eastern Land Association,
235 ; his boy in Knox's charge,
238
Jay, John, Knox's letter to, 159
Jefferson, Thomas, Secretary of
State, 212
Jersey Line, mutiny of, 140
Jones, Paul, 126

K

King, Rufus, 199
Knox, Henry, General and
Secretary of War ; the ances-
tors of, 2–3 ; parentage in
America, 4 ; apprenticeship
in Boston, 5 ; boyhood, 6 ;
witness of Boston Massa-
cre, 7, 8 ; loses two fingers,
13 ; his books from London,
16 ; downfall of business, 18 ;
his letter to Longman, 19 ;
serves in an artillery company,
19 ; in a grenadier corps, 22 ;
courtship and marriage, 22–24;
flight from Boston, 30 ; meets
Washington, 32 ; appointed
colonel, 34 ; expedition to Ticonderoga, 38 *et seq.;* meets
John André, 41 ; letter to
Washington from Norwich,
Conn., 51 ; describes panic
in New York, 56–57 ; letter
describing embassy from Howe
to Washington, 58 ; criticises
the army, 70 ; at the crossing
of the Delaware and battle of
Trenton, 79 *et seq.;* appointed
brigadier-general, 81 ; describes battle of Princeton, 83
et seq.; advises march to
Morristown, 86 ; advises

Knox, Henry—*Continued*.
public works at Springfield, Mass., 87 ; and a military academy, 88 ; lays out defensive works for New Jersey, 88 ; threatened to be superseded by Ducoudray, 91 ; describes Howe's operations in New Jersey, 97 *et seq. ;* announces British entry into Philadelphia, 107 ; describes battle of Germantown in letter to Gen. Artemas Ward, 109 ; advises against assault on British in Philadelphia, 113 ; visits Boston, 114 ; in Philadelphia, 119 ; describes battle of Monmouth, 119, 120 ; his ventures in privateering, 128 ; at Camp Pluckemin, 130 : letters to General Lincoln, 133–134 ; at Hartford, Conn., with Washington and Lafayette, 136 ; member of the André court - martial, 137 ; complains of difficulty of obtaining military supplies, 142 ; attends military conference at Wethersfield, Conn., 143 ; letter on " water-gruel government," 147 ; his activity at Yorktown, 155 ; account of Yorktown surrender, 159 ; appointed major-general, 162 ; letter from Greene to, 162 ; commissioner for exchange of prisoners, 164 ; confirmed major-general, 166 ; headquarters at West Point, 167 ; letters about the unpaid army, 169 *et seq.;* action on Newburgh addresses, 173 *et seq. ;* proposes Society of the Cincinnati, 175 *et seq.;* enters New York, 178 ; leaves West Point for Boston, 187 ; treats with Penobscot Indians, 188 ; Secretary of War, 189 ; describes Shays's rebellion, 194 ;

his ideas of a general government, 200 ; explains Massachusetts' position on the new Constitution, 204 ; sends General Greene's son to France, 206 ; letter concerning Lafayette's son, 209 ; letter to Rev. David McClure, 209 ; Secretary of War in Washington's administration, 212 ; advocates a national militia system, 213 ; domestic expenses in New York, 215 *et seq. ;* advocates building of a navy and coast defences, 224 ; in the suppression of Whiskey Rebellion, 227 *et seq. ;* resigns his office, 229 ; fixes his home at Thomaston, Me., 232 ; his land speculations, 234 *et seq. ;* his industrial enterprises, 239 ; his distinguished guests, 241 ; member of the General Court and Governor's Council, 242 ; copper-mining schemes, 243 ; early deaths of his children, 247 ; affronted by being ranked by Hamilton and Pinckney, 250 ; death and funeral, 256 ; last will and testament, 257 ; anecdotes and personal traits of, 259 *et seq.*

Knox, Mrs. Lucy, birth of first child, 50 ; leaves New York in a panic, 56 ; her criticism of Connecticut people, 60 ; at Valley Forge, 117 ; letter from Benedict Arnold to, 129 ; death of infant daughter, 134 ; birthday letter from her husband, 148 ; at Mt. Vernon, 157 ; receives news of Yorktown surrender, 158 ; death of, 257

Knox, William, carries on his brother's business in Boston, 89 ; joins him in Philadelphia, 106 ; sent to Mt. Vernon

Knox, William—*Continued*.
with news of Yorktown surrender, 158
Knoxville, Tenn., 223

L

Lafayette, General, joins the American army, 102 ; visits Hartford, Conn., with Washington and Knox, 136 ; ordered to Virginia, 142 ; his affection for Knox and Greene, 189 ; revisits the United States, 190 ; his son named for General Washington, 209
Land patent, the Waldo, 234
Lauzun, Chevalier de, 153
Lee, Charles, appointed major-general, 32 ; in command of the Southern Department, 53; suspicious conduct of, and capture by British, 77 ; reprimanded by Washington at the battle of Monmouth, 123 ; end of military career, 124
Lexington, beginning of troubles at, 29
Lincoln, General Benjamin, at defence of Charleston, S. C., 132–133 ; Knox's letters to, 133–134 ; receives British surrender at Yorktown, 158 ; Secretary of War, 183 ; resigns his office, 184 ; collector of customs at Boston, 215 ; financial dealings with Knox, 237
Long Island, Americans entrenched on, 56 ; battle of, 62 ; retreat of Americans from, 63

M

Machias, Me., naval engagement near, 44
Maclay, William, 221
Maine, wild lands in, 235
Marshall, Chief Justice, estimate of Knox's character, 260

Massachusetts, action on the new Constitution, 204 *et seq.*
Middlebrook, N. J., American camp at, 96 ; Knox writes from, 97 ; return of army to, 132
Military academy, Knox advises establishment of, 88 ; Knox's, at Pluckemin, 130
Militia system, national, Knox advises, 213
Monmouth, battle of, 119 ; Washington reprimands Lee at, 123
Montgomery, Richard, appointed brigadier-general, 32 ; death of, 50
Montpelier, Knox's house at, cost of, 233
Monvel, Monsieur, 235
Morris, Gouverneur, commissioner for exchange of prisoners, 164
Morristown, American army encamped at, 86 ; winter quarters at (1779), 80, 134
Morton, Mrs. Sarah, poetry of, 48
Mount Vernon, Washington at, 188
Mutiny, of Pennsylvania line, 138 ; of New Jersey line, 140

Mc

McClure, Rev. David, 209
McGillivray, 223
McHenry, Secretary, 225

N

Naval victories of Americans, 127
Navy, Knox advises building of, 224
New York, military operations around city of, 49 ; American retreat from, 66 *et seq.* ; great fire in (1776), 69 ; Washington proposes new operations

New York—*Continued.*
against, 143 ; evacuation by British, 178 ; seat of government removed from, 225

O

Ogden, Colonel, 169
Osgood, Samuel, 212
Otis, Harrison Gray, 12, 265

P

Paddock, his artillery company, 20
Peace, commissioners from England, 117 ; treaty signed, 163 ; the establishment of, 181 *et seq.*
Pennsylvania line, mutiny of, 138
Penobscot, I n d i a n s, Knox's treaty with, 188 ; visit Montpelier, 240
Percy, Lord, 28
Pepperell, Governor William, 234
Philadelphia, Howe sails from New York for, 101 ; American army enter, 102 ; panic in, at approach of British, 106 ; evacuation of, by British, 118 ; Knox enters, 119 ; Harry Jackson in, 121 ; French and American armies m a r c h through, 122 ; seat of national government in, 225
Philippe, Louis, 241
Pickering, Timothy, 225
Pinckney, C. C., ranks Knox, 250 *et seq.*
Pluckemin, N. J., fête at, 130
Pomeroy, Seth, appointed brigadier-general, 32
Princeton, battle of, 83
Privateering, Knox's ventures in, 127
Putnam, Israel, appointed major-general, 32 ; at New York, 54

R

Randolph, Edmund, 212
Revere, Paul, patrol in Boston, 27 ; midnight ride, 29 ; furnishes bell for Knox, 244
Rivington, James, ships tea to Knox, 15 ; Tory pamphlets from, 17 ; his printing-office wrecked by Americans, 50
Rochambeau, General, arrives in America, 135 ; visited by Washington and Knox, 143 ; his army marches to the Hudson, 145
Rochefoucauld, Duke de, 241
Rutledge, Edward, 64

S

Saint Croix River, disputed boundary at, 189
Saratoga, victory of, 111
Schuyler, Philip, appointed major-general, 32
Shays's rebellion, 193 *et seq.*
Springfield, Mass., Knox advises works at, 87
Springfield, N. J., fight at, 135
Spencer, Joseph, appointed brigadier-general, 32 ; major-general and his brigadiers, 54
Stirling, Lord, 54 ; taken prisoner, 62
Stuart, Gilbert, his portrait of Knox, 13, 259
Sullivan, John, appointed brigadier-general, 32 ; taken prisoner, 62 ; charged with errand by Lord Howe, 63
Sullivan, William, his pen picture of Knox, 261

T

Talleyrand, 241
Thomas, John, appointed brigadier-general, 32 ; at the siege of Boston, 45 ; death of, 50

Thomaston, Me., Knox fixes his residence at, 232

Thacher, Dr. James, describes American retreat from Long Island, 63 ; march to Virginia through Philadelphia, 152 ; estimate of Knox's character, 260

Ticonderoga, Knox's expedition to, 38 *et seq.*

Torpedo, Bushnell's, 68

Tonnage of American ships, 242

Treaty (of 1778), with France, 116 ; peace, with Great Britain signed, 163

Trenton, battle of, 79 *et seq.*

Tryon, Governor, flight of, 50

Trumbull, Governor of Connecticut, 33

Trumbull, John, proposed purchase of his paintings, 244–245

V

Valley Forge, painful march of American army to, 114 ; celebration of French treaty at, 116 ; Mrs. Knox at, 118

Vose, Captain, Knox's factor at Montpelier, 241

W

Waldo, General Samuel, 234

Ward, General Artemas, Knox reports to, 30 ; appointed major-general, 32 ; in command at Dorchester Heights, 45 ; Knox's letter to, describing battle of Germantown, 109 *et seq.*

War, Secretary of, salary of, 186 ; continued office of, 192 ; functions of, under new Constitution, 212, 213 ; discussion of emoluments of, 217

Washington, Fort, capture of, by British, 73 ; General Greene's letter concerning surrender, 74

Washington, George, appointed commander-in-chief, 31 ; meets Knox, 32 ; letter to Governor Trumbull, 33 ; to President of Congress, 34 ; friendship for Knox, 36 ; enters Boston, 46 ; at Harlem Heights, 69 ; warns Gov. Livingston, of New Jersey, 76 ; crosses the Delaware into Pennsylvania, 77 ; recrosses the stream and drives the British out of Trenton, 78 *et seq.;* protests against Knox being superseded by Ducoudray, 92 ; order against bounty-jumpers, 94 ; reprimands Lee, 123 ; compliments Knox at Monmouth, 124 ; thanks from Congress, 124 ; camps at White Plains, 124 ; attends fête at Pluckemin, 131 ; visits Rochambeau at Hartford, Conn., 136 ; deals with Pennsylvania and New Jersey mutineers, 140–141 ; sends requisitions to Knox for "capital operations," 142 ; impressive call from a Pennsylvania patriarch, 154 ; in Virginia, 156; at siege of Yorktown, 161 ; compliments Knox on artillery service, 162 ; letter on disaffection of army officers, 168 ; action on the Newburgh addresses, 172 ; enters New York, 178 ; farewell to officers, 178–179 ; advises Knox of Lincoln's resignation of office, 184 ; retires to Mount Vernon, 188 ; presides over Constitutional Convention, 202 ; President, 212 ; leaves public life, 246 ; death, 252

West Point, celebration at, of the Dauphin's birthday, 157 ; Knox in command at, 180

Wethersfield, Conn., conference
    at, 143
Whiting, Rev. Thurston, 263
Whiskey Insurrection, 227 *et
    seq.*
Wooster, General David, 32

Y

Yorktown, British position at,
    154 ; siege of, begins, 155 ;
    surrender of, 158